Rope Boy

For Leni
and Stephen Dillon too,
in the hope that he will also
love the mountains

Rope Boy

A life of climbing, from Yorkshire to Yosemite

DENNIS GRAY

Vertebrate Publishing, Sheffield
www.v-publishing.co.uk

Rope Boy

Dennis Gray

 Vertebrate Publishing
Crescent House, 228 Psalter Lane, Sheffield S11 8UT, United Kingdom
www.v-publishing.co.uk

First published in Great Britain and the United States in 1970 by Victor Gollancz Limited.
This edition first published in 2016 by Vertebrate Publishing.

Photographs Dennis Gray's collection unless otherwise credited.

The quotation from *Bagpipe Music* by Louis MacNeice is reprinted
by kind permission of Faber & Faber. The maps of Gauri Sankar and
Mukar Beh are reproduced by kind permission of the *Alpine Journal*.

Dennis Gray has asserted his rights under the Copyright, Designs and
Patents Act 1988 to be identified as the author of this work.

This book is a work of non-fiction based on the life, experiences and
recollections of Dennis Gray. In some limited cases the names of people,
places, dates and sequences or the detail of events have been changed
solely to protect the privacy of others. The author has stated to the
publishers that, except in such minor respects not affecting the
substantial accuracy of the work, the contents of the book are true.

A CIP catalogue record for this book is available from the British Library.

ISBN 978-1-911342-22-9 (Paperback)
ISBN 978-1-910240-91-5 (Ebook)

Every effort has been made to obtain the necessary permissions
with reference to copyright material, both illustrative and quoted.
We apologise for any omissions in this respect and will be pleased
to make the appropriate acknowledgements in any future edition.

Produced by Vertebrate Publishing Ltd.
Printed and bound by Lightning Source.

Contents

Introduction

'Lowliness is young ambition's ladder.'
(Julius Caesar)

The West Riding of Yorkshire is an area of remarkable contrasts: squalid industrial belts, sprawling villages, high moorland littered with gritstone out-crops, idyllic dales. To the casual visitor the industrial areas will probably appear dirty and oppressive, but let him probe beneath the surface of daily life and he will find a quality of existence rare for such an environment, reflected by the inhabitants' love of choral singing, brass bands, cricket, fish and chips, and of the dales, moors and rocks of their native Riding. Despite appearances, anyone living here is ideally placed to become a climber, a fact highlighted by the many West Riding mountaineers who, from modest beginnings on small gritstone outcrops, have progressed to the great mountains of the world.

I was born in October 1935, in Leeds, a manufacturing city with one redeem-ing feature – the ease with which it is possible to reach open countryside to the north. My father was a Dalesman from Wharfedale and my mother Liverpool Irish. My father followed an unconventional profession as a club and stage entertainer, and my sister and I grew up in an atmosphere of show business talk, among club and theatre people – singers, musicians, comedians and the like. My early memories are of piano singsongs, nights spent in station waiting rooms, artists rehearsing in our sitting room, of easy laughter and tears.

My parents had met when my father was on tour and although a love match their marriage was often in stormy waters, if not actually on the rocks. We lived in a large, broken-down Yorkshire stone house in one of the poorer districts of Leeds and, partly because of my parents' open-handedness, partly because of a large sitting-cum-rehearsal room, our abode was a centre for many local artists. My mother was the happiest of women, usually singing as she worked at her household chores, generous and kind and always prepared to sacrifice herself for her children's sake but, true to her Irish temperament, was not to be argued with if roused or annoyed. Our family knew poverty and occasional riches, according to the bookings on my father's engagement calendar. Some weeks we lived mostly on bread and dripping or bread and sugar, other weeks we lived like lords. My father, as a true man of the stage and generous to a fault, immediately spent or lent what he earned. My sister and I learnt at an early age to fend for ourselves and were used to travelling. My sister took up singing professionally at fifteen, but I hated the entertainment business and never wanted to follow in my father's footsteps.

When I was eleven and a pupil at Quarry Mount Primary School, I joined the local Boy Scout troop in Woodhouse, another of the poor quarters of Leeds. Occasionally the Scouts planned a hike, and the month I joined a Sunday walk was to take place over Ilkley's famous moor. This was early in 1947 and to most of the boys in the troop such an outing was an adventure, since none of their parents owned transport and a few of them had never been out of Leeds.

We were instructed to catch the first bus from Leeds to Ilkley. On the appointed day I caught what I thought was the first bus, a few stops from its starting point, but to my disappointment none of my fellow Scouts was aboard. I reasoned that this must be a duplicate bus and that doubtless they would be waiting in Ilkley when it arrived. An hour later, at journey's end, I was again disappointed; none of my friends were there and I wandered the streets looking for signs of them without success. I had obviously missed them, but I knew that the route planned was up to Ilkley Moor and on to the Cow and Calf rocks, the popular viewpoint looking over Wharfedale; from there they would go back by a roundabout route over the moors to Guiseley. If I hurried I might cut them off by going direct to the rocks by the road instead of crossing part of the moor.

I ran as fast as I could up the steep hill road, arriving breathless at the Cow and Calf; after a rest I began to search for my companions. At the side of the rocks furthest from Ilkley is Hangingstone Quarry, much frequented by rock climbers, and into this I wandered in my search. There was no sign of the Scouts, but a group of climbers stood gazing intently up at the opposite quarry wall. Most small boys are inquisitive and I was no exception. Clutching my bottle of lemonade, haversack on back, I nervously edged up to the crowd to see what held their attention.

A tall, athletic, white-haired man was balanced on what appeared to me a vertical, holdless face. Nonchalantly he pulled a handkerchief out of his trouser pocket and blew his nose, to the delight of the watching climbers, and reminding me of a stage acrobat. He began to move upwards, and this was somehow immediately different from a stage show; his agility, grace of movement, control and, above all, the setting high above ground, with no apparent safety devices, sent a thrill through my young body such as I had never before experienced. I had read about mountain climbing but my reaction hitherto had been indifference. One of the group whispered to a newcomer 'It's Dolphin!' as if this would immediately make clear why they were watching. The knot of climbers murmured their approval as the white-haired man reached the top of the rock face, and from the efforts of another of them to follow on a rope thrown down to him, it was obvious that Dolphin must be a gifted climber. The face was only forty feet high but to me it could have been three times that height. I forgot all about my hopes of meeting my fellow Scouts and sat watching for hours. Always Dolphin was the most impressive and I gazed in wonder as he moved up vertical walls and fissures with speed and ease; his mastery held me spellbound. Then suddenly I saw him and some others changing into running shorts, replacing nailed boots with gym shoes, parachute jackets with vests, and before I realised what they were at they had disappeared on to Ilkley Moor.

Although shy, I ventured to ask one of the remaining climbers a few questions about his sport and in particular about the man who had impressed me so much. Good-naturedly he explained some of the techniques involved in rock climbing and told me that I had been watching 'Arthur Dolphin, the best rock climber in the area'. I thanked my informant, looked around once more for the Woodhouse Scouts, then set out across the moor to find my way to Guiseley and a bus home. Walking along I suddenly startled myself with the idea 'I would become a climber like Arthur Dolphin'. Up to that moment my ambition, like that of every other small boy at Quarry Mount School, had been to become a cricketer and play for Yorkshire; this was now relegated to second place in my future hopes. My next realisation was equally disturbing – I didn't care about missing the Woodhouse Scouts; the unexpected revelation of the sport of climbing had been worth my trouble.

Once the desire to climb is implanted in a person, it is extraordinary to what lengths he will go to achieve his objective. I have known people sacrifice their livelihood, ignore family obligations, drop career chances in order to learn to climb. Luckily for me, despite my youth it was not difficult to find someone to take me climbing, for in our Scout troop one of the older boys, John Collins, did climb and owned a rope. He was a regular visitor to Ilkley and Almscliff Crag and I badgered him into taking me with him to the Cow and Calf rocks on his next visit.

Climbing in 1947 was vastly different from what it was to become only a decade later. The country was still recovering from the aftermath of war, rationing was a feature of everyday life, and the standard of living for the majority was low. Equipment was rudimentary or homemade, and most of the climbers were dressed in ex-war department surplus – camouflage trousers, parachute-brigade jumping jackets, berets and so on. If they owned a rope it was of manilla, hemp or sisal, and few had boots made specially for climbing; most had walking or ex-war department boots, nailed with Tricounis, clinkers or triple hobs. In dry weather, gym shoes were occasionally worn, especially for tackling hard climbs, but the majority climbed in boots most of the time. Few climbers understood the use of running belays, mainly because of the lack of karabiners on the market; the few there were had ex-war department as their point of supply and would never have passed today's stringent UIAA (Union Internationale des Associations d'Alpinisme) tests. It used to be said at that time that 'if there had been no war, British climbers would have had to go naked, dressed only in the coils of their ropes'.

My first climb at Ilkley with John Collins and another local climber known as Lazarus was the *Long Chimney* in Rocky Valley, an edge on Ilkley Moor not far from the Cow and Calf rocks and Hangingstone Quarry. Though one of the longest climbs at the rocks, over fifty feet, it is relatively easy, but paradoxically graded Very Difficult. So impressed was I by this ascent, so difficult did I find the chimney, that I nearly went back on my resolve to become a climber. I could not face attempting another climb that day; my nervous energy had been utterly spent and I preferred to watch other people from the safety of the ground. One good thing about extreme youth is that setbacks are easier to overcome and, despite my poor performance and obvious lack of natural ability, a fortnight later found me back at Ilkley determined to make another attempt.

This is roughly how I started to climb. Sometimes I went to Ilkley by myself, sometimes I was so disappointed with my efforts that I nearly gave up. I was small and my arms were weak and I would go home discouraged, but after a week or two I would be back at the rocks, to try to do better. Surprisingly, despite the popular opinion that climbing was highly dangerous, my mother always encouraged me; I could rely on her for bus fares, but often I walked part of the way to save money. This was not unusual; some of the climbers I knew in my boyhood, married men with families who had to work six days a week, walked over the moors to Ilkley after finishing on Saturday, to bivouac under the stars in the longed-for contact with the world of mountains. They would climb on Sunday, then walk back on Sunday night, ready to begin work again on Monday morning. Some of them had a brilliance in climbing ability I shall never forget, and how many times could their story be repeated throughout the industrial north? The summit of their ambition was to visit the Lake District or North Wales, to them 'the real mountains', for their summer holidays. There was then no holiday pay so these excursions had to be scraped and saved for by such economies as walking to climb at weekends instead of paying for public transport. The horizons were limited but there was then a spirit of adventure and camaraderie that has since almost disappeared – inevitable when the numbers who climbed became enormous, familiarity with greater mountains commonplace, and our own homeland hills thoroughly exploited.

After I had been climbing for several months I decided I must buy a rope. We were going through a lean patch at home so all I could afford was forty feet of two-inch-thick sisal, known to us as 'barge rope'. This was actually what it was for – tying up barges – but as it had a breaking strain of several hundredweight and I only weighed six stone I was happy to use it climbing and roping off. One did not expect to have to hold a falling leader; if he did fall and escaped serious injury, he felt lucky and shamed by his miscalculation, the prevalent attitude being that the leader should never fall and if he did he was in high disgrace, not a hero.

Through my visits to the Cow and Calf rocks I got to know many of the local West Riding climbers and I also became aware that there was much more to climbing than its mechanics. To some of the climbers it was a way of life, a philosophy amounting almost to religion, and through them I read books which they felt expressed the essence of this attitude: *Mountain Craft* by Geoffrey Winthrop Young, Smythe's *The Spirit of the Hills*, Shipton's *Upon That Mountain* and, most important of all, Mummery's *My Climbs in the Alps and Caucasus*. Though Mummery had been dead for over fifty years, he was the man to whom they felt akin; he was in line with the spirit of the new age which exulted in the sheer freedom to be found in climbing.

In July, 1947, I won a scholarship to grammar school and said goodbye to Quarry Mount Primary School with its many boys in clogs and some in near rags of clothing. My interest in climbing now became even more engrossing and every weekend found me at Ilkley or Almscliff Crag.

Almscliff, a gritstone outcrop near Pool-in-Wharfedale, though boasting climbs of only modest height, in the twenty-five to sixty foot range, is one of the oldest of climbers' playgrounds. Some of the greatest figures in British climbing history have been pioneers here and regular visitors included Slingsby, Ingle, Dent, Frankland, Botterill, Smythe, Dolphin. To climb constantly at the crag is to be in contact with the history of rock climbing as it developed on such outcrops.

Almscliff provides steep and rounded climbing of an unusually strenuous nature and initially I found this too much for my small frame and preferred Ilkley with its incut holds. Not for nothing do the locals pun it as 'Armscliff' and even today the crag boasts some of the steepest and hardest of outcrop leads to be found anywhere. Gradually I improved in arm and finger strength until I could manage the easier Almscliff courses, and from then on it became and has remained my favourite outcrop climbing ground. Arthur Dolphin was supreme there when I first visited the crag and to see him in action was to see him at his best. It was a difficult place to reach, lying off the main bus routes at that time, but it had its group of devotees who would bicycle or walk most of the way from their home to this outcrop, and soon under the spell of its unique climbs I was one of them.

About a year after I started climbing, John Collins and I, with another local climber, decided to visit Laddow Rocks, the most northerly of the Peak District gritstone escarpments, at Whitsuntide. We caught the train to Greenfield from Leeds, then walked over the moors to Laddow. Even though it was a bank holiday there were no other climbers about – in those days there was still plenty of space, and queuing to climb anywhere in Britain was unheard of. We had a memorable holiday, doing most of the easier routes, and I particularly remember the *Long Climb,* which was near the limit of my ability. It was the first time I had bivouacked and I lay between a groundsheet and a couple of blankets looking at the stars, wondering at the grandeur of it all and thrilled to be at last what I considered a real climber. Our equipment would be laughed at by today's young climbers, but we survived, and returned feeling as proud as if we had been on an expedition to the Himalaya.

At grammar school I was disappointed in the work; the teaching methods seemed wholly based on the dictum 'little boys should be seen and not heard'. I suffered liberal beatings and spent most of the time copying, copying, copying out of endless books. Eventually my interest was killed in all but two subjects, art and English literature, especially poetry; the rest bored me, and I could not accept teachers who taught by might instead of reasoned example. Climbing was what I looked to for escape from this dull routine. At times I was desperately unhappy at school, though I was never without good and loyal friends, but the futility of it all seemed unbearable. I do not mind being alone and I used sometimes to go off by myself and think for hours. Slowly it was dawning on me that school was just one part of a huge system, a sausage machine for turning out a certain type of person, a conventional being who would do as he was told without question, swallow society's values whole, take up a profession that was 'safe and respectable', believe that all was well with the world, that change would be bad, and the rest of it. It was neither teachers' nor pupils' fault, we were all cogs in the same machine. As we grew up I watched my school friends accept society's ideals, yearn for fast cars, money, money, money, power to beat each other in the game of life, to be a success in the popular idiom. I wanted no part of this; I sat and dreamed of the freedom to be found in the hills.

1 The Bradford Lads

'From Hull and Halifax and Hell good Lord deliver me.'
(Dalesman's Litany)

Towards the end of the 1940s there emerged from one of the industrial areas of the West Riding of Yorkshire an unusual group of climbers who, because most of them lived in the Bradford region, became known as 'the Bradford Lads'. Unlike other groups of that period, they never for one instant looked upon themselves as a club nor considered becoming one. They were rebels against the established order of the climbing world and did not want rules or regulations to curtail their freedom, nor did they wish to ape the club ideal which they despised. Without formal ties, they were held together solely by their desire to climb.

Most of them came from a working-class background and discovered, like hundreds of others, an escape from the grime and smoke of their city environment in the surrounding countryside. They found their way to the Cow and Calf rocks, to Almscliff Crag and other local outcrops, and there, as I did, they learnt to climb, slept out rough, met other enthusiasts, discovered the mountain life. Some of them found in climbing and its surroundings a deep and significant meaning, a philosophy of life, as well as a sport that gave them a motive for living.

When I met the lads at the West Riding outcrops, they had already begun to form a group and, despite my youth, I soon became conscious of being an accepted member. Initially the numbers were small and fluid, but once a hard core had established itself, fresh recruits joined in from many northern areas, especially during the last period of their existence as a group. The outstanding feature of the Bradford Lads was the individualism of the members. Radical in outlook, they were against everything that smacked of authority. Everyone had grown tired of the restrictions imposed by the war; we looked for freedom in our climbing and were not to be stopped in this quest.

The original members of the group were Alf Beanland who, despite appalling health, with asthma and tuberculosis, was out climbing at every opportunity; Peter Greenwood, then a young teenager but full of the drive and aggression which were often to lead him into trouble, but which helped him to pioneer some of the finest climbs in the Lake District; the brilliant Drasdo brothers, Harold and Neville; Don Hopkin and Ernie Leach, two climbers of wide experience; Billy Boston, Jim Lyons, Bob Sowden, Fred Williams; Doug Hayes, propounder of the theory that when the sun was out, basking in it was more important than climbing; and finally Marie Ball, the only female member of the group. Marie could lead Very Severes, hold her own hitch-hiking or hill walking, and could handle anyone, including the arrogant looking for a fight.

Later, especially in the period of Lake District activity, many other West Riding and Lakeland climbers[1] became part of our scene, among them Arthur Dolphin, then in his early twenties and already famous in the Lake District and his native Yorkshire for his feats of pioneering. Born at Baildon on the edge of Ilkley Moor, he came from a well-known sporting family, especially of cricket players, and was himself an all-round sportsman and athlete and ran for his county. His physical appearance was somewhat ungainly; he was tall and gangling, his complexion is best described as albino, and his hair was unusually white. During the Bradford Lads' era, he lived in Leeds and worked as a metallurgist. He had begun to climb as a schoolboy just before the outbreak of war, and during the war had been confined to local gritstone outcrops where he had made a brilliant series of first ascents, particularly at Almscliff Crag. Several of these climbs were of a new level of difficulty for their period, and gradually he was transferring to the Lake District the standards he had developed on outcrops.

At the beginning of this epoch I was a small boy in the lower school of Leeds Modern School. Fired with an enthusiasm which astonishes me today, I managed with little or no money to walk or hitch-hike to local outcrops which the lads were visiting. My equipment consisted of a pair of ordinary boots nailed with triple hobs, a blanket sewn up to make a sleeping bag, a newly purchased hemp rope and an ex-army rucksack. I shivered away many Saturday nights in barns or fields but it was worth it to me then, it was the contact with mountains and nature for which I yearned.

Most of the lads had to work a six-day week when they began climbing, but the five-day week came shortly after the group's inception, and it was surprising how many of them managed to move into the trades thus favoured. The extra free day opened great possibilities for the working-class climber, although poor prospects and less pay were often the price of this prized concession. Being at school gave me many advantages; I had long holidays and every weekend free from Friday afternoon till Monday morning. I spent most

---

1. Others were Jack Bradley, Mike Dawson, Frank Cartwright, Mike Hollingsworth, Syd and Irma Theakston, John Ramsden, Tom Ransley, George Elliot, Mike Dixon, Terry Parker, Pete Whitwell, Pete Shotton, and two infamous characters known as the Moon and the Pale Man.

of school time reading climbing books instead of attending to the lessons. School bored me more as I grew older. I am afraid I was a difficult problem, and always my reports reflected this disinterest and unwillingness to work at academic subjects.

About the time the five-day week began, we discovered the possibilities of hitch-hiking. Although there were few vehicles on the road and petrol was rationed, what vehicles there were would usually offer a lift. This was the fillip needed to get the lads away from the limited horizons of local climbing; slowly we spread our wings to visit centres further afield, and tackled hill walks such as Marsden to Edale in the Pennines and the Three Peaks in the Yorkshire Dales. Walks of this length were beyond my stamina, and I still remember the round of the Three Peaks made in 1949 by a group that included Jim Lyons, Billy Boston, Alf Beanland and myself. We started in Dent and finished in Settle, a distance of more than twenty-six miles, over some of the roughest country in the north. I was thirteen and the effort made me ill for a week; my legs were so stiff that I couldn't play in an important school cricket match, in fact I gave up the game from that date. Cricket seemed small beer compared to the reality of moors and rocks.

From the days when I began climbing aged eleven, until I was thirteen, I attempted nothing harder than Difficults and Very Difficults; I was not strong and was small for my age. Slowly I worked through the easier-graded climbs on local outcrops, wearing triple hobs, using no running belays but climbing carefully and belaying well by accepted standards. Individual members of the Lads acted as mentors, particularly Alf Beanland whose patience and good humour I shall never forget. We all wanted to extend our experience, and from reading about mountains I wanted to be able to call myself a mountaineer. I listened with awe to stories of climbing in high mountains, and read and reread the only textbook on climbing I could afford, John Barford's *Climbing in Britain*. It cost me one shilling in 1947 and I still have this copy, more than twenty years later.

The Lake District has always held a special appeal for me, and in my earliest climbing days the very name was a symbol of mountaineering. Our hitch-hiking experiences had shown that it was possible to get to the Lakes even if one couldn't afford normal transport expenses. It was approximately a hundred miles from home, but if you had time enough to spare, sooner or later you were bound to reach your destination. I had plenty of time, thanks to school holidays, and at Easter, 1949, with two slightly older boys I made my first visit to what we considered then the real mountains.

We reached Langdale safely and set out to walk from there to Wasdale Head; from books we understood Wasdale to be the centre of climbing, the home of British mountaineering. Many years before this had been so, but now our information was sadly out of date. During the march it rained and snowed, our route finding was poor, and we moved so slowly, weighed down by immense packs, that we had to bivouac for the night on Allen Crags near Great End. When we finally reached Wasdale it lived up to our expectations; the Easter bank holiday was over and no other climbers were in the valley. Climbing was carried on at a leisurely pace and we were more in love with the mountains than the rocks; we climbed *Kern Knotts Chimney* and the Napes ridges but it was the walk up Great Gable and Scafell which meant most to us. On returning to Langdale later in the same week, this time in a single day, we climbed White Ghyll Slabs, some routes on Scout Crag and Middlefell Buttress. We were utter novices and to us it was all pioneering; we had no guidebooks and found our own way, and many were the difficulties we encountered.

After these first trips I thumbed my way to the Lakes for all vacations. Unfortunately, one of these visits was cut short by tragedy. Christmas, 1949, was roughly the first Lakeland gathering of the Bradford Lads, and after hitch-hiking from Yorkshire we assembled at what in the years to follow was to be our headquarters – Wall End Barn, near the farm of that name on the Blea Tarn road leading out of the Langdale valley.

On Christmas Eve a large party of us set forth to climb on Gimmer Crag via Middlefell Buttress, the latter a good way to avoid the monotony of the walk out of the valley to reach the high crags. We had decided to climb *Ash Tree Slabs* and *'D' Route*, and on reaching the crag we scrambled round its base to the north-west gully. The Langdale guidebook was long out of print and our knowledge scanty; we went too far up the gully looking for the slabs and were thus on the scene when a young girl, a member of an unroped party scrambling up *Junipall Gully*, fell off. She bounced from ledge to ledge, then out over the cliff face to land with a dull thud on a rock in the bed of our own gully. We climbed up to her and it was immediately evident that there was no hope of her surviving. She was about fifteen years old and had been beautiful, this much was obvious from her fine hair and delicate features, now horribly contorted. One of our party ran off for a rescue stretcher while Alf Beanland rendered first aid, but it was to no avail and a short while later she died cradled in his arms. There was no scream, not much blood, but it was a terrible moment. A sad party carried down the stretcher that evening. I stayed far to the rear; too small to be any use in carrying, I was loaded with spare equipment and truthfully glad to be in this secondary role. The last part of the girl's fall had been about sixty feet through the air and her body had arched before impact. This sight was to stay with me for months, and I used to wake in the night, nerves taut and expectant. The accident upset me seriously; I packed my rucksack and hitch-hiked home next day, unable to stomach the thought of climbing again that Christmas.

Petrol rationing ended at Whitsuntide, 1950, and from then on the growing number of vehicles on the A65 between Yorkshire and the Lakes catered for an ever-growing number of hitch-hikers. It was not uncommon, late on a Sunday, to see a dozen climbers spaced out along the Ingleton road at Kendal, trying to stop a lift. The twenty-mile stage, Kendal to Ingleton, was crucial – it was a lift or walk, for there was no other transport on that road of a Sunday.

Often the most enjoyable aspect of hitch-hiking was the telling of travellers' tales. Anyone who has hitch-hiked will testify to the uncertainty of that form of travel and many were the stories on this theme. Neville Drasdo, after a long wait at Ingleton on a journey north, flagged an aged woman at the wheel of an equally ancient vehicle. The car stopped and, despite a heavy load of farm produce, chickens, eggs and so forth, took Neville and his rucksack aboard. The vehicle was set in motion again by its driver but a hundred yards along the road it hit a bump, jolted and rolled over on to its roof, amidst a breaking of eggs and squawking of fowls. 'Don't worry, this often happens!' gasped the old lady from her upside-down position. Other vehicles arrived on the scene and the car and occupants were pushed the right way up to continue their journey, shaken but without further incident.

Tactics are important for hitch-hiking; it is no use being tenth in line behind a queue of nine other would-be hitchers. In one Bradford thumbing story, a driver who had stopped to offer a lift was surprised by a figure leaping out of a roadside ditch and into the back seat of his car before the bona fide hitch-hiker had the chance to run up and claim his lift. 'I've been lying in that ditch for over an hour!' confessed the wet and muddy tactician.

None of us ever refused any kind of lift. The slowest on record was Billy Boston's five-mile journey in a gypsy's horse-drawn caravan late one evening in a midwinter snowstorm. I managed to hitch-hike to the Lakes for twenty-five consecutive weekends in 1951, and Ernie Leach set a record for the lads with thirty-five consecutive weekend journeys.

Our climbing was centred on Langdale because it was the easiest for us to reach; once in that valley we took up residence at Wall End Barn. This ancient building was on the most generous scale and could accommodate dozens of climbers; people used the barn instead of camping because they couldn't afford tents. Originally the place was reasonably clean and tidy but when the climbing population boomed a short while later and the number using it increased enormously, conditions became definitely insanitary and even unhealthy. The floor was covered with bracken which slowly disintegrated to dust and was rarely replaced; it was always dark and in winter cold and draughty in the extreme. However, it was a shelter and catered almost exclusively for climbers; there friendships were made and visiting climbers passed on information about their rocks and learned off the Wall End regulars about new routes and recent developments in the Lake District. At the barn I first met Nat Allen, Joe Brown, Mick Noon, Pat Walsh, Ron Moseley, Vin Stevenson, John Cunningham and a score of other young climbers who were to leave their mark in the years ahead.

There was real character in that climbers' slum, it was a finishing school of an unusual type. Philosophies were expounded and politics discussed, one learnt blues and folk songs well ahead of their popularity; songs were written, one or two by myself, and some by men of talent, such as Alan Bullock, which I heard many years later sung on the BBC and in bars. There were no rules or regulations and things often went out of control; sometimes fights broke out, and only its damp stopped the place burning down on several occasions. If a climber and his girlfriend stayed together in the barn, and many did, it was solely their affair. As long as the farmer had his one shilling a night per head, he left young climbers, often in their dozens, to run their own affairs.

The barn was famous, and even infamous, and eventually it was closed, partly by outraged opinion, but there was a free-wheelery about Wall End which was lost forever with the closing of that refuge. The climbing scene was the poorer for its closure, and the replacing of this type of accommodation with organised campsites, although perhaps necessary with the vast increase in numbers, robbed Langdale and the Lake District of something it has never since recaptured.

When the Bradford Lads began their regular Langdale weekends, there was no up-to-date guidebook to help their explorations. We gleaned what we could from various sources, Fell and Rock Climbing Club journals which gave details each year of new climbs; from Arthur Dolphin, co-editor of the proposed new guide; from other less-reliable sources who often proffered us misleading advice and inaccurate information.

The Lads soon had a number of climbers capable of leading the harder routes. I myself found that wearing plimsolls my standard shot up. I could lead the easier Very Severes and on my fourteenth birthday led *White Ghyll Wall*, with Alf Beanland as second encouraging me every foot of the way. After the roundness of Almscliff Crag, Lakeland climbing seemed comparatively easier.

Peter Greenwood soon emerged as a brilliant rock climber; without the usual lengthy novice period then held necessary he made for the hard climbs from his first day out. He had outstanding gymnastic ability and partly because of this he emerged from some lengthy falls which seemed inevitable with his approach to life and climbing. He cared little for reputations or tradition; full of drive, he was always prepared to have a try. His impulsiveness sometimes frightened me, but I knew him as a kind and generous person underneath and often found myself included in his plans for hard climbing, despite my tender years.

Peter heard a rumour that *Kneewrecker Chimney* on Raven Crag was *the hardest climb* in Langdale. That was enough for him, and the next weekend, despite a covering of snow, found us roping up at what Peter guessed to be the start of the route. We had the cliff to ourselves, it was a beautiful midwinter's day, but with a cold wind. It was late afternoon as Peter climbed the first two pitches in one run out; our arrival in Langdale had been delayed by blocked roads and we had to hurry if we were to complete the climb before dark.

Following Peter I thought the route was too easy to be the right one, but on joining him at a large stance, my doubt was dispelled. He was belayed under a hanging chimney capped by an overhang – the pitch we had heard lauded f or its difficulty. I have done the climb several times since but it has never again seemed so intimidating. We had no description of the route, but Peter's attitude was if others could get up a piece of rock, so could we. His theory usually worked well, but on this occasion he climbed easily to the roof and then stuck on a small ledge under the overhang closing the chimney. Here, unknown to us, the correct way swings left, but Peter tried to exit directly over the capstone. Several times he nearly managed it, several times he narrowly avoided a fall. For over an hour he was stuck there but typically refused to give in. It grew dark, the wind shrieked outside the chimney, a surprise squall burst upon us and it began to snow.

Completely fearless, Peter decided he would leap into a nearby tree, and called down to this effect. This would have been a creditable feat for an Olympic athlete, and if he missed the tree he would go out into space. 'No! No!' I pleaded.

'It's only a few feet away,' he yelled through the snow.

'Have one more look,' I insisted; my hands were dead with cold and I couldn't have held a long fall. It was so dark I could hardly see Peter, but I was relieved to hear him mutter something about having a last attempt to get up. He worked high under the roof once more, but this time, as a kind of afterthought, lent to the left, his hands curled over snow-covered holds, and somehow he held on long enough to swing round and stand up on easy ground above. It had been a close thing. My own efforts to follow were puny to say the least; liberal assistance from above is the best description.

Next morning Peter and I met Arthur Dolphin and Jack Bloor who had motorcycled up from Leeds and were just setting out to climb. Arthur was impressed by Peter's achievement. His eyes twinkled as he listened to our adventures; it was obvious that he admired the drive of the new generation – hitch-hiking to the Lakes, sleeping rough in barns, tackling hard climbs in bad conditions. He was one of the few people from the older, university climbing tradition who could bridge the gap between the new wave and the established organisations. Although shy and retiring, once barriers were broken he did his best to inform us about climbs and offer advice.

'No,' he told us, '*Kneewrecker*'s not the hardest climb in Langdale. I think that title goes to *Kipling's Groove*. It has the finest pitch in the valley and is the most serious to lead.'

Arthur and Jack made off towards White Ghyll, leaving Peter resolved. 'I'll try *Kipling's Groove* as soon as possible,' he confided. 'If Arthur says it's the best climb in Langdale, it must be!' Arthur was the only man I ever heard Peter talk of in such a manner; like myself, he hero-worshipped him as a person.

Some weekends money shortage made it impossible to visit the Lake District; hitch-hiking cost nothing, but we could not always afford to buy food and other requirements. Many of the lads still worked on Saturday mornings and were restricted to local crags; among them (Neville Drasdo for instance) were some of the best rock climbers of the group.

On Sunday nights, if it was humanly possible, we met at Tommy's Cafe in Otley between Leeds and Bradford. This was Mecca to the Bradford Lads, and inside its then-murky walls plans were hatched for new climbs, stories bandied round and the next week's venue decided upon.

One Sunday night in the winter of 1950, the door of the cafe swung open and in came Harold Drasdo, obviously the bearer of news. He had just hitch-hiked from Langdale where Joe Brown had repeated *Kipling's Groove*, placing a piton in the climb to protect the hardest moves. This was a bombshell. Brown putting a piton into a climb previously led free? We couldn't believe it. I already thought him the finest rock climber ever to emerge in Britain. In fact, there were mitigating circumstances. The weather was bad, and Joe had climbed straight up from the bottom of the cliff, originating a new direct start under the misapprehension that this was the correct route. It is harder than the original line which traverses in from the right higher up; Brown knew the start to be comparatively easy and so, on arriving at the true crux of the climb, he placed a piton. This proved unnecessary for he found the climb relatively straightforward, but the action once taken was irretrievable; the piton could not be removed despite the efforts of his second, Pete Greenall, and there it remains to this day. It was the only miscalculation of its type I have known Joe Brown make.

The Bradford Lads were having no excuses and plans were made to remove the piton immediately. Dolphin was their hero and *Kipling's Groove* then his finest climb. It had already been repeated safely by a member of the Creagh Dhu Club. Brown's ascent was a red rose affront! A little later Peter Greenwood, seconded by Fred Williams, led the climb and spent a long time trying to hammer out the piton or break its head; it was – a trademark of Brown – well placed and hard to move, and in the end Peter stormed up the climb, refusing to clip into the offending ironmongery. But *Kipling's Groove* was never again the same climb. Arthur Dolphin led it once more without the piton, but few leaders who have come after him have elected to ignore this safety aid. The top pitch is a long and serious lead, and several leaders have fallen and been held by the piton; without this protection someone might have been killed, so despite ethical considerations, the ends have justified the means.

Nylon rope had begun to replace hemp and manilla, and nailed boots were giving way to the Vibram rubber sole. But the biggest change of that period was perhaps the new willingness to tackle hard climbs in bad conditions, of which our excursion on *Kneewrecker Chimney* was an example. Earlier descriptions of hard climbs contained such phrases as 'For a dry, windless day in rubbers'. Now there were climbers who would tackle anything in any conditions, encouraged by their faith in superior equipment. Joe Brown was working miracles in Wales and the Bradford Lads were doing their share in the Lake District. Perhaps the finest effort of this kind by the lads was the ascent by Peter Greenwood and Harold Drasdo of the Very Severe *Deer Bield Crack* in a genuine winter blizzard.

Deer Bield, though a relatively small cliff and easy to reach from Grasmere, is impressively steep and north facing with little sunshine. At that time it had two classic climbs, the *Chimney* and the more famous *Crack*. Between them lay the unclimbed *Buttress*, considered the last great problem of the area. It had been attempted many times by many parties; in 1951 Arthur Dolphin produced the solution with what, I feel, was the first climb in the modern idiom in the Lakes, an ascent of outcrop standards of difficulty combined with poor protection.

A month after the first ascent Peter Greenwood and Fred Williams repeated the *Buttress*, a performance carried out in pouring rain, wearing socks over gym shoes. Peter fell off the last pitch, the crux, when a flake he was laybacking came away; he had a long fall but was well held by Fred, despite the latter being pulled off his meagre stance and swinging clear himself. Peter finished the climb but for once was awed by events.

Later, Deer Bield yielded several new routes to the lads and, inevitably in that period, to the Rock and Ice Club. Peter Greenwood, Jack Bradley and I discovered the *Dunmail Cracks* climb but were driven off by bad conditions; Peter returned with Dolphin to complete the route, and Harold Drasdo pioneered his fine climb, *Hubris*.

At Whitsuntide, 1951, with Peter Greenwood and Fred Williams I paid my first visit to North Wales, where we met Arthur Dolphin. They were climbing the hardest routes in the Llanberis area, too hard for me. The highlight of the holiday was Clogwyn Du'r Arddu. I was so impressed by this cliff as we approached it over Maen Du'r Arddu that I daren't attempt anything. I watched Arthur lead a large party up *Sheaf*, and Peter and Fred climb *Bow-shaped Slab* without the normal lasso approach. Dolphin missed the route on *Sheaf* and climbed high up the *White Slab*; only the arrival of some Welsh regulars who corrected his mistake stopped what would have been an outstanding lead on the upper part of the slab. Arthur rounded the holiday off by leading *Spectre* with ease, seconded by Ken Tarbuck who opened our eyes with his rope techniques. I climbed the *Direct Route* on the nose of Dinas Mot, and left Wales vowing to return as soon as possible.

Clogwyn Du'r Arddu had enthralled me and also scared me stiff, no cliff I had seen or climbed upon was so beautiful or impressive. A new Llanberis guide had recently been published, written by Peter Harding in a style which suited my own tastes. It included quotations, detailed history, sweeping judgements: 'The boldest lead on British rock' (*Great Slab*; Colin Kirkus); 'A marvellous piece of route finding' (the *Sheaf*; Cox and Campbell). It may not have been objective, but it was informative, and is unequalled by any rock-climbing guide which has appeared in this country since. The more I read of 'Cloggy', the more I realised its unique place in British climbing history.

Jack Bloor, a close friend of Dolphin, was keen to climb on the cliff and he asked me if I would like to attempt *Longlands* with him, as this was the easiest major ascent. Jack, though overshadowed by the brilliant Dolphin, was no mean climber and, like Arthur, a runner of prominence. I had recovered from being scared by Cloggy and didn't hesitate, and we left Leeds on Jack's ancient ex-war department motorcycle.

When we arrived in Llanberis Pass it was raining, but Jack refused to go back empty handed and being a fifteen-year-old rope boy I had no alternative but to accompany him. *Longlands* in the rain was adventurous by current standards; rumour had it that 'you needed a week of fine weather before climbing on the west buttress of Clogwyn Du'r Arddu'.

We reached the foot of the rock and roped up. The massive folds of the cliff, the drip, drip, drip of water down the first pitch, a swirling mist, the screeching gulls which had come inland from bad coastal weather, all induced a feeling of tension, heightened by the lack of other human beings. I was relieved when Jack started; he climbed the first pitch in relaxed style and bade me follow. It was a revelation to find that, despite all we had heard, the climbing was straightforward and nowhere too difficult for us to manage, even in the rain. Jack dealt with the Faith and Friction pitch and although this made me ponder, once I plucked up the confidence to move it was not too bad. Soon we reached the overhang. Jack decided to let me try to lead this famous problem for, although I was small and slight, I had strong fingers and for the final difficulty on *Longlands*, this is what you need. I must confess to getting into a bit of a tangle; I climbed the overhang safely but my rope kept catching on the projection itself. Jack followed rapidly, then led through to the top. I joined him and we stood on the crest, wet through but happy. Today's novices who do routes like *Longlands* almost as soon as they start to climb will never know what it meant then to complete one's first Cloggy route.

Joe Brown and Merrick (Slim) Sorrell spent their summer holidays in the Lake District that year, and I spent some time in their company. It was already obvious that Joe was a phenomenal rock climber; he repeated *Deer Bield Buttress* and was impressed enough to declare that it was nearly as hard as *Diglyph*, a route he had pioneered on Cloggy on the same day as Dolphin had solved the *Buttress* climb. Memories of those days are of light-hearted jesting, horseplay and laughter; climbing was merely a part of mountain life. Joe was no fanatic; at times he was hard to equate with his performance on the rocks. He played second fiddle to Slim in important fields – practical jokes, building bridges, eating competitions, wrestling and romance. Joe was king of the land of nod, his forte was sleeping; he trained on sleep and I believe still does.

In retrospect most climbers would agree that Joe Brown, Arthur Dolphin and John Cunningham were the outstanding rock-climbing pioneers in 1951, and their example was responsible for the rise in standards and certainly inspired their contemporaries.

In the Lake District the Bradford Lads discovered crags unknown to their predecessors, some by systematic exploration, others by chance. Chance led to the discovery of the *Sword of Damocles* on Bowfell by Peter Greenwood and myself. One day of mist and rain we were doing the *Plaque* route on Bowfell Buttress; the mist cleared for a brief moment and across the gully to our left we glimpsed a crag seamed by deep grooves between impressively steep walls. 'Are there any climbs on that lot?' Peter demanded.

Although the youngest of the group I was an expert by this time on climbs and their whereabouts. Leeds Reference Library has a fine collection of mountaineering books and it was there I spent my midweek hours instead of doing schoolwork. 'No, I don't think so,' I said. 'It's too high for the *Cambridge Buttress*, that's lower down.'

'Let's go down and have a look at it,' Peter suggested when we reached the top of our climb. We went down the gully and stood underneath the crag, awestruck by its deep central groove. It was raining and cold and we couldn't get started into the bottom of this most obvious line.

'Too hard, I think, today, Pete?'

For once Peter agreed. 'Must tell Arthur about this. My God, what a find!' I was sworn to secrecy, and Peter returned later with Dolphin and Don Hopkin, and this strong party of the Lads produced from our chance find the famous *Sword of Damocles*.

Although we had our ups and downs, the standard of living was rising for the majority, and motorcycles began to replace the overloaded and slow hitch-hiking method of travel and soon became an obsession. Everyone who could raise a deposit acquired a machine. Needless to say, the number of crashes was fantastic; climbers and motorbikes are a dangerous formula. The stories at

Tommy's Cafe were more about the roads than about the rocks.

Jack Bradley, later to be a successful businessman – dare I say it? a millionaire – bought a racing machine with side-car frame. This often transported five stalwarts, usually with Frank Cartwright, alias 'The Egg', leaning from the pillion in the best TT style at an alarming angle, head just clearing ground on acute bends. The 'Brass Band Box' was a thrilling outfit to ride upon, and it had its crash. One night, at a particularly difficult bend, the Whoop Hall, it turned over with its five passengers. Harold Drasdo, who was riding in the large black box like a coffin which Jack had fitted to the side-car frame, used to tell the story with enthusiasm. Jack, cornering at speed, had called to them all to lean to the right instead of to the left; this unbalanced the machine and it turned over. The marks on the road where it had bounced along were obvious for a long while after the smash, but all escaped from the disaster with minor injuries.

Peter Greenwood was perhaps the maddest driver and had several miraculous escapes. On one occasion he misjudged a bend and went through a hawthorn fence at seventy miles per hour, to be revived by a passing motorist with a brandy flask and with no injuries but cuts and bruises. The machine he was driving was described as looking like a pram, so battered had it become.

My own experiences were dangerous. Five weekends running I accepted lifts to the Lakes, to end each time hitch-hiking home or in hospital after a crash. Harold Drasdo hit a wall in Langdale and fractured a wrist; Frank Cartwright hit the back of a car in Borrowdale and had a write-off the first weekend after buying a new machine; Alf Beanland, who was unmechanical to say the least, fell asleep driving along the road. In each accident I was on the pillion. To be fair, it was not always my driver's fault. In Frank Cartwright's accident, a car turned right without warning just as we overtook at twenty-five miles per hour.

On the fifth weekend of the series, a party of the Lads were riding in a convoy of six motorcycles. Without warning we came on a sharp bend, the leading machine, on which I was a passenger, skidded and deposited driver and myself on a grass bank with a jolt. This had a chain effect on the five riders behind us and one after the other they crashed. With great skill the pilots of each bike avoided other machines and bodies; one landed on the bank beside us, others went into a fence and two bodies cleared the fence altogether. Some farmhands scything grass behind the fence must have thought they were hearing the biggest pile-up in motoring history – grinding gears, screaming engines, squealing brakes, shouts, curses, rending metal – an impression no doubt heightened when two bodies, hurtling as if shot from a cannon, landed in their midst. Again there were no serious injuries, but the price to skin, clothes and machines was high.

After five smashes in five weekends, the lads decided I had become a jinx. The last driver I had ridden with had never so much as missed a gear, let alone crashed, before I climbed on to his pillion. No riding for me in future!

But the next weekend Peter Greenwood came to my rescue; he was not superstitious and was willing to give me a lift. I could even drive if I liked; little things like licences and my being underage didn't bother Peter. I doubt if he had a licence himself at that date. He made no allowances for wet roads, ice or snow and let nothing slow him down. We set out early on Saturday morning and before we reached Ingleton it was raining and sleeting; needless to say, we came off before we got to Kendal, and by the time we reached Langdale my nerve had gone completely. We hadn't hurt ourselves but I was so scared that I hitch-hiked home again first thing on Sunday morning. This was slower than riding with Peter, but I felt infinitely safer.

The lads were now travelling all over the British Isles to climb, and were among the first English climbers to realise the potential of Ireland, with new routes in the Mournes and Donegal. Scotland was popular with the group, and I had made friends with some of the younger members of the Creagh Dhu Club, in particular Mick Noon. The attitude of this unique Glasgow club was much to my liking; they knew poverty and had no illusions, they were high-spirited and their horseplay was sometimes outrageous, and they had courage and drive.

Mick invited me to visit the Cobbler with him, and I hitch-hiked north to meet him at Killermont bus station in Glasgow. He was waiting with a crowd of other Dhus who looked like the original *No Mean City* gang instead of a group of Scotland's best climbers. But these men of the Creagh Dhu were friends, and despite exaggerated stories about their roughness I knew they were good company. Mick whisked me on to a bus to Arrochar; as we drove through Glasgow I could appreciate the initiative of working-class climbers in escaping from their awful environment. It appeared to be a sea of slums and saloon bars, terribly depressing, but there was nothing depressed about my gregarious Glaswegian friends who joked and sang all the way to Arrochar.

We plodded up the Cobbler and spent an educative hour bouldering on the Nairnan stone, working at severe problems most of which were ascended with speed and ease by John Cunningham. Mick and I then had an enjoyable afternoon on routes on the Cobbler cliffs. I had a fright on a climb called the *Cat Crawl*; leading a pitch with rounded holds my boots slipped off the greasy rock, I slid down a couple of feet and snatched a hold as I was about to fall, somehow staying in contact with the rock. I was lucky. If I had fallen, I should have gone a long way as the pitch was totally unprotected.

That evening was an experience. More and more Dhus arrived as the day progressed and finally Hamish MacInnes; at this first meeting it was obvious that here was a rare character. We took up quarters in a derelict hut on the mountainside, after some persuasion on a padlock. Every Dhu sported a flat cap, and accents were so thick I could barely follow the conversation, but it soon became apparent to me that if the Dhus took a dislike to anyone it went deep.

However, they were not shy of telling stories against themselves, and I laughed until tears flowed at the misfortunes which had befallen Porridge, Sunshine, the Monster and co.

MacInnes was laying siege to a large unclimbed ceiling, undoubtedly the first major artificial climb in Britain. As befitted a man nicknamed MacPiton, he was armed with every conceivable aid known to climbing man at that time, many of which I had never seen and have never seen since. Despite a generous offer from one of his aides or gnomes to accompany them next morning on what would undoubtedly be 'the most important ascent in the history of the Cobbler, nay, of British mountaineering', I said goodbye and set forth to hitch-hike to Glencoe, to meet Neville Drasdo.

Neville and his brother Harold were Glencoe enthusiasts, and Neville had persuaded me that climbing in the Lakes or Wales must be inferior to this northern outpost. I arrived at the impressive Pass of Glencoe to find Neville in residence at Cameron's barn on the edge of the Inverness road. I had barely removed my rucksack before he had me walking up Buachaille Etive Mor to climb the Rannoch Wall. We ascended *Agag's Groove*, then did a Very Severe which yielded easily to gritstone hand-jamming, and decided that we had the measure of the wall. Next day came a shock when we elected to climb the *Red Slab* on the same face; it was graded Severe in rubbers and proved so difficult that we nearly had to retreat. On the crux pitch there was little protection and it was a long lead with the second poorly placed. Neville finally led this with a determined effort; after following him I could only suggest that Scottish standards seemed to vary widely. The Rannoch Wall is a superbly open place, and the *Red Slab* gave me a respect for Scottish climbing which has remained ever since.

One of the lads, Mike Dixon from near Leeds, had joined forces with an Aberdonian climber, Bill Brooker, and between them they made several outstanding first ascents in Skye, including the *Crack of Dawn*. Mike's enthusiasm was infectious and he convinced Billy Boston, Ernie Leach and myself that we should go there for our holidays in 1951. It was a long hitch-hike from Leeds but I had plenty of time, thanks to school summer holidays. I enjoyed travelling to the misty Isle, for Scotland was romantic and exciting to me then. My route took in Ailort and Morar, and on the way home I visited Kintail, Loch Ness and the Great Glen. The north-west couldn't fail to impress anyone who can see, but it was the characters I met on the road who enthralled me. They didn't think it strange that a young boy should be on the road; like them I was one of the travelling people. I met tramps and hawkers, tinkers and gypsies, and even long-gone berry-pickers. It was educative, to say the least, for my fifteen-year-old mind. One gentleman of the road took me poaching with him, fishing in a private loch where we were nearly caught. We escaped with our spoils, and the best part, as in so many Creagh Dhu stories, was lighting a fire and cooking the catch; fish has never tasted better.

The weather on Skye was atrocious, but there was at that time the comfort of the MacRaes' barn to offset the damp conditions. We had a happy time in Glen Brittle, enlivened by meeting Mike Dixon, Bill Brooker and another young Aberdonian, Tom Patey. Tom, then only a teenager, was a medical student in Aberdeen. It was obvious that he intended great things, and it was not surprising that went he on to impressive Alpine and Himalayan ascents. A man of many and varied talents, he kept us amused with his thoughtful wit, musical abilities and interesting stories.

In spite of the weather we climbed a respectable number of routes, including the *Cioch Direct*, *Amphitheatre Wall*, *White Slab* and so forth. Notwithstanding Skye's rain, bogs and midges, the interplay of mountain and sea views, mists swirling in corries, sunsets, the blueness of the sky on our single good-weather day, the roughness of gabbro, the jagged Cuillin ridge and the green of Glen Brittle, all vividly impressed themselves on my young mind. For many years I was afraid to return in case reality should prove that my boyhood memories were.

In 1952 I started to work, leaving school in despair and disgrace. I was given employment by a Leeds firm of printers who intended to make an executive of me, but I cared little for such promises. Some of the Bradford Lads were anti-work, anti-authority, antisocial even, and I was one of these. We wanted to be free of society's strictures, to climb and travel, to bum around. One of the Lads grew his hair shoulder-length, gave up work when he felt like it, went wherever fancy or fortune took him; George Elliot anticipated the beatnik philosophy in this country by many years.

I read *Annapurna* by Maurice Herzog when it was published and was filled with admiration for the adventure, but it seemed too far from our mountain reality in 1952 when working-class boys didn't go to the Himalaya. Greater influences were *Cannery Row* by John Steinbeck, Davies' *The Autobiography of a Super-Tramp* and, most important, *Always a Little Further* by Alastair Borthwick. This was 'our' book, written about the climbers and outdoor people of Scotland during the grim depression years in the 1920s and 1930s. Somehow they had managed, without money and with little food and equipment, to escape to the mountains, to use their wits in overcoming terrible material difficulties. We saw ourselves as their modern counterparts and understood the veiled message of the stories that if you wanted to climb and explore, all you really needed was the will.

The Lads as a group were now at the height of their powers and 1952 was the year of their best achievements. That summer Peter Greenwood teamed up with Arthur Dolphin. We began to visit Scafell regularly, walking from Langdale, and on successive weekends in May Arthur and Peter made two new routes on the East Buttress, *Pegasus* and *Hell's Groove*, which have since been dubbed classic. Peter got up the first pitch of *Hell's Groove*, which had defeated earlier parties, by one of the most gymnastic pieces of climbing I have ever seen, and this spurred Arthur to solve the rest of this famous course. I sat and watched the whole ascent, sunbathing with our basking team led by massive Doug Hayes. They were a group within a group; without ambition they only climbed when sunbathing was impracticable and their motto was static relaxation.

None of us could afford cameras and few, if any, photographs exist of those eventful days, but I can still see Dolphin as he confidently worked his way up the cliff face, his white hair making him easy to follow. His control and skill were unforgettable.

The discovery of Raven Crag in Thirlmere, untouched and bristling with overhangs and vegetation, switched the focus of attention to that valley. The nearby Castle Rock in St John's in the Vale was combed for unclimbed rock; Harold Drasdo and Don Hopkin pioneered a fine route which they called the Barbican. During this climb Harold noticed the possibility of a direct route up the steepest section of the face.

Harold Drasdo, although not physically powerful nor endowed with high natural ability, was the best technician and most tenacious leader among the lads. Once he got to grips with a problem he would go on trying until he was successful or exhausted. He was also a master of the new and revolutionary protection techniques of utilising carefully placed and contrived running belays.

Secretly, Harold made plans for the new direct route on Castle Rock; with his brother Neville he gardened part of the climb and got up the first pitches. He then took me into his confidence and asked me to second him on the actual ascent, mainly because one of the first items I had bought with my earnings at work had been a nylon rope! It was only medium weight but 150 feet long, and the new climb would obviously need what was then an unusual length of rope.

We hitch-hiked separately to Thirlmere, keeping our plans secret in the best climbing tradition, and spent the night in a barn near the crag. From the scree leading to the base of the cliff, Harold pointed out the line he hoped to take; I was impressed. The morning was unusually bright, with autumn beginning to show over the Vale of St John and away down the valley into Thirlmere.

We tied on under the North Crag, the largest face of Castle Rock, and Harold set out. Looking up the face I secretly hoped his enthusiasm would be thwarted before he had got too high. He climbed quickly, first across a small slab, then bridging up a steep groove where he placed several running belays with his usual expertise. Soon the first lead was accomplished, with Harold already high up the face and belaying himself to a fine yew tree.

The North Crag is uniformly steep and overhanging; its bold aspect is barely equalled in Lakeland. But Castle Rock is a most deceptive cliff, its overhangs and the gangways which cut through them often give the feeling of extreme climbing even when in fact the standard is relatively easy. There are often large incut holds as I discovered when I followed Harold, to join him at the tree.

'From here,' he proudly announced, 'we employ an unusual method. First we climb the tree to its top branch, then launch ourselves at the overhang above, and climb it direct.'

'No kidding!' I gasped.

'Actually it's easy. We came this far the other week, our kid romped up it!' Harold assured me.

I hastily belayed and watched Harold shin up the tree and then from its topmost limb do exactly as he said – launch himself from the swaying mass on to the overhang. A short struggle and he was on a ledge in the middle of the overhanging upper face of the cliff. Here out of a fissure in the rock grew another tree to which Harold made fast. A feature of Castle Rock are its trees, which grow in the most unusual places; so I thought as I struggled with the yew. I was then sixteen and still undersized, and from the highest branch I couldn't reach any holds on the overhang above my head.

'Get the tree moving,' commanded Harold. Obediently I got the tree swaying out from the rock face, arched under my body. Without intending to move, I suddenly catapulted upwards from the tree and found myself clutching the overhang, my fingers curled on incut holds.

'Give me a tight rope!' I yelled.

'Can't, it'll pull you off, it's running sideways,' came the reply. 'Get a knee on.'

I scrabbled at the rock, hanging over a hundred feet of space. Just as my strength gave out, I swung right on to better holds and managed to get a knee on a ledge. 'Phew! I nearly came off,' I croaked as I joined Harold. 'Where to now?'

'Up there.' Harold pointed to a narrowing gangway which disappeared on the overhanging face to our left. 'Then round the corner, on the other side of the overhang. It's only vertical round there,' he added, tongue in cheek. He was always the optimist, capable of convincing himself and everyone else of the feasibility of any plan, especially in bad weather. A great man for the melodramatic, he was savouring every moment of our struggles.

Looking up the proposed finale, I wished again that my leader might be turned back. Roping off appeared preferable to what was above our heads. But Harold had reconnoitred carefully on his previous visits and set off again with confidence. He went up the gangway in good style, and where it merged into the face reached the base of a flake; this appeared loose but Harold confounded my opinion by laybacking up its edge and then fixing a running belay round its whole girth. He jammed himself behind the flake for a rest, looking down on me like a bird of prey, then swung round the corner of the overhang and on to the vertical face out of sight. Communication became difficult. First the rope was dragging at him, then it moved more freely through my hands, then it stopped. He had come to a niche, perhaps seventy feet above, and was trying to rest. I could hear him shout something about 'no alternative', then the bang, bang, bang as he placed a piton; another shout: 'Watch the rope!' and he was moving again. Inch by inch the coils ran out, then the last few feet went at a gallop and he was on top.

I followed with great difficulty and arrived at the top full of admiration. 'Dras' later had the satisfaction of seeing his new climb, which we named 'the *North Crag Eliminate*', become another classic of the Lake District.

By 1952 it was obvious that the Rock and Ice Club was the outstanding group of climbers in Britain. There was a friendly attitude between all the groups of active young climbers, and on our visits to Wales we were always made welcome by the Rock and Ice on their home ground in Llanberis Pass. Through this contact we kept abreast with their latest new routes.

Each year Joe Brown's prowess became more incredible; he is truly a genius of rock climbing. He provided my most vivid memory of that year, on the day we refused to climb despite the long hitch-hike to Wales and the waste of precious mountain time.

The rain was driving horizontally across the pass as we cowered in our rude shelter, the road menders' hut, alas no more. This was forbidden by the law and at least one of the Rock and Ice had been arrested for staying there. But that small shed of tin and wood was our only shelter, providing a home to many an impecunious climber, and there we clung on, living in squalor, in spite of persecution, happy amidst the boulders below Dinas Cromlech.

We settled down to a day of cards, playing 'Sergeant Major' and telling stories. Alfie Beanland, my companion, was in his element as a raconteur of irresistible humour. Late in the afternoon the door was heaved open, knocking aside the jamming boulders intended to exclude the police and other intruders, and revealing Joe Brown and P.H. White, known to us as Gee-Gee. They were dripping with water, soaked through but looking smugly happy.

'Get wet hitch-hiking?' we asked.

The imperturbable Brown: 'No, climbing.'

Mild interest from the card players: 'Where?'

Brown: 'Ogwen.'

'The Slabs?'

Brown: 'No, *Suicide Wall*.'

'*Suicide Wall*?'

Brown: '*Suicide Wall*.'

'Jesus! What was it like?'

Brown: 'Hard.'

'What was it like, Gee-Gee?'

'Like Joe says. Hard.'

Such was the graphic description we received of what was then the most difficult climb in Wales.

Harold Drasdo and I had discovered a big line on Dove Crag in the Lake District; we had tried it and failed. I mentioned this to Joe and he and Don Whillans, his equally brilliant climbing partner, came north and completed the ascent of *Dovedale Groove* which was to go unrepeated for nearly ten years. In those days there was still plenty of space and so many obvious big lines waiting to be climbed that one didn't mind passing on information to friends.

Among my own climbs in North Wales that summer were *Bow-shaped Slab* on Cloggy and *Slape* on Clogwyn y Crochan, but I think the best was *Central Groove* on Llech Ddu which I did with Don Hopkin who led most of the way, wearing clinker nails in pouring rain.

This was the era of the Bradford Lads' bus trips; in winter they were better than hitch-hiking, safer than motorcycles, and nearly as cheap. One of the lads was fully occupied planning and organising these riotous affairs, which became over-publicised; often we were joined by other people wanting away at weekends – potholers, hikers, travelling salesmen, skiers and even, on one occasion, escaping criminals. Usually our clients left our bus declaring: 'Never again!'

On one occasion the high jinks brought the law on us. Our horseplay in a cafe at Ingleton had upset the proprietor and the removal of his six-foot 'CAFE' sign resulted in our arrest at Kendal, stopped by the police with a Chicago-style roadblock. The removers of the sign intended to replace it on the return journey, but it was hanging down the centre aisle of the bus and we were caught red-handed. The police were understandably not keen to have a busload in their cells, and the local inspector asked the culprits to own up. But our antisocial faction soon had him crimson with anger with their facetious remarks. He threatened and blustered and in the end pleaded that a single culprit should confess. Peter Greenwood magnanimously declared he would own up; this didn't suit the boys and one by one they disputed his claim: 'It wasn't him, it was me!' The inspector quickly recorded Peter's name and address and thankfully made off into the night, clutching the sign and the confession and ignoring shouts of 'Flog him!' 'Bring back the birch!' defiantly hurled after him. Peter was duly fined ten shillings at the next assizes and the episode made a fine story for the Wall End regulars.

Another famous bus trip left Leeds at Easter bound for Ben Nevis; one of the Lads was working in a brewery and with the profits of other excursions he bought vast quantities of half-price beer for us. We took delivery of this on the pavement outside the GPO and the loading of it in City Square, Leeds, during the rush hour caused a sensation. Six hefty climbers with ice axes had to guard it while the bus found somewhere to park. The ale occupied every nook and cranny of the vehicle; soon under its influence a sing-song was in progress and the overloaded bus carried the happiest group of climbers to head north for a long time.

We elected to go to Scotland via the Lake District; on the way Jack Bradley and Peter Greenwood decided to go for a sail on Lake Windermere. Laughing and singing, we searched for a craft; Peter and Jack climbed aboard a large rowing boat, a hefty push and off they floated. It was raining slightly and a strong squally wind was blowing. 'Help!' came a voice from the lake, very sober now.

'Row back in!' we yelled.

'We can't, there's no oars!' This caused consternation; there were outsiders with us who didn't want to wait, didn't want the police, refused to let us call out the lifeboat. In the end, the problem was solved by dumping their rucksacks at the water's edge, shouting this news to the drifters, and driving on. Peter confessed later that it had been miserable in the boat, but after a few hours they had drifted close enough to wade ashore and subsequently enjoyed a good holiday in the Lake District while we suffered abominable conditions in Scotland.

When bus trips faded in popularity, back came the inevitable motorcycle and another clash with the law. A fringe member of Lads, an antisocial character known as the Pale Man, not wanting to be left out as a road-burner stole a new and particularly speedy motorbike. None of us knew the machine to be stolen; the culprit even acquired a forged logbook to prove his ownership. Many months after the theft the police traced the bike. George Elliot had borrowed it to run a friend home when a police car began to chase him with wailing siren as George sped along the open road towards Bradford. George decided he would show the police some fast driving and accelerated away from his pursuer. A general police alert was put out and more and more squad cars joined the chase; it became, in George's words, 'a real laugh'. He rode into Forster Square railway station, intending to shake off his pursuers by driving through the yard and out by the goods entrance, but some well-meaning citizen blocked the escape with his car and George, pillion passenger and machine were arrested.

George was surprised to hear the machine had been stolen and protested his innocence. The bike belonged to the Pale Man and he was with the Lads at such and such a place. The police checked on this but the Pale Man had disappeared. They let George and his passenger go, pending further enquiries, but the machine was taken into custody. This action was considered an affront by some of the Lads; what a great scheme it would be to steal the bike back from the police! This our commando faction did, after much plotting and scheming, by wheeling it away under the noses of the law. The spiriting away was no easy task as the tank of the bike had been drained, and it was a tired expedition which, after wheeling it several miles, carrying it over walls, pushing it up hills, gave it back to the Pale Man.

When retribution finally came, it was swift. The Pale Man was caught brazenly riding the stolen machine and many of the Lads were implicated. Some had swapped parts for their own bikes, one had crashed the stolen motorcycle, there was no licence, no insurance. I myself had driven it down the Langdale valley a few times, and had once been spotted with three passengers aboard.

So many climbers attended the ensuing trial that it was like Wall End Barn. The magistrate had a difficult job, annoyed by cries of abuse from the spectators' gallery; he sent the Pale Man to jail, fined several of the Lads and cautioned others, and ended by clearing the court. I was not called before the court because of my youth; the decision upset me, for the publicity of the case ensured fame for the guilty and innocent. It was with genuine disappointment that I missed the ordeal.

One of my best holidays was spent with Alf Beanland at Ogwen. Alf had greatly improved in health. When I first knew him I several times thought he was going to die in his asthmatic spasms, and when he was ill with TB I visited him and found him hardly able to talk. Now he was full of high ambitions; he had already done many of the classic ascents of Zermatt and Chamonix and was building up his experience for the *grandes courses* of the Alps.

Alf believed in speed on easy routes and broken ground and often soloed climbs, maintaining that a climber should be capable of soloing nearly to his leading standard when roped. Another of his practices was descending climbs. On one of our days together we soloed thirteen climbs, including several Severes and one Very Severe. I followed immediately behind the thin-chested and asthmatic Beanland, a human spider in appearance, long limbed and tall, and many years my senior. I baulked at route fourteen – *Alpha* on Glyder Fach – and in fact had difficulty following on the end of the rope Alf threw down to me. Once on the top I expounded at length my lack of enthusiasm for Alfie's theories, to the mockery and laughter of my mentor.

During this holiday we met Chris Bonington who had hitch-hiked from London. He had recently left school and was burning with enthusiasm for climbing. He teamed up with a friend of ours, Mick Noon of the Creagh Dhu, and we decided to go out together next day on Tryfan. The weather was bad, but Alf and I arranged to meet Chris and Mick on Terrace Wall and set out ahead to climb *Munich*, the route pioneered by the Austro-German climbers who visited Wales in the 1930s.

The rock was wet and greasy and mist swirled in the deep gully. I suggested retreat but Alfie was bubbling with good spirits. I have never since climbed with anyone who could inspire me to effort as he could; I had absolute trust in him and had only to think of his struggles with indifferent health to try the harder. He coaxed me into leading climbs I would not have led with any other person; I led through with him on *Bow-shaped Slab* and led him up *Unicorn* on Carreg Wastad and on many other climbs then considered hard leads, although at that time I was sixteen.

I found myself up the first pitch of *Munich* and taking in his rope before I had time to argue further. We went on slowly but comfortably, then came down to the Terrace Wall to meet the others. There was no sign of anyone else on the mountain; perhaps they hadn't bothered? 'Good Lord!' ejaculated Alfie as we sat eating a tin of pears. 'There's a lot of blood about, and it looks fresh to me.' It was all over the terrace we were sitting on; I felt uneasy, for blood sometimes makes me faint. It led off the terrace and on to the descent route towards Ogwen.

'We ought to go and see what's happened,' I volunteered. We raced down the blood trail to Ogwen Cottage; whoever it was had at least got down successfully.

Other climbers told us that Chris had fallen off *Scars Climb* and had been rushed to hospital. As he said later, he had started laybacking up a crack and when it closed in, he had tried to keep laybacking instead of climbing the wall to the side of the crack. He had fallen over sixty feet but had been held by Mick Noon who had himself been badly burnt by the rope on the neck, of all places. When Chris returned to us that evening, he looked like an Eastern potentate with his head heavily bandaged; he had several deep cuts and abrasions but mercifully was not seriously injured. Next day he insisted on following us up some boulder problems, using one good leg and a walking stick. Alfie wryly prophesied, 'With enthusiasm like that, he'll either end up dead or famous!'

In 1953 news came of the ascent of Everest. This meant as little to us personally as reading *Annapurna* had to me, and for the same reason: no working-class climber had taken part and for most of us even the Alps were beyond our means. But later this event was to have great significance for some of us. From the profits of the Everest film, from books, from lectures and so on, came the money to set up the Mount Everest Foundation. The Foundation provided much of the financial support for the expeditions I myself subsequently took part in.

As the summer approached I climbed a lot with Arthur Dolphin, who was preparing for a long Alpine season. He had recently become engaged to Marie Ball, the only woman member of our crowd. They intended to live in the Lake District after their marriage when Arthur returned from the Alps. They hoped to set up house on the Cumberland side of the mountains, and Arthur had accepted a post with the Atomic Energy Authority at Calder Hall. He was in the process of writing a new guidebook to the Scafell group, and had in mind many new ascents on the East Buttress. I spent midweek evenings in his company, bouldering and gritstone climbing, and at weekends climbing difficult routes or flogging over Lakeland peaks. I have never since been with anyone who stood so much above the pettiness of lesser beings, completely without jealousy or rancour.

In July I went with a group of the Lads to Wales, to camp at Cloggy and Llanberis Pass. I remember the fight we had on *Pigott's Climb*, the wetting on *Pedestal Crack*, the bloodletting on the holly tree on the *Ivy Sepulchre* of Dinas Cromlech and the thin edge of *Phantom Rib*. We left after ten days' enjoyable climbing, a close band of friends, but never again were things to be the same for the Bradford Lads.

Next weekend I was just leaving home on Friday night to go climbing when the shock came: banner headlines in our local paper saying, 'Yorkshire climber killed in Mont Blanc range – Arthur Dolphin falls to his death'. It couldn't be true. To my youthful hero-worship Arthur was indestructible. But there was no mistake. Killed on an easy descent on 25 July 1953, Arthur Dolphin, whose skill and grace on steep rocks had made me want to climb, was dead.

I hitch-hiked to Langdale and tried to hide my feelings when I met the rest of the Lads. At once I fell out with Peter Greenwood, whose regard for Arthur was as deep as my own. Peter picked on something I said, trying to cover the tragedy with empty words, and only the intervention of an older and wiser climber saved a bitter row.

We didn't realise it then, but this was the end of an era. The Lads were sent hither and thither by fate. Peter Greenwood moved to live in Keswick, then founded a successful business in Carlisle; Jack Bradley started to build his business empire; Harold Drasdo, Neville Drasdo, Alf Beanland, Billy Boston and others studied and struggled their way into colleges and universities. George Elliot joined the Merchant Navy, Don Hopkin moved to Morecambe to better his job prospects and to be nearer the Lake District. My age group had to face the disruption of National Service for two years. When my time came for registration, I had to decide whether to get it over with or be deferred. I should have registered as a conscientious objector, but I was too naive to pass any examining board, for my objections were easier felt than expressed. I decided to go into the army immediately and forget objections and deferment. I wanted to hate my forced servitude and, as Harold Drasdo had warned me it would, it taught me how to hate properly.

Arthur Dolphin's death affected us all but we never talked about it. I did see Marie a lot until I reported for the army and again immediately after my demob. Typically Arthur had gone back to the foot of the south face of the Géant to collect his and his companion's equipment from the place where they had bivouacked before their successful ascent. Initially, he fell only a short distance but a sharp stone pierced his skull and brain and he then rolled hundreds of feet down easy ground. Completely unselfish, he was the best influence a young person could ever have. I shall never forget my good fortune on the day I walked as a small boy into Hangingstone Quarry to see for the first time this white-haired athlete in action – a knight in shining armour.

2   The Rock and Ice – Past: A Gentleman's Gentleman

'Oh, wherefore come ye forth in triumph from the north?'
(Macaulay)

A curious fact about British climbers since the war has been that, with the no-table exception of the Bradford Lads, when two or more of them go regularly to the hills together they form a club. At present there are more than 160 clubs affiliated to the British Mountaineering Council and dozens of others outside that body. This situation is unparalleled in world mountaineering, for most other countries have national clubs broken into sections for administrative pur-poses. Our system has disadvantages and is often criticised, but it has helped to foster the mixture of individualism, parochialism and eccentricity from which has sprung the post-war progress and achievement of British climbing.

Most of our established clubs had a traditional and conservative attitude, and some still looked for social qualifications from prospective members as well as climbing ability; to many young men starting their mountain careers this outlook was repugnant. In return, many members of the established clubs viewed with open distaste the post-war rush into the mountains by youth, in retrospect an understandable reaction, for their clubs had carved for them-selves little empires or spheres of influence, and the sudden influx of tyros from a different social background, with a complete lack of respect for existing memberships and traditions, threatened a preserve which had once belonged to them alone.

Later, changing social and economic conditions swept away prejudice and barriers, to bring about a marriage of new and old, age and youth. But the new-wave climbers of the immediate post-war years would not have been happy amidst the stuffiness and formality of traditional clubs, so they formed associ-ations of their own making, with few rules, a small intimate membership and no social qualifications, held together by activity in the mountains. This type of club already had successful forerunners in the first mass outdoor move-ments during the depression years of the 1920s and 1930s; these, of which Glasgow's Creagh Dhu is an outstanding example, had established a tradition of initiative, endeavour and hard physical living amongst the hills: not tough by choice but through sheer financial necessity.

Typical of the early post-war years was the now defunct Valkyrie Club.

It had its origins in the long-established Derby Mercury Cycling and Outdoor Club, rooted deep in the working-class movements of an earlier generation. The Mercury has produced from its membership Olympic cyclists, national basketball players, amateur boxing champions, skiers of renown, and climbers who have written their names indelibly in the annals of the Peak District and elsewhere. From this last group came the impetus to form the Valkyrie; based on Derby, with a clubroom in that city, it had a meteoric rise in the climbing firmament, its reputation being built on first ascents by many leaders and also on a leavening of men who may not have been front-rank climbers but who excelled in all-round sportsmanship, from gymnastics to cycle racing. This was to be expected of an offshoot of the Mercury which organises the famous Dovedale Dash cross-country race, produces a professional-standard pantomime each winter, and has seen members collecting medals at the Empire Games.

The Valkyrie quickly grew from strength to strength; it could have dominated British rock climbing, but equally swiftly it brought about its own demise, beset by the difficulties and organising problems which face any small and active club of personality. It had a short energetic life and pointed the way to a mode of living and hard climbing which was to be an inspiration and yardstick for many young aspirants.

The Rock and Ice Club was formed in Manchester during the summer of 1951. It has been said that it was the direct successor of the Valkyrie, but this is not correct. The real connection between the two was more tenuous; several people were members of both, and the clubs were related more by contacts than by imitation. It is true that the Manchester club followed the same pioneering tradition, but it was no more the direct successor than were half a dozen other small clubs into which the Valkyrie membership dispersed.

The formation of the Rock and Ice Club was the work of Ron Moseley, Doug Belshaw, Merrick (Slim) Sorrell, the Greenall brothers, Pete and Ray, Pete White and Joe Brown; it rapidly developed standards and climbing initiative uniquely its own. Joe Brown, always an individualist, was against belonging to any club; he had joined the Valkyrie because of friendship ties, and such ties again made him agree to go along with the others in the foundation of the new club, thus unwittingly becoming the symbol of its future greatness. With Joe Brown in its ranks the group quickly became legend. The first new member was Don Whillans who joined in September 1951; in October Don Chapman, Don Cowan, Nat Allen and Dick White were admitted. The first three, like Brown and Sorrell, had been Valkyrie members but their membership of the new club meant much more than the continuation of successful partnerships; Nat Allen and Don Cowan in particular had good Alpine experience and they helped to nurture amongst the Rock and Ice the wider horizons of alpinism.

The year 1952 brought further able climbers into the club in the persons of Eric Worthington, Les Wright, Norman Rimmer, Thos Waghorn, Don Roscoe and Eric Price. By the end of 1952 the club was at full strength and from then onwards, until its disbandment in July 1958, only a small number of new members were admitted, which was a reason for its eventual downfall. Ron Cummaford was made a member in 1953, Alan Taylor in 1954, and in 1955 Joe (Mortimer) Smith, Fred (Neddy) Goff, and Peter Hoy, who died tragically a few months later in Malta on National Service. In 1956 Johnny Sutherland joined, and lastly Vin Betts.

Officials elected at the club's first AGM were honorary secretary Doug Belshaw, honorary treasurer Ron Moseley, meets secretary Slim Sorrell, committee Pete White, Joe Brown and Don Whillans. Contrary to opinion, the club was a properly constituted body from its inception and associated itself with the work and ideals of the British Mountaineering Council; from 1952 onwards its name appeared in the list of clubs furnished by that body, but it was precluded from membership because of its small size.

Although the club had a constitution and elected officials, it was from the first lighthearted and spontaneous, with little or no organisation; club meets, for instance, were often impromptu affairs based on the prospect of making new routes at any particular crag or centre. The Rock and Ice leaders had a cunning eye for the advantages offered by the new equipment now on the market – nylon rope and slings and reliable karabiners – and were ahead of others in using these aids to protect a lead and thus to enable them to go much nearer their limits on hard pitches.

To some observers the club's reputation was built and earned by just two of its members, two climbers of genius, Joe Brown and Don Whillans, but as an independent outsider who knew the club throughout its existence, I feel that this is not correct. Whillans and Brown may have been the arrow's tip, but the weight behind the head was often the work of other members. The Rock and Ice was as harmonious a whole as any climbing association can expect to be; outstanding climbers are rugged individualists, but with the odd exception there were no major disputes.

My own first contact with the Rock and Ice as a club, though I had known individual members for a long time, was at Easter, 1952, when the club organised a bus trip to Glencoe. At the last minute there were vacant places and through Slim Sorrell I managed a lift. My own destination was Ben Nevis but through travelling on that bus I learnt something of Rock and Ice activities and plans. My seat companion was Don Whillans; although I had met him once, this was the first time I was in the company of the Salford hard man. The young Don Whillans gave an even younger Yorkshireman some strong words; I had not at that date met his equal for spikiness or caustic wit and was completely disarmed by his manner. Don was then a teenager, but his assurance, confidence and solid common sense belied his years. Although small, he had immense shoulders and forearms, and a shock of fair hair crowned a face which had north-country realism as its very expression. His movements spoke of physical power and fitness which in maturity were to be the springboard of a great mountaineer.

I first met Don at Whitsuntide, 1951, when I was walking down from Clogwyn Du'r Arddu; he was walking up on his own, and as we drew level he stopped in his tracks and stared hard at me for a moment. Perhaps he couldn't believe such a babe in arms to be a climber; I looked younger than I was.

'Ahh-doo,' he slowly came out with as greeting. I stood transfixed, unable to catch the utterance of this pocket-sized Hercules.

'Ahh-doo!' he slowly reiterated.

I could see his temper rising and stammered a 'Hullo', then turned and bolted down the Llanberis track.

'Bleeding stuck up!' I heard him spit out as I took flight. I was not allowed to forget this incident when we met again on the bus.

Over the years when I came to know Don better, as a close friend, I realised he was a man of many moods and talents, a larger-than-life character who shapes his own destiny and has no illusions about fame or his own or anybody else's worth. About climbing he is ruthlessly honest and has never cared a fig for popular opinion. Such attributes plus his example and climbing genius have made him the most talked-about climber of his or any other generation. Stories about his exploits abound, some true, some half true, some mere fabrication. I could fill a book with incidents that have occurred while I have been with Don, both climbing and on other occasions when arrogant or argumentative individuals have met with sterner resistance than they bargained for. Most of the stories are not mine to tell and would best be recounted by the one person in a position to judge their truth, Don himself. But there is a story for which I can vouch and which does concern me as well as Don and other Rock and Ice personalities.

Towards the end of the Rock and Ice era most of us had improved our standard of living sufficiently to be able to afford four-wheel transport; as a rising young executive I had a large van, the biggest vehicle among us, which frequently carried a load of members. We used to race each other over parts of the drive to the crags, and my van carried a bugle which my passengers would blow at any of our friends whom we happened to overtake. Others too had means of announcing their presence on the road; Joe Brown, for instance, had a hunting horn. However, on this occasion we were not racing our friends but were returning home late on Sunday evening after a weekend in Llanberis Pass. My passengers were Mortimer, Doug Verity, Don Whillans and his wife Audrey, and I was driving along between Cerrigydrudion and Ruthin when the incident began. On a particularly hilly and twisty bit of road, a motorcycle combination with a large sidecar overtook me on an acute bend, then cut in so violently that I had to brake hard to avoid hitting its back end; the driver turned and gave us a rude sign! That was enough, and we shot after him. On the next straight of the road I overtook him and as we roared past Doug Verity leaned out of the window and blasted at the driver with our bugle; watching in the mirror I saw him nearly fall off his bike with surprise. A short way on Morty and Don, keeping lookout through the back windows, reported that the combination had caught us up and was about to overtake again, and urged me to go faster to avoid this ignominy. But the challenge was not to be staved off and again we were passed on a sharp bend, the driver shaking his fist at me, then cutting in and forcing me to brake hard once more. This was more than enough! On the next straight, my engine at peak revolutions, I overtook, and as we screamed past Doug gave him another blast on the bugle. This cat-and-mouse game went on for several miles until finally the motorcycle, which was high-powered, with a last defiant gesture from its helmeted and leathered driver, left us trailing and zoomed away.

Half an hour later we stopped in Ruthin for tea; as I was pulling on the brake a hand suddenly shot through the open driving window and grabbed me round the throat. I had just time to catch a glimpse of the biggest man I have ever seen, in black racing leathers and crash helmet, towering above the van. His hand was immense and he had me at his mercy. Don immediately grasped the situation and aimed a punch through the window at my assailant which the motorcyclist simply countered by blocking it with my head. The back door of the van was locked, Morty and Don couldn't get out that way and, to make matters worse, had been sitting for comfort's sake in their stockinged feet. Doug Verity charged round the offside of the van, with Don and Morty following through the passenger door. Doug grabbed the driver's spare arm; he is well over six feet but he only came to the giant's shoulder and it was all he could do to hang on to his arm. Don leapt into action, punching like the proverbial steam engine, but the driver in his protective leathers was unaffected and continued squeezing the life out of me and wrestling with Doug. Morty ran behind the man and kicked his backside – to no avail; in his stockinged feet Morty's kicks made no impression.

'Give me my boots, Audrey, and I'll give him a dose of Timpson!' Don rushed back inside the van. 'Mortimer, look after my watch!' he ordered, unstrapping his most prized possession. All this came to me through a haze; I was going under, the inside of the van was spinning and my face, Morty declared afterwards, resembled the bird which was forced to say 'Uncle!' Don dived out of the van once more, bootlaces trailing, but ready for the fray. Wham! He landed into the giant's shins with his climbing boots, the colossus grunted in pain and let go of my throat. Don, now in full temper, battled with this freed hand while Doug kept up his strife on the other; Morty kept running behind the driver and kicking his bottom, still in his stockinged feet. Eventually I managed to climb out of the van and asked the giant who the hell he was and what the hell was his game. At this he stopped fighting, Doug relaxed his hold but Don continued his aggression, dancing about like a fencing master, throwing punches and kicking out with his feet.

'You tried to drive me off the road, you're a crowd of maniacs,' he shouted between swatting at Don as if he was a fly. A crowd had gathered at a safe distance; this was livelier than chapel and all were obviously enjoying the battle.

'You cut in on me first,' I insisted.

'What was that noise you were making as you overtook me?' he demanded.

'Take off yer leathers and I'll fight yer,' growled Don, with Audrey holding on to his shoulders, trying to calm him down.

'You'll fight me! You'll fight me!' roared the giant in astonishment, then he rocked with laughter. 'I could handle you lot with an arm behind my back, you're a lot of runts!' Slowly turning on his heels, he disdainfully walked to his machine, kicked over the motor and roared away up the road, never to be seen by us again.

Although I am of a pacific nature, always ready to appease, abhorring violence and in any case too weak physically to get involved in it if possible, I wouldn't have missed that evening's episode for the world.

In January, 1954, I was called for two years' National Service in the Royal Army Pay Corps. The idea of wearing a uniform and being regimented disgusted me, and it was with reluctance and a heavy heart that I bade farewell to the Bradford Lads and reported to the Corps Infantry Training Centre at Devizes. The weather was unusually severe that winter and on the open ground of Salisbury Plain most of our training activities were hit by blizzards. The stupidity, bad organisation and lack of imagination were unbelievable, and our whole training dissolved into farce. Whatever was organised – drill, rifle range or physical training – always ended in a disorganised rabble buffeted by raging snowstorms. Our commissioned officers were still fighting the First World War and our non-commissioned officers were just as bad; if only the taxpayer could have seen how his money was being used! The Pay Corps enlisted recruits from many avenues of civilian life; besides the expected numbers of pay clerks and accountants our platoon had men from society's more unusual occupations, such as a Welsh opera singer, a professional boxer with knock knees, a trumpet player from a dance band and a jockey, among others. Between us we formed what our sergeant could only declare was 'the living end'. It was copybook of what one expected of service and training in the army under non-commissioned rank and resulted in the firm opinion that such a type of National Service was the biggest time-waster ever devised for the young men of this country; I was pleased when National Service was abolished, and I hope it is never reinstated in that form.

At the end of the fourth week of training our platoon was paraded in front of the company officer, who read out detail about a posting in Manchester for which he wanted volunteers. I had been warned by friends of the three important rules to ensure an uneventful army life: always to occupy the middle rank on forming up into platoon, to register as a Catholic whatever my beliefs and, most important of all, never, ever, to volunteer for anything. Volunteers on this occasion had to meet certain requirements: grammar school and school certificate; then there was another mention of the magic name, Manchester, home of my friends the Rock and Ice, Mecca and Jerusalem combined to any luckless climber soldiering on Salisbury Plain. I wavered a moment, struggling with my conscience, others were putting up their hands; I stuck up my hand with the rest and was promptly accepted.

My change of fortune from the rigours of basic training to the homely delights of Longsight, Manchester, was a miracle to me then. I was installed in a civilian billet, looked after by an elderly landlady and her charming daughter, and worked in an office from 8.30 a.m. to 5.30 p.m. Conditions in the Manchester Pay Office were the equivalent of civilian employment; my immediate superiors were Civil Service personnel and they had little respect for army bull and regulations.

My first night in Manchester I set out to locate the Rock and Ice; it was a Tuesday evening and I knew that the club met on Tuesdays at Ronnie Moseley's parents' house. At this weekly meeting members discussed plans for holidays, drank pints of tea and made transport arrangements for the following weekend; it had become a feature of Rock and Ice life and members who lived outside the district, such as Nat Allen, fifty-two miles away in Derby, had been known to make the journey to be present.

I had no idea where Ron lived except that it was in Levenshulme and I tramped round that Manchester suburb till late in the evening, stopping passers-by and enquiring if they knew anybody called Moseley. I had almost given up hope when I ran into someone who knew Ronnie personally and directed me to his home in Broom Lane.

Timidly I knocked on the door; from within came hoots of laughter, sure evidence the Rock and Ice were there in force. Ron answered the door and stared in disbelief at me in uniform. 'Good Lord, young Dennis in a monkey jacket! Not another Pownall's commando? Come in, come in!' Moseley's grin was ear to ear as he ushered me in; he had done his National Service in the Pay Corps too and had worked in the Pay Office at Longsight; his billet had been his parents' home and he had held the mysterious post of unit artist. We were known locally as Pownall's daisy commandos because the building we occupied had been the Daisy Works, belonging to the firm of Pownall before requisition by the War Office.

In the Moseleys' back room one could hardly move for members of the Rock and Ice, some of whom I hardly knew. However, I was pleased to see Joe Brown, the ever-present cigarette in hand, sitting like a Buddha in the middle of the throng and telling one of his hair-raising stories, to the accompaniment of comment from the audience. I have deliberately used an Eastern figure to describe Joe; he has always appeared to me to have a slightly oriental manner, perhaps acquired in the Far East during National Service. His physical appearance is powerfully Sherpa-like and his poker face would on occasion do justice to any Asian. Once Joe is among close acquaintants and relaxes, he is a raconteur of talent, but no person or topic was sacred amongst the group and although Joe might enjoy a special position in climbing he was as actively ribbed by club wits as any other member.

Rock and Ice taste in humour and repartee was essentially its own, and to appreciate it one had to be an initiate. This sometimes annoyed outsiders when they could not understand the appropriateness of certain comment nor, for that matter, the exact meaning of the club's descriptive slang – 'ninny', 'drink of water', 'ta ta' are typical examples. Ambitious or pushing types were disconcerted to find themselves referred to as 'a big drink of water' when they failed to live up to expected standards.

Joe hesitated in his delivery as I entered; he studied me for an instant, then grinned: 'Put another brew on!' The Rock and Ice were addicted to tea and drank gallons of it, heavily milked and sugared; certain club members had proud reputations for brewing and could prepare tea of a good standard under any conditions. Ray Greenall was chief club brewer and was even known later as 'Anderl the Brew'. Few of the club drank alcohol; no one could afford it if climbing was to come first. After pints of tea enlivened by stories, plans were discussed for the coming weekend. I was welcomed as a new recruit and it was assumed that I would be in on any scheme decided upon.

'Let's get out the pegging gear and go to High Tor,' suggested Ron, a leading pioneer in artificial climbing. The suggestion was accepted and arrangements made for getting to Matlock and High Tor – by motorbike, by hitch-hiking, by public transport; we would meet in the fields under High Tor, to bivouac for the night despite it being February.

Joe then declared to the meeting that as he was becoming famous it was time he had an official gentleman's gentleman; in the absence of more suitable material this young gentleman freshly arrived from White Rose territory would make a fine appointment. Its terms were roughly that Joe would teach me how to become a wily old bird like himself, while I in turn was to act with dignity and represent his interests. Just what I was to do I never found out, but I did make a lot of tea, carry many ropes, and give a deathblow to Brown's property-repairing business by acting as his labourer on some of his contracts. However, the arrangement suited me and thus I became gentleman's gentleman to Mr Joseph Brown, of Longsight, Manchester.

Ronnie briefed me on the other meeting places of the club in Manchester: Wednesday was Palais night and Thursday the YMCA. The Palais night was at the Levenshulme Palais de Danse; only one or two of the club ever danced, the rest sat in a corner and drank tea and talked climbing above the noise of the band. Several times Rock and Ice members had been restrained by burly chuckers-out while attempting to demonstrate moves on the latest new routes on the dance hall pillars. The YMCA was the central branch in Manchester of which I don't think any of the club were members, but its position and excellent lounge with a buffet service for the inevitable tea made it the ideal meeting place for the whole club, as some people could not get to other midweek gatherings. They had been visiting the YMCA for so long that the staff there thought them god-fearing, paid-up members whom they greeted by first names as they entered the door. I hadn't any money so I couldn't attend other Rock and Ice gatherings that week; I didn't wish to mention this and made the excuse of working late at the Pay Office. It was the early hours of the morning before the meeting broke up, but those who didn't live in Levenshulme never bothered about catching buses, they would walk home.

Joe came back with me towards my billet to find its whereabouts; from my description he couldn't understand where it was in relation to his own home. It turned out to be just round the corner from his mother's house and so, with instructions to report there on Friday night in time for tea, we parted.

On Friday, without equipment of my own, I reported as arranged; Joe had just arrived from work and was covered in white lime after a day of cementing. When the meal his mother had prepared had been disposed of, a leisurely session of talking and tea followed; finally Joe decided it was time to pack the food supplies and equipment. The provisions consisted of tea and steak; Joe at that time was a red meat man and his mother had bought enough steak to last every meal of the forthcoming weekend.

We boarded a bus to Stockport, then the last bus from Stockport to Matlock; for some reason I cannot explain, wherever we travelled we always caught the last possible bus. Ron Moseley, Eric Price and Thos Waghorn were at the Matlock meeting point, shivering in the cold evening air. We walked out of the town and headed down the road to High Tor; below that prominent limestone bastion we climbed over spiked iron railings into a field beside the Derwent and prepared to bivouac. Although it was one o'clock in the morning, water was obtained out of that highly polluted stream and tea made. We then settled down for the night and I lay awake, shivering away the hours that followed in a borrowed sleeping bag, considering it probable that these Rock and Ice hard men would kill me off with their assumption of my ability to rough it. I was pleased when darkness gave way to light and provided me with an excuse to get up and start cooking. Ray Greenall arrived as I was lighting the stoves; his transport had let him down and he had been forced into hitch-hiking to Matlock through the night, snatching a couple of hours' sleep in a field en route.

After breakfast we walked to the base of High Tor loaded down with equipment. One of the Rock and Ice maxims was that your equipment must be the best you could afford. Joe, for instance, had not a penny to his name but owned pounds in value of rope alone; every copper he could spare was spent on equipment. One of my jobs was to carry ropes and I proudly staggered up to the cliff with three 150-foot overweight nylon ropes of a quality on which I had never before climbed.

High Tor was more or less a virgin cliff at that date. It is an impressive limestone sentinel jutting proudly out of the northern hillside above the Derwent valley; on this my first visit, its smooth walls and large overhangs held me in thrall. At the base of the Tor we roped up, Joe, Ron, Ray and myself, and Joe shot up a hundred feet of free rock climbing without much protection, which the rest of us found the limit of our ability in the icy conditions. There has been a generation of climbers since the Rock and Ice era who have expressed amazement that this Manchester group could have been such a dominant force as they were in the 1950s; it was this ability to climb hard in bad conditions which above all else was responsible for their reputation. Few could equal it then, perhaps only a handful could do it now.

The polluted water we had been drinking began to take effect. Our leader was doubled up on his stance as I joined him, on arrival Ray Greenall had a green pallor, I also began to feel sick and dizzy, but our last man, Bergfuhrer Moseley, was having none of this softness and was not to be deterred. Ron was overshadowed in extreme rock climbing activities by Joe Brown and Don Whillans, but on his day he was the Rock and Ice's most determined climber. Ron was then a draughtsman and artist and in later life his scraperboard drawing made him a national reputation; his art is the touchstone of his character, which is complex and sensitive. He was more affected by the vagaries of form than any climber I have known. At his best he was capable of making new routes of the highest merit and difficulty, for example the *White Slab* and *Moss Groove* on Clogwyn Du'r Arddu; when off form he might have to struggle on easy climbs. However, his drive was always his own and inner-motivated, and typically on High Tor he took over the lead from our stance, to tackle a series of overhangs which would have deterred most other climbers of the period by their looseness, if not size. The rock would necessitate artificial climbing from here to the top, which was what Ron most enjoyed and delighted in overcoming.

Artificial climbing is a slow process, especially on a first ascent; each piton has to be carefully placed and hammered home into a crack. Soon Ray and I, who were holding the leaders' ropes, were bored and chilled to the marrow, perched on a stance buffeted by icy winds. Ray decided to give me lessons in the new dance craze from America, the rock and roll; hanging from our belay pitons we jumped and jived about, tensioning on the ropes, oblivious of Ronnie who was just then surmounting an overhang. A piton came out as our leader moved over the roof lip but Ray and I were too intent on our dancing and singing to notice that our front man had parted company with the rock and was slowly being lowered into space. Our gyrations were rudely interrupted by a string of invective from Ron, hanging twenty feet away from the rock and let down by our slack ropes to nearly the level of his start two hours earlier.

A hail came from the ground; it was Joe who had descended and made some cure-all for our stomachs: a billy of tea. We dealt with first things first by hoisting the billy on a hauling rope, leaving Ronnie hanging in space, purple with a combination of anger and strangulation. This important job safely accomplished, we threw out a rope-end and pulled our leader back into the rock, then we sat drinking our tea while Ron called us every name he could lay tongue to. Suddenly he started to laugh; it was always difficult for him to maintain anger for long, and we let out further slack to enable him to climb down to join us. It began to snow, so Ron decided to abandon the route and return on the morrow to finish the climb. We called it a day and gleefully roped down to ground level, Ray and I pleased by what in our estimation had been a huge joke.

At the edge of the High Tor railway tunnel we found a derelict hut not far from the cliff; it was a filthy place and filled with black smoke every time a train roared by a few feet away. Cleanliness was the least worry of the Rock and Ice, the important thing was a night's lodging for free; if it cost nothing any shelter would suffice. We soon occupied the hut, and more and more members began to arrive; some had to work Saturday mornings and did not manage to get out till late afternoon. By the time it was dark so many bodies had squeezed in that I was having difficulty in breathing. Last to arrive was Nat Allen from Derby and with his joining the party a hilarious evening was assured; among club wits he was supreme. Being the youngest I was ribbed mercilessly, and Joe saw to it that I was kept busy fetching water, lighting stoves and cooking, but I didn't mind for I ate an enormous meal at my master's expense.

After eating, the evening resolved itself into a game session. Some of the Rock and Ice games required thinking prowess, such as 'Sergeant Major' or 'Black Anna' (card games), but most of the entertainments were physical feats of balance or strength: press-up competitions, pull-ups, hanging by fingers from a nail driven into wood. Each member had his forte: Joe was an expert at bottom skipping – sitting on the ground and skipping over a rope passed under the bottom; Thos Waghorn could put both his legs behind his head in yoga fashion; Moseley could achieve nearly thirty pull-ups, Whillans could leap almost his own height from a standing start, Eric Price completed eight pull-ups on pinch grips only. In later years the outstanding performer was Mortimer Smith who pound for pound was the strongest person I have met climbing; he could press up sixteen times with my ten stone on his shoulders, and I once saw him press up ten times with a fourteen-stone man on his back. When Morty grew to maturity the game sessions were never dull, for it was impossible to guess what his strength might achieve until his turn to try came along.

Rock and Ice competition was at its keenest on boulder problems and members would drive each other to the limit over such feats. Surprisingly, neither Joe Brown nor Don Whillans had the monopoly here; Eric Price for instance would often burn off the whole club and be as resoundingly congratulated for his efforts as ever was a major first ascent by more famous members.

Sunday morning we rose early and several climbing parties were formed. I found myself back on yesterday's ledge holding the tenacious Moseley's rope, and alongside me again was Ray Greenall; we hung from the belay once more with teeth chattering, but forbidden to engage in any further dancing antics. It began to snow and my keenness evaporated. Our leader continued his slow upward progress until he reached a cave, whereupon Ray and I decided 'we didn't wish to be famous after all' and elected to 'replace ourselves with lustier men from the reserves'. At this, the usual Rock and Ice comments floated down the rope, 'You're a couple of ninnies!', 'Just big girls!', but I was thankful to allow more able club members to take over rope-holding and eventually follow Ronnie to the top of the crag.

All too soon it was time to catch the bus back to Manchester. The journey was an experience; the other passengers were treated to a running farce which of course broke the rules of normal travelling behaviour. Joe had ripped his trousers and so, with hints that he appeared indecent, he borrowed a pair and proceeded to change; however, both his own tattered pair and their replacements were whisked from his hands as he was halfway through his changing act, leaving him standing in the aisle in brief underpants. The trousers were flung from member to member before the embarrassed Brown managed to regain his seat and finally intercept the garments. The comment of older passengers was typical of the fact that we soon forget our own youth and condemn any but conventional behaviour; they wrote us off as 'Manchester Teddy boys'.

From then onwards, weekend followed weekend with the Rock and Ice. The more I saw of the club the more impressed I was by its climbing prowess; nearly every member was an outstanding performer in his own right and those who were not front-rank leaders had other qualities which often complemented the stars' performances. The approach was essentially light-hearted and in keeping with my own previous experience. Detractors of the Rock and Ice at that time and later were either motivated by envy or by misunderstanding of the nature of the club's outlook. Charges were made of secretiveness, extreme competitiveness and even unfriendliness; these had no basis in truth. I was from another area, from a different group, but I was welcomed with open arms and treated with kindness and friendship.

Other people were building reputations for the Rock and Ice and claims were made that could not be substantiated, but it was no doing of their own. They never made extravagant claims, and some of their climbs were never recorded and other leaders have subsequently claimed the routes as first ascents. They had no illusions of grandeur and other climbers who had, if they met Whillans for instance, were often disturbed by his uncompromising judgements. But newspaper and other mass media were looking at this time for heroes from the changing social patterns of Britain in order to interest the public at large in new activities and to capture the attention of a massive new sector with great spending power. This demanded personalities with background and culture values of their own, and the Rock and Ice supplied the demand to perfection. The cheap characterisation of the group as 'the climbing plumbers' (Joe Brown, Don Whillans, Nat Allen) was typical of the various images thrust upon the club.

The climbing world was guilty of equally false characterisations, though of a different kind. Often the Rock and Ice were known as 'the little men' despite the fact that only Ron Moseley, Joe (Mortimer) Smith and Don Whillans were below average height and the club's ranks contained more tall than small men. Wild theories were put forward by pundits as to why this group should possess a high degree of skill; physical build was seized upon and it was decreed that all outstanding climbers would be, perforce, small and powerfully built with a high strength to power weight ratio. Another theory was that they owed their success to gritstone training, and it was decided by the same judges that no climber of brilliance would emerge in future who did not have this kind of outcrop experience. Others sought an answer in more intangible terms; perhaps the Rock and Ice possessed special and secret abilities or techniques? Joe Brown was credited by some with having invented and refined hand jamming; this is untrue. As a thirteen year old I watched Arthur Dolphin hang by one hand from a jam, he had learnt it off climbers who had learnt it off climbers! The hand jam is used in one of the climbing areas of Austria, and a friend from that district tells me that his enquiries show it to have been used there for fifty years. Within the Rock and Ice such appraisals were laughed at, but there is no doubt that other climbers could not see through such facile judgements and tended to accept a false image.

Another irritating characterisation foisted on the Rock and Ice was that members were all known to each other by colourful nicknames. True, there were many such labels but this was no more a facet of the Manchester club than of other similar groups both before and since. The Creagh Dhu had their

Porridge, the Monster, Sunshine among a rich crop of pseudonyms before the Rock and Ice group existed with their Villain (Whillans), Baron (Joe Brown), Count Neddy Goff (Fred Goff). The Bradford Lads used such labels too. Always their origin stems from a familiarity with a person closer than his formal name. I have a mania for nicknames myself, possibly from reading Damon Runyon at an impressionable age, and was responsible for those by which several climbers are generally known – Fred the Ted (Brian Fuller), Gnome (Terry Burnell), Pin (Ian Howell) and Tubby (Alan Austin) among them. This practice of address by nickname was misinterpreted again and again in press articles and even in a recent climbing book; reporters and writers appear to believe that anyone with a nickname must be a member of the Rock and Ice Club. Many climbers with little or no connection with them have appeared in articles about the Rock and Ice.

The plain fact about the Manchester club was that it possessed a galaxy of talent out of proportion to its size, in high mountain ranges as well as in Britain. But its members did not deliberately set out to achieve anything; their prime motive was enjoyment, and the fact that so many of them had been born and brought up in close proximity to one another gave the group its basic ties.

The Rock and Ice leaders were men of outstanding skill and daring but they were also fortunate in having their share of good luck. Many members had miraculous escapes from motorbike pile-ups, survived long falls, escaped in bad mountain conditions by the skin of their teeth – but they did survive. Throughout its whole existence, the original club did not sustain a single serious climbing injury; this speaks for itself – they had good luck but always it was allied to great skill. They had learned, like most others of their generation, to climb the hard way, either with friends who were novices like themselves or by finding the rocks and hills alone and working up through easier-grade climbs. It is difficult to imagine our new-style outdoor pursuit centres, with their climbing instruction courses, producing the type of climber found so richly in the Rock and Ice; they might be superior technically but I doubt if they would possess the same degree of spontaneous enterprise or individuality.

After I had been in Manchester a short time Ronnie Moseley raised the question of my joining the club. I declined, supported in my argument by Joe Brown. My youthful associations with the Bradford Lads still held me in honour; I was anti-club, feeling such membership an unnecessary tie, and I wanted to remain a free agent. Joining a club, even the Rock and Ice, was against my principles and it was obvious from Joe's support that he sympathised with my viewpoint.

I think the closest I came to injury with the Rock and Ice was on the day in North Wales when Joe Brown and I made the second ascent of the *Red Wall* of Craig y Rhaeadr in Llanberis Pass, of which Don Whillans had made the first

a short while before. We had with us a large and heavy motorcyclist, owner
of a Vincent HRD 1,000 cc, who had frightened Joe and me to death by giving
us a lift, wearing our rucksacks and other equipment, through Llanberis Pass
and its hairpin bends at speeds of eighty miles per hour. We had nearly fallen
off the back of his machine on one bend and even Joe had screamed in fright.
I could see that the motorcyclist would have to pay us back for this liberty and
was glad not to be in his boots.

We ambled up to the base of the cliff and surveyed the wall; it looked
steep and impressive and of course, to add spice, it was wet. Soon Joe had
climbed the first pitch which was a rising traverse rightwards over an ever-
increasing drop; the climb moved out from the wings of the crag on to the wall
which ran up the highest part of its face or thereabouts. The rock was running
water and Joe told the motorcyclist to be careful, as the latter set out to follow
his lead, and that the rock was greasy. The fellow was no expert, more of a
dabbler, so we put him between us in order to give him security from front and
behind. Despite his bulk of fifteen stone he moved lithely on the first moves
of the pitch and seemed comfortably in control when suddenly, with no
warning, he shot off into space. Both Joe and I were belayed and we clung on
grimly and stopped him swinging across the rock face, then lowered him back
to terra firma.

'Just a careless slip,' he informed me on returning to his starting point.
'Perhaps you would like to have a try while I rest?'

With a shuffle-type set of traversing moves, including two thin moves,
I managed to join Brown on his stance. A slip would have been easy; it was,
as Joe said, very greasy.

I changed places with Joe at the belay, a flake high and to the right of our
stance, stuck out on the wall over a clear drop. Joe set off up the next pitch,
moving so quickly that I could hardly pay the rope fast enough. Having found
a good belay he instructed me to bring up the motorcyclist.

The bulky man set out across the initial traverse once more. I took in his
rope and watched apprehensively, fully aware of the difficult task I would have
to hold his fifteen stone if he swung into space with no back rope to keep him
steady. This time he proceeded cautiously until he reached his previous high
point; he was nearly across the first difficult section when, with a shout,
he slipped off the rock again and the next instant the world spun round me as
I too shot into space. When I realised what had happened I was hanging head
first down the crag, suspended from the belay flake. The weight of the cyclist
had pulled me off my ledge though somehow I had managed to keep hold of
him, and I was being slowly suffocated by his large body hanging from mine.
Joe had the rope between us tight; I was terrified of being cut in two but
I could not have let the bulky fellow go if I had wished, for the rope he was
hanging from was wound round me in a cocoon. Joe, always calm and

unruffled in any rock-climbing situation, mechanically shouted instructions. 'Lower him off,' he ordered, and somehow I managed to do this. 'Now I'll pull you the right way round' came his voice out of a spinning void. With liberal assistance from his rope I regained a vertical position; the rock face seemed to be revolving and the walls of rock to be expanding, and from my upside-down position the ground seemed hundreds of feet away instead of the eighty or so it really was. I had lost all perspective and it was a while before the scenery stopped spinning. Again, with help from above, I managed to swing back on to my belay ledge, where I collapsed into its bilberry recess completely exhausted.

This performance had burnt my hands slightly and bruised my ribs badly. I was certain my ribs were fractured and lay shaking with fright at my condition. The motorcyclist decided against all my pleading to have one more attempt. Joe was enjoying the show immensely; this would teach the man to scare us with mad driving antics. 'One more move and you would have made it,' he lied to the heavy spaceman. I was too weak to protest further and clung grimly on to our connecting thread. This time he stuck actually in the middle of making the first hard move – he couldn't step up, he couldn't go back. Fear overtook me again and I begged him not to fall off. Suddenly one of his hands snaked off the rock and seized the rope.

'I'm going to swing off!' he declared hysterically.

'Grab the rope with both hands! He'll hold you!' shouted down Joe.

'No, no, no!' I sobbed, but slowly he peeled off, swinging into space like a trapeze artist. Off into thin air I followed him, snatched by this millstone pulling me after him as if I was paperweight. Things were not quite as bad this time, and I kept the right way up. Fright gave way to temper and I jettisoned the tumbler as fast as I could, taking care not to burn my hands any more. Joe pulled and I swung back on to my ledge; it was with relief that I heard the motorcyclist declare he would 'leave it for another day'.

Whether it was the effort of holding his falls or that the climb is really so difficult, I don't know, but the rest of the way to the top of the *Red Wall* I found so hard as to be my limit, and I've never been back for a second attempt. My ribs were sore for many weeks afterwards and it turned out to be a lesson for both the motorcyclist and myself. Joe had to accept a lift back to Manchester with him, no other transport being available. As I hitch-hiked home the same evening I chuckled gleefully at my luck – I had only bruised my ribs but Joe on the back of that driver's Vincent HRD might end up in a mortuary!

In 1954 the Rock and Ice were planning a meet in the Alps and it became more important than ever to cut down on expense, especially travelling costs. The most inexpensive but strenuous way into the hills was Ron Moseley's method of cycling. To save money for the Alpine holiday Ron attempted to persuade other members to follow his example. One Tuesday evening at his parents' home, after drinking more tea than usual, several people agreed to make an attempt, and I volunteered to travel by bus with all the heavy equipment.

On Friday evening only three of the Rock and Ice appeared on bicycles: Ron who owned one, Ray Greenall on a younger brother's and Joe Brown on his niece's. The rest of the club had mustered alternative transport and escaped to Wales. Moseley with his usual enthusiasm had planned a tough weekend – cycle to Hayfield, walk over Kinder and Win Hill to Stanage Edge, climb and sleep out there, and on Sunday night walk and cycle home again.

I caught the bus as arranged, carrying all the equipment. Although eighteen, I was still travelling half-fare, for I possessed the original baby face. Goodness knows what the conductor made of me; however, as I had the cheek to insist on being under fourteen, he issued me with a half-fare ticket, muttering something about 'the strongest thirteen-year-old hiker I've ever seen carrying so much stuff'.

The bus roared by the cyclists pedalling steadily along; Joe cheekily gave a rude sign and the others yelled abuse as I was carried past. It was a different story a few hours later at Hayfield. A super-fit Moseley came streaking into the turn-around bus terminus, pedalling like Fausto Coppi, but it was a long time before Joe and Ray appeared. Ron was the object of bitter reproofs all weekend, Joe referring continually to the fact that his was a lady's bike and not a sports model like Moseley's.

The weekend resolved itself into a typical outing. By Sunday evening I was out on my feet as we returned from Stanage over the Kinder plateau; Ron with burning enthusiasm had insisted we climb late at Stanage and darkness caught us amidst the peat bogs of the high moors. Joe and Ron were far in the lead as Ray and I struggled along in their wake, falling continually into peat hags, streams and bogs. My right boot disintegrated and the sole fell off, and I became so tired that I was for lying down in my tracks and going to sleep. In such circumstances, the surface hardness of Rock and Ice characters soon gave way to practical aid. Ron and Joe waited and took over most of the equipment we were carrying. Ron was always the first to offer assistance and several times he helped in like manner on similar long tiring flogs. Coming down off the moors to Hayfield we lost the way; in the valley we could see a light and headed straight down the hillside towards this beacon. When we were nearly at the bottom two figures, armed with shotguns and holding ferocious barking dogs, loomed out of the darkness. In unfriendly tones we were informed that the land was private and we trespassing; there was no right of way hereabouts and if we didn't go back where we had come from, they would turn the dogs on to us. The thought of turning round and slogging up to where we had been was more than I could contemplate; I was exhausted and my heart sank completely. Joe with his silken tongue started to work on the gamekeepers, trying to persuade them to let us pass, appealing to their better nature, bringing to bear many obscure arguments. It has always amazed me that Joe is known generally as a shy, retiring person with little to say for himself. Retiring he may be, but few can better him in argument once he is personally involved. Slowly he melted the ice between us and the keepers, cigarettes were lit, confidence established and in the end the men came to show us the best way down to Hayfield. We parted friends, their last comment being that we were not the usual type of Manchester lout they had recently been catching damaging the estate; we were welcome any time on their part of the moor! I have often cursed Joe Brown for a persuasive tongue when I have found myself doing things I never intended, but this was one occasion when it was a blessing.

I was pleased I did not have to cycle back to Manchester like the others and thankfully waved them off as they set out to ride home. Later I passed them on the bus. Joe was so far behind that I never expected him to reach Manchester that night; he looked dead beat pedalling along in his climbing boots. They did all complete the course, Joe and Ray arriving back in the early hours of the morning. Joe declared that from then on cycling to the crags was out for him. His body just wasn't the right shape for pedalling long distances and in any case his niece would not allow him to use her machine again as he had broken the saddle!

The Alpine season of 1954 saw the Rock and Ice in Chamonix in force. They repeated some of the hardest existing routes and Brown and Whillans made a difficult new ascent, the west face of the Blaitière. Their success meant more to British mountaineering than any event in the Alps since the war; others of their contemporaries had made good ascents before them and more recently our young alpinists have improved on their performance, but the efforts of the Rock and Ice in the 1954 season proved to be a spark which ignited a new and revitalised British alpinism.

There was a memorable Rock and Ice meet in Wales on the return of the club from Chamonix; Slim Sorrell, his wife Dorothy and I travelled down specially for the event, and Slim, who was often the instigator of club activities on the wilder shores of life, decided that a stone fight would make a fitting way of celebrating our friends' return. Sides were picked and climbing forgotten as the battle raged through Llanberis Pass; at one point the Down Pass team drove the opposition nearly into the village of Nant Peris at the bottom of the Pass, and the high point of the Up the Pass side was the Cromlech Bridge, a distance between the two of several miles! By sheer good luck no one was injured, and it was with relief that stones were dropped and a truce agreed on Sunday evening to allow most of the club to return home for work on Monday morning. Joe, Slim and I decided to stay on for a week; I was supposed to be on special duties away from the Pay Office and took French leave.

The weather was bad so we decided to move into one of the climbing huts which abound in the vicinity of Llanberis Pass. None of us was then a member of any orthodox club, but the hut we moved into belonged to a club who were acquaintances of ours and we were sure they wouldn't mind us staying there, in their absence midweek. In pouring rain we spent some frightening days on Clogwyn Du'r Arddu, led by Joe up climbs we would have had difficulty in leading on a dry summer's day. Joe and all the Rock and Ice had a thing about the cliff at that time and would sooner climb in the rain on Cloggy than in the sun on inferior cliffs elsewhere. It had become their preserve and on its walls and slabs they had acted out some of their greatest feats, changing the Welsh rock-climbing scene, making the greatest crag of Snowdon and a bunch of Manchester climbers synonymous.

During the week we joined forces with three other well-known climbers, Pete Hassall, Trevor Peck and Peter Biven, who were camping until the torrential rain washed them out and they too moved to join us in the hut. With a party of this size it was time to put into practice a long-nurtured plan to have an eating competition.

The competition would be decided by the number of bowls of stew eaten, and was mainly the brainchild again of Slim. The stew was made in a baby's tin bath which we had found, and among other ingredients contained twenty-eight pounds of potatoes, six pounds of carrots and four tins of stewed steak; it took four primus stoves to supply the necessary heat and most of a day to prepare. Slim decided that on account of my size and youth I should be given an advantage by eating out of a smaller bowl, at which Joe protested hotly, 'A gentleman's gentleman can eat stew as well as anybody else, and in any case I'm betting on him to win for I've got great faith in his ability to eat stew.' Slim reluctantly replaced my bowl with one of equal size to everyone else's and the contest began.

Each contestant used different tactics according to his personal eating habits: some gobbled the bowl of stew as quickly as possible, then took the rest allowed between each bowl; others ate slowly and never took any rest. I favoured the latter method and patiently shovelled down the stew which was delicious. Slim, the biggest and strongest contender, was the first to collapse, stopped short by hiccups when only on his third bowl. The most difficult task from then on was not to laugh, as Slim was determined that neither Joe nor I should win; he pulled faces, danced about and tickled us while we ate. By bowl five the pace was beginning to tell, and Joe fell off his chair in one of his uncontrollable fits of laughing. This affected all the company but me; I ploughed steadily into the stew and one by one the others gave up. At bowl seven I was declared winner and gained a reputation as a stew-eater which lives on to this day.

Joe was now so famous that wherever we climbed he was eyed as if he were from another planet. His reputation meant little to us and we had many amusing incidents, especially in the presence of Slim who was merciless in drawing others on to make fools of themselves. During the week we met at the Cromlech boulders some young climbers who were typically misinformed. Joe was struggling a little with a difficult boulder problem when these young lads came up to Slim and me, who were standing by to field Joe in case of a slip, and started talking about their hero, Joe Brown, who even then was up on Cloggy soloing a hard new climb in the bad conditions because no one was good enough to second him. Bit by bit Slim drew from these youths enough legends to make any egotist happy. But Joe was wincing and red with embarrassment as he completed his problem to the comment from one of the tyros 'Joe climbs that one no-hands!' He could take it no longer and disappeared as the eulogy continued; in the end Slim and I collapsed in hysterics. It is easy to be superior; actually they meant Joe no harm, and perhaps we should have put them right.

At the end of 1954 life began to change radically in the Pay Office. We had many officers drafted in from combat regiments and they could not accept the slack discipline and existing manner of working. The office was attacked one night by the IRA; three drunken Irishmen kicked down the front door and from then on one would have thought we were serving on Dunkirk beach instead of in Stockport Road, Manchester. Many of us had to forsake our beds at night to march round and round the office, carrying wooden clubs, and after a second foray by the IRA, the same three drunks kicking in our front door, we were armed with loaded rifles – loaded, I must add, with blank ammunition.

By chance I discovered that I possessed a slight bent for cross-country running and began to run in occasional races. Slowly I improved until I started to run for the corps and in the army championships, which the corps won by a comfortable margin for we had two English national team members.

Cross-country running and then track running dominated the rest of my service life. It was a way of escaping the endless extra guard duties at night; instead of such irksome tasks I was away running at meetings throughout Great Britain. I remember a painful encounter with Joe Brown in the summer of 1955, after his return from the successful ascent of Kangchenjunga: 'What is a gentleman's gentleman doing running about the countryside instead of climbing?' I tried to explain my difficulties but to no avail, and I took a terrible verbal beating from the Baron.

One evening I was out training on the roads outside Leeds, on special get-fit leave for an inter-command event. I was panting up a steep hill; by then I considered myself a bit of a man on the hills and was putting heart and soul into running up that hill as fast as I could. Suddenly I was aware of another runner panting behind me. I put on more and more speed but I couldn't shake him off, then he passed me in a long, loping stride which appeared slow and easy. He waited at the top of the hill, and before I could get my breath back was asking me who I was and who did I run for. Then he introduced himself as Eric Beard. At first I didn't take to him and thought him too pushing, but as I came to know him better, I realised this was extreme good humour and boisterous spirits. Long-armed and equally long-legged, he had tremendous potential as a long-distance runner and was slowly climbing the ladder of athletic fame.

From then on, we trained together whenever I was home on leave, and as he lived close to my parents he often came to our house to meet my climbing friends. Beardie, as he was known to thousands of hillwalkers and climbers, then had his sights on the marathon race, and worked during the day as a green-keeper on a golf course simply to enable himself to have enough opportunity for training. He was completely dedicated, and had already packed in several higher-paid jobs, such as being a tram conductor; he had been voted Leeds number one conductor for courtesy and attention by the travelling public!

His ambition was to build up a team of road runners for the many events then springing into athletic calendars. Through him I joined the Leeds Athletic Club and began to compete in some of the road events, although still officially a junior. We ran in the Windermere to Kendal road race, the Oldham Hopwood Trophy Race and so forth.

On my demobilisation in January 1956, and subsequent return to Leeds, I introduced Beardie to climbing and the Rock and Ice. Although never an extreme rock climber, he quickly developed mountaineering keenness and love of the hills, and his athletic prowess found a new outlet in feats on the British mountains which have made him famous amongst mountain and hill racers. At the time of his death in November 1969,[1] he held the records for the Welsh 3,000s, the round of the Mountains of Mourne, the Skye Main Cuillin Ridge, the Cairngorm 4,000s, Ben Nevis to Snowdon summit via Scafell Pike, walking or running all the way. His greatest feat was breaking the Lakeland Fell record in 1963 when he covered eighty-eight miles, climbed fifty-six summits and made 33,000 feet of ascent and descent in just under twenty-four hours.

Eric Beard's biggest disappointment was the forced abandonment of his marathon career – in his first race at this distance he suffered a bad injury. This occurred in the 1958 Doncaster to Sheffield marathon for the northern counties title, for which I was acting as his manager and driver. For the first fifteen miles he was in the leading bunch of runners, then unaccountably he began to fall back, complaining of leg pain. I imagined this must be the cramp which is prevalent in long-distance road races and, thinking it was a spasm and would pass, I urged him to keep running. At eighteen miles he collapsed, and I drove him in an agony of pain to hospital where X-rays revealed to our astonishment a fractured fibula. He had run many miles with a fractured leg caused simply by the pounding on the road. This finished his racing career for a while and

---

1. See Chapter 7.

turned him to the mountains. Although like myself never an official Rock and Ice Club member, he soon became one of the boys, his singing and joking making him one of the characters of the group.

Demobilisation ended my dual career of gentleman's gentleman and soldier to HM the Queen, and I returned to my beloved Yorkshire. Of our old climbing group, the Bradford Lads, only Alf Beanland and John Ramsden were in touch with me. They had discovered a brilliant protégé of my age, twenty years old; his name was Eric Metcalf, now to be known as Matey for short. Matey had parts of his fingers missing on one hand but this was no handicap; I found when we met that he was as able a rock climber as my friends claimed, and as easy to get on with as his nickname suggested. Soon we were out together every weekend and began to visit Wales regularly; we kept in touch with the Rock and Ice, particularly Ron Moseley, Ray Greenall and the club's new recruit, Mortimer.

I found that my running activities had made me very fit; my climbing improved with a sudden surge, and between us Matey and I accounted for many of the then existing hard Welsh climbs. My keenest memory of that summer of 1956 was an ascent, the fifth, of the *Cenotaph Corner* of Dinas Cromlech, later to be known as 'an easy day for an old lady' but then considered about the hardest lead in Llanberis. Why this downgrading? Was it so overestimated? Taking into account today's higher standards, I still believe the route in its pristine state to have been every bit as hard as it was claimed to be. When we climbed it, the crack was filled with vegetation, it was still wet despite a heatwave, and bridging the top of the corner to place the pitons (not then in position) was precarious to say the least; the landing at the top of the corner was accomplished by swinging over the lip clinging to earth sods of dubious reliability. I have done it a couple of times since and agree that it is not the same climb now it has been thoroughly cleaned.

At home I worked hard in the printing industry, passing exams, studying at art college and printing school. I had ambition and was quickly promoted by the firm I worked for; on completion of my studies in 1957 I was in charge of my department, with older men under me and the promise of what was termed 'a great future'. At this time I felt no conflict between my love of the mountains and my job; at weekends I climbed and midweek I studied and worked. I was deeply interested in graphic art, printing processes and athletics as well as climbing.

Around this time the first cracks appeared in Rock and Ice solidarity. Joe Brown returned from the brilliant success of the Muztagh Tower expedition and he, like several other members, was courting and thinking of marriage. The single-sex atmosphere of Rock and Ice climbing was changing; women were appearing on the scene in ever-increasing numbers, and some of them were good enough to shatter the notion that no woman could climb to the club's standard. Slim Sorrell's wife, Dorothy, was a wonderful climber before being struck tragically by paralysing polio, a woman took part in the sixth ascent of *Cenotaph Corner*, and many of the Rock and Ice discovered that their girlfriends or wives could hold their own on the mountains as well as they could.

The club had to change to meet these new circumstances; one could not continue forever to doss out in the open or five or six men to a tent. In any case a hut had been acquired above Llanberis, an amazing place with a minimal rent, and a comfortable haven in bad conditions. But hut ownership can soon be a cause of friction, and this one brought about the first real disagreements in the club. The place had to be looked after, younger members and friends, including myself, took delight in horseplay, throwing tea leaves, water fights, and wives and girlfriends were not impressed by such antics, and there are the problems of the responsibility for keeping the hut tidy, and of administration. I have myself observed that as soon as any small club obtains a hut in the British mountains, either its climbing activities fall off or the hut is neglected and quickly abandoned. Soon the Rock and Ice surrendered their hut in favour of personal accommodation once more. Every member could now afford a tent, and for a while the difficulty of club organisation was staved off.

In the summer of 1957, several Rock and Ice members, plus myself, decided on a holiday in Cornwall. I had never climbed anywhere but in traditional mountain centres or on outcrops, and such a change seemed a good idea. Joe Brown had married and he too felt the need for a change of holiday. A large party of us assembled at Bosigran, near St Ives. I was immediately impressed by the Cornish scene; besides the superb granite climbing there are the beaches, swimming, the ever-changing moods of the sea, and often the sun.

We had gone to Cornwall determined to catch a shark. Affluence had enabled us to equip ourselves with an ex-war department twenty-two-man dinghy and a ten-man inflatable life raft – a far cry from a few years earlier when the lot of us had hardly been able to afford food for a weekend's climbing. Launching these craft nearly caused a drowning. Our group was joined by Peter Biven and Trevor Peck who were old hands in Cornish sea matters, and Joe Brown, Peter Biven and I tried to swim out with the ten-man raft. We cut through the breakers and out into the Atlantic, then climbed on to the raft, only to be hit by an extra big wave which capsized us. I had tumultuous, upside-down visions of a green and blue churning tunnel and in I sank, along with the other two. Joe and I surfaced and swam back to safety through the breakers while the raft was carried ahead of us to shore. Peter Biven was nowhere to be seen. He must have been under a long time, and we were relieved to see him emerge from the waves after what seemed like an eternity; when he finally beached, he had a lump like a coconut on his head through hitting a submerged rock. It had been a narrow squeak, but we were not then fully aware of just how dangerous our activities were; climbers have discovered since sea-cliff climbing became popular that the sea can be as serious an objective danger as the mountains.

Finally, bolstered with a larger crew from the reserves, we managed to float the dinghy out and, armed with a home-made harpoon tied to the end of a 150-foot overweight nylon rope, we set out to hunt the basking shark reported to have been seen further down the coast. Joe was soon seasick and the rest of the boys fed up. We sailed for hours down the coast, never saw a shark, and finally had to beach miles from our starting point. Carrying the dinghy back on a van roof caused endless traffic jams as we couldn't deflate it!

We did some fine climbs in Cornwall, including *Suicide Wall* on Bosigran; this I remember as a superb route with good position and climbing. During the ascent Joe spotted a new climb to the right and pioneered a strenuous line which he called *Bow Wall*. Altogether the holiday was enjoyable, it had been a surprise to see the Rock and Ice beside the seaside. They had devised some hair-raising adventures for themselves, especially when the twenty-two-man dinghy sank with all hands and one of the boys was only rescued by repeated diving attempts by the rest, trapped as he was inside its enveloping folds.

Don Whillans had been away in 1957 as a member of the Manchester expedition to the Karakoram Himalaya. During the attempt on Masherbrum, which was unsuccessful, the young Cambridge climber Bob Downes had succumbed to pulmonary oedema. Bob was one of the few from his background that the Rock and Ice had taken to; he had gone out of his way to meet them on their own terms and I remember how genuine had been his enjoyment and happiness at the success of another climber. On one occasion, when I had led an ascent of one of the hard Llanberis problems, he whisked me away for a celebratory drink. I always think of him as Puck with a wistful grin.

During that winter I climbed a lot with Mortimer Smith, Ron Cummaford and Don Whillans, and plans began to be made for a club meet in Chamonix in 1958. I made up my mind to go, and Eric Beard also decided to join the party. Joe Brown thought that he too would go, and a scheme evolved for Mortimer, Don, Joe and myself to climb together as two ropes of two. I began to look forward very much to the Alpine meet.

Easter 1958 was a tragic occasion for the remaining members of the Bradford Lads. Alf Beanland against all odds had slowly fought off his illnesses, had finished a college course and was teaching art in Birmingham. By now he was a seasoned alpinist with many major ascents behind him, and with John Ramsden was planning even bigger things for the summer. At Easter he went to Ben

Nevis with two Birmingham friends. Alf had set out to repeat *Zero Gully*, one of the hardest ice climbs in Scotland. When they were quite a way up, with Alf leading, the ice avalanched, bringing away a large rockfall and killing the three climbers outright.

The news reached me as I was coming home in high spirits from a memorable Rock and Ice meet in Wales. We had climbed on Cloggy plastered in snow and ice, slid on boulders nearly the full distance down the Snowdon railway, and Mortimer, Don and I had climbed one of the hardest Llanberis problems, *Surplomb*, in the rain. Don had given an entertaining exhibition by bridging, facing out, up and down the top chimney crux pitch to demonstrate how easy a method this was of climbing it.

And now Alfie Beanland was dead. I wondered for the first time whether climbing was worth the risk. Alf had been a good friend to me, he had taught an awkward little boy how to climb, had shepherded me up many an ascent, and had always made me laugh, and anyone else in his company. He had loved life and people. For a while after his death, I was not sure that such sacrifice was worth the rewards. First it had been Arthur Dolphin, now Alfie, two entirely different personalities, the technician and the artist; I had been lucky to know such men. Later it came to me that this perhaps made the risk worthwhile; only by being a climber, only by knowing the mountain life, would I continue to meet such people.

The impermanence of life and human institutions was further borne in on me by the disbandment of the Rock and Ice Club in July. When it came about, Joe Brown, Mortimer Smith, Don Whillans and I were in the Alps; the first intimation we had that the club had ceased to exist was by reading about it in the popular press. The action had been taken above the heads of my companions. The headlines blamed girlfriends and wives as the cause of the club's downfall, but this was not true; it was the work of time; everyone growing older, social conditions changing, members going off in other directions, seeking different paths in life.

Joe was philosophical about it and declared it inevitable, Mortimer was not pleased, Don was outraged. He was one of the club's keenest supporters, and the manner of its disbandment struck at the loyalty which is so striking a facet of his personality. It was a good job that the members responsible were not in Chamonix then, otherwise irreparable harm would have been done to many close friendships. I was only slightly affected; I felt it was a pity, but although I had gone around with the club for many years, I had never joined and was still a member of no climbing organisation.

The demise of the Rock and Ice underlined the difficulty of keeping an energetic small club alive once the officials who have nursed it along feel in need of relief. Ron Moseley and Doug Belshaw had remained in office throughout the club's existence; they wanted replacements, none was forthcoming so they ceased to look after its affairs. However, most members and their friends continued to climb together, and there was little or no difference in practice.

All the same, the disbandment of the original Rock and Ice Club did mark the end of seven years of outstanding achievement; they had set new standards, they had extended horizons and, most important of all, they had always enjoyed themselves.

3   Alpine Apprentice

'Stories of falling ice, of long hauls up to the huts, of bivouacs and endless traverses under the crushing load of enormous rucksacks; of unimaginable ice falls; of blizzards, fog and exhaustion – to say nothing of mountain sickness ... '
(Hermann Buhl writing of the Alps)

The return to the Alps after the chaos of war was a slow and in some cases painful process for British climbers. The first post-war generations had to face material and other difficulties which, for some years, forced upon our mountaineers a cautious and not over-ambitious programme of ascents. The renaissance of alpinism in this country came first from groups of university climbers, then, as money conditions improved, from the new type of small and energetic clubs.

The British climber found himself at a serious disadvantage at the beginning of this revival, due mainly to language difficulties and the consequent lack of guidebook information. An important innovation was the founding of the Alpine Climbing Group in 1952, with the express aims of bringing together those interested in high-standard alpine climbing, the spreading of modern information and techniques, and the provision of alpine guidebooks in English. The first president was the late Tom Bourdillon, member of the successful 1953 Everest party, who died tragically at the height of his powers in 1956, on the east face of the Jägihorn. To his example, more than to most others, is owed the subsequent high standards attained by British alpine climbers. In company with Hamish Nicol he made the first ascent by any party from this country of a modern *grande course* when they repeated the north face of the Drus in 1950. From this success can be traced the beginning of a more ambitious approach by our climbers.

Slowly the numbers visiting the Alps grew throughout the late 1940s and the early 1950s, and by the time Joe Brown and Don Whillans made the first ascent of the west face of the Blaitière they had become considerable. Despite this growing interest in climbing abroad, my own ambition was still limited to Britain; I could not afford to go to the Alps as salaries and grants were poor for management trainees. It appeared to me impossible to save enough money to travel abroad as well as climb every weekend in our homeland hills. The only way for me to get to the Alps in the early 1950s would have been by hitch-hiking, and this seemed impracticable simply because of time considerations. The fortnight's holiday I was allowed each year seemed too brief, but later Mortimer Smith proved this judgement wrong. As an apprentice with two weeks' holiday he hitched-hiked from Manchester to Chamonix and back, starting out with £12 in his pocket and returning, after climbing five routes and buying a new pair of Continental boots, with £2 left of his original stake. He was, however, one day overdue at work and almost had the sack!

In September 1955, I did get my first opportunity to see mountains abroad when during my National Service I went to Austria to run at Innsbruck and Salzburg. I managed to travel during my stay, and a first excursion took me down the Inn valley to Kufstein and up into the Wilder Kaiser range to see the Kaisergebirge, the classical school of Austro-German rock climbing, an impressive limestone group of toothy summits set above dizzy white walls. I had no companion and wandered alone into the mountains where I found many climbers and walkers around. Most spoke English and everyone was friendly and inquisitive, for a British climber was rare in their mountains. After a night in one of the many climbing refuges, I had an enjoyable scramble to a minor summit with a young Austrian. Although I had to return to Innsbruck that evening, I had seen enough to make me want to return to those steep limestone cliffs and jagged summits, amongst which many great alpine climbers found happiness and renown.

While I was in the Tyrol an Innsbruck youth invited me to go on a wine smuggling expedition with him, over the border into Italy. I have since learned that this is almost a national sport; nonetheless, it is a crime that carries serious penalties. Karl had borrowed a Volkswagen bus which carried us over the Brenner Pass to a small Italian village near Vipiteno. There, he proceeded with my help to load the vehicle to the roof with casks of wine. In those days I never drank anything stronger than water, and as we spent the whole afternoon drinking wine I was drunk and nonchalant when we set out to cross back into Austria. Karl had obviously made this run before: when we arrived at the Italian border a couple of wine casks were offloaded, no questions asked, and we sped on our way. The story was different at the Austrian customs post; the guards were clearly not in on our act, perhaps they were fresh arrivals? The evening air became alive with armed men who surrounded the vehicle and proceeded to bash away at it with rifle butts, plainly searching for hidden compartments full of contraband. We were then formally arrested. Karl gabbled explanations fast, but the guards couldn't understand what I, an Englishman speaking no German, was doing in an Innsbruck bus smuggling wine. They evidently thought they had caught an international smuggling ring and I was led off to a small cell and locked up.

Around midnight the cell door was unlocked to reveal a grinning Karl, accompanied by an officer of some kind. We could go free! The two of us climbed back into our bus, still filled with wine casks, and set off down to Innsbruck like participants in an alpine rally. Karl kept laughing aloud about the incident; in any country it helps to have friends in high places, and as far as I could understand my companion's father was mayor of Innsbruck. The next day I was what athletes as well as climbers refer to as 'off form'.

At the end of my time in the Tyrol I got permission to visit the Dolomites. Another athlete, a mile runner of promise, and I went to Cortina d'Ampezzo via Misurina. Before reaching that lake we came to a place on the road where it is possible to see, many miles away, the north faces of the Tre Cime di Lavaredo. We decided to run up and have a closer look and set off at a steady jog towards those famous rock walls. This became a severe lesson in judging scale; it is a long way from the Dobbiaco road up to the Tre Cime and we arrived, despite months of daily training, somewhat shattered. We had guessed our goal to be only a mile away, not the many miles it turned out to be. I was to find subsequently that altitude affects me severely; even 7,000 feet above sea level makes a difference until I am acclimatised. On arriving at a good vantage point under the north faces, I was sick! Besides retching, I was awestruck by the Dolomite walls. But jogging down, I quickly recovered and began to increase our pace until we were literally racing. I was no match for the miler on the run-in, up the final stretch of road to our transport; he later became national champion at his chosen distance.

We enjoyed our stay near Cortina. I came to like Dolomite scenery and life immensely; it was Valhalla for me for the next few years. I find the Dolomites the most attractive mountains of the Alps, with their snow-streaked spires, ridges and towers, their yellow and red rock faces in contrast with the green alps, rushing waters and whispering woods below. The Dolomites enjoy a finer climate than most other Alpine regions, and their people combine the Austrian zest for life with the Italian love of singing. When the time came to return to Manchester and my army unit, the idea of leaving such mountains for a galling and worthless service life was hard to bear. I almost chose to go absent without leave, but if I had missed the transport home I should have been in serious trouble. I had no money and was sufficiently a realist to understand that, with demobilisation a few months away, to kick over the traces would only prolong the agony for myself. Regretfully I climbed on to the train at Innsbruck to be carried away from the Dolomite fairyland and back to army routine.

I could not afford to visit the Alps on demobilisation in 1956, and in 1957 I went on the Rock and Ice meet in Cornwall. This may have been foolish, but when one has only a short holiday each year any place which offers a new experience with a minimum of time wasted on travelling is perhaps worthwhile. The summer of 1958 arrived; the Alps were not to be denied. By now British Alpine climbing was firmly on its feet; high levels of competence had been achieved by a respectable number, and a small elite was tackling the most difficult ascents, headed by Don Whillans as the outstanding British alpinist of his era.

Overflowing with anticipation and trepidation I joined Joe Brown, his wife and Mortimer Smith for the journey to Chamonix, travelling by train to meet Whillans who had gone out ahead of us. Joe was recovering from a fractured leg, injured while running scree below a Welsh cliff, and was limping visibly. I had fourteen days' holiday; less travelling time this allowed ten days in the mountains – not long when the vagaries of Mont Blanc's weather take a hand.

At Chamonix, Don Whillans was at the municipal campsite, just down from the fourth successful ascent of the south-west pillar of the Petit Dru (Pilier Bonatti). The bad weather during this climb and an injury to one of the party had made it into an epic ascent, and Don decided he needed a rest before climbing again.

Joe, Morty and I elected to start out immediately, to try to snatch a climb as a threesome; afterwards Don would meet us and we would combine into ropes of two. Before setting out Morty and I wandered the streets of the town, with me sightseeing and both of us purchasing food supplies. Chamonix was not as I had imagined it; it wasn't beautiful, more a Blackpool amongst mountains was my impression, but the view towards Mont Blanc and the Aiguilles made up for the brashness of man.

We caught the last train to Montenvers, loaded with equipment and food, including enough loaves to stock a bakery. My companions pointed out the sights as the train climbed through the woods while a group of merry French climbers belched a garlic accompaniment. At Montenvers we moved into a woodcutters' shelter known to mountaineers as Chalet Austria and as usual housing that country's young and impecunious climbers. We were warmly greeted by massive Walter Phillip and the youthful Richard Blach from Vienna who had taken part in the Petit Dru climb with Whillans.

Although Joe was not a hundred per cent fit, he was only interested in routes he considered worthwhile and vetoed any suggestion of a training climb. He had a thing about Alpine climbing: the first climb of the season is uncomfortable because of acclimatising and fitness problems, everybody suffers, so one might as well have an unpleasant time on a good climb as a poor one and have something to show for the effort. He wanted to start with the north face of the Grands Charmoz, immediately above the Mer de Glace. With other Rock and Ice members he had already been a long way up the face before bad weather forced retreat upon them; a fitting climb to limber up on, he decided. The Austrians became interested and said they would come along too; British climbers appeared to be in favour with them after their experience on the Drus. Walter Phillip, no mean climber himself, spoke of Whillans with respect as 'the great climber'.

This was my first evening among high mountains and I wandered out with Mortimer above the Mer de Glace to watch the sunset. Across the glacier the Drus were on fire, with the back-cloth of the north face of the Grandes Jorasses blooming in the alpenglow. Above our heads soared the sombre north face of the Charmoz, and behind and around were the Aiguilles, with the Republique like something out of a space programme. The scene frightened me, I could not say why; it also had qualities inadequately called beauty and mystery. My fears were partly composed of lack of confidence, partly of something intangible and primeval. I have sometimes envied companions untroubled by such feelings. Many of the best mountaineers I have known never appear to see mountains in terms other than rock, snow and ice in large or small quantities – the arena for their activities. They never seem to feel incompatibility with a mountain environment, nor the contact with an inexpressible force which I have sometimes felt so overwhelmingly that it has brought an almost uncontrollable fear.

The longer I gazed at the Charmoz the steeper appeared its north face. 'It looks a bit tough, Morty,' I ventured, pointing upwards.

Joe Smith, small, good-natured and physically powerful, was always cheerful and he grinned optimistically, 'Don't worry, it'll rain tomorrow!'

We woke at 2 a.m. to a rattling of pitons and ice-climbing equipment; our Austrian friends were ready to depart. 'Ve shall see you on ze vail,' declared Walter, disappearing into the night with Richard on his heels. We simply turned over and went back to sleep, to wake much later to the clank, clank of returning pitons and the drumming of rain on the roof of the chalet. The weather had, as Mortimer predicted, taken a turn for the worse and Walter and Richard had been forced to retreat. Later that day found the Austrians declaring 'Not only are British climbers good climbers but also sound judges of weather conditions.' We did not disillusion them; to get our party out of bed at two o'clock in the morning would have been impossible, even in the finest conditions in Alpine history.

Whillans arrived in the evening from Chamonix; he was keen to climb the west face of the Petites Jorasses, a recent new route which was being lauded for its difficulty and beauty by valley mandarins. The north face of the Charmoz was abandoned in favour of this objective.

The weather was bad again next day, so we decided to wait twenty-four hours before leaving for the Leschaux hut and our proposed climb. The day was spent lazing and working at climbing problems on the walls of the hut during which occurred an incident which provided some hilarity. Mortimer succeeded in climbing a ferocious no-feet-to-be-used problem, simply on arm pulls. None of our Austrian friends plus another of their countrymen, Diether Marchart, nor we three British could climb 'Mortimer's Wall', all of us failing to achieve the one-arm pulls to grab the roof. Don nearly made it with a gymnastic contortion but cannonaded off down the slope below the hut and almost disappeared over a precipice. At this moment a party of British climbers came along the path beside the hut. Their leader eyed us with contempt, then declared in nasal scouse: 'Wait till Brown and Whillans get here, they'll show you bloody Austrians how to climb!' He was amazed at the retort he received and disappeared down the Montenvers track, with a Whillans riposte cleaving the air, as if Mont Blanc itself was about to avalanche on top of him.

Next morning, bright and early around midday, we set out in improved weather for the Leschaux hut. Our route lay up the Mer de Glace and once down on to this, my first Alpine glacier, I began to understand a little of what Alpine climbing is. Our speed was swift, not exactly a race, but it felt like one. Don and Joe disappeared over the horizon, leaving the apprentices to follow on leisurely. Morty, though only a teenager, was already an alpinist of experience; as we stomped along he reminded me he had endured 'more bivouacs than you have hot dinners'. When we caught the others up again they were in the middle of the Leschaux glacier below the north face of the Grandes Jorasses, gazing up at the *Walker Spur*. The possibility of switching plans to this route was discussed. There had not been a British ascent, but continental climbers had built such a mystique about this climb that it had an unbelievable aura of difficulty. We vacillated; the weather was unsettled, and I pointed out I was an Alpine novice, yet to make an ascent. 'Be a good route to start on!' Joe declared. In the end we turned away and climbed the snow slopes leading to the ruins of the old Leschaux hut, destroyed some years before by an avalanche. In the Alps we preferred to sleep in bivouacs when climbing, and disused woodcutters' huts or camping in valleys. We simply could not afford other accommodation.

The ruined hut proved an excellent shelter; enough of it remained to accommodate the party, and its situation was majestic. I had been impressed the previous evening at Montenvers, but that paled in comparison with our new surroundings. The Leschaux is one of the wildest and most beautiful cirques in the Alps, with unparalleled views to the north face of the Grandes Jorasses. At the head of this basin lie the Petites Jorasses, dwarfed by their neighbour but nevertheless fine in their own right. This new situation again invoked in me a feeling of fright combined with anticipation, an impression heightened as we turned into sleeping bags at sunset, in preparation for a dawn start on my first serious Alpine climb.

Next morning we were off at first light, keeping together up the wide stretch of glacier till we reached crevasses and some bare ice. Don and Joe carried hammer axes, Morty and I only piton hammers; none of us carried crampons as the Petites Jorasses is a rock-climb, and the apprentices found one slope of bare ice tricky. When we reached the foot of the rock we had not decided who was to climb with whom so we tossed a coin for partners. The two leaders were to shout and Morty and I were the prizes; Joe won Mortimer, Don had to be satisfied with me.

Don and I started out first, following a steep, cracked dièdre which went up as far as eye could see, cleaving the 2,000 feet of granite above our heads. Overcoming altitude has always been a difficulty to me and I still didn't know how slowly I acclimatise; as we gained height I felt dizzy and had to inform Don I was about to be sick. Don can be a difficult person to come to terms with in a valley, but on a climb there is something of a Quixote about him. He was worried about me, and when I began retching he insisted we go down. The two Joes were starting up as we rappelled back to the bergschrund. My nose began to bleed slightly and, as well as vomit, some blood was coming out of my mouth. This visibly impressed my companions, and all agreed I had to go down. I declared myself able to descend alone and set out down the Leschaux glacier. The others saw me safely through the worst crevasses, then roped up as a threesome to complete their ascent.

Going downhill I soon felt better and stopped to watch as the others climbed the dièdre, three tiny dots on a wall. The west face of the Petites Jorasses is reminiscent of a cock's comb; the fault they were following lost itself in over-hangs long before the serrations of the comb were reached. I concluded I had been ambitious in trying this as a first Alpine climb but was near to tears as I started moving again towards the ruined hut. When I got there I decided to go on down to Chamonix to see if Eric Beard had arrived. He had left home at the same time as I had but was hitch-hiking instead of travelling by train.

I soon located him at the campsite, for if Beardie was in residence every-body seemed to know him. He was keen to start climbing so, loading up with further food supplies, we walked up to Montenvers and Chalet Austria in the late evening. Next morning found us en route for the Leschaux in time to be there well ahead of our friends' return from their climb. Marching up the glaciers, roles were reversed; I was the guide with Beardie the novice. Typically his pack weighed seventy pounds; among other items he carried ten pounds of potatoes to make a monster stew on arrival. I have never laughed so much on a glacier as walking up the Leschaux; Beardie fell into three crevasses, toppled over half a dozen times and staggered about as if drunk. He was merely awed by the mountain spectacle and couldn't concentrate on where he was going. By the time we reached the hut ruins he was covered with cuts and gashes and had a new nickname – Alpine Clown. When the west face party got back from their successful ascent, Don took one look at him, demanded who had been knocking him about and offered to 'have a do at 'em!'

Back at Chamonix we couldn't make up our minds on our next objective. Joe Brown was suffering agony with his bad leg but wanted to climb the south-west pillar of the Drus, Mortimer wanted to climb the west face of the Petit Dru,

Don the east face of the Grand Capucin. I could see that whichever route was selected would be a good opener to my Alpine career. Eventually I set out for the Capucin with Don, while the two Joes headed for the south-west pillar.

Don and I ambled up the Mer de Glace in the late afternoon, avoiding tourists and crevasses, and climbed into and out of the Géant icefall, to bivouac 150 feet up a rock buttress in a comfortable niche overlooking the glacier. We cooked, and as evening closed in settled down for the night. This was my first bivouac in the Alps and I sat gazing at the stars long after Don was snoring beside me. It now seems incredible that modern equipment should have so completely revolutionised a night out in high mountains in the brief span of time since that date, when a forced bivouac was to be feared, especially in bad conditions. On this my first night out, despite good weather I found the undertaking uncomfortable, yet in retrospect it was romantic. Mountaineering authors often describe at great length the deep and significant introspection which they indulge in during bivouacs. I have never reacted deeply at such times; it is only afterwards when I am warm and comfortable in the valley that the memory of the scene floods me with a genuine response. At the time I am too aware of my skin to probe into the unconscious.

When we awoke next morning the sun was already high overhead. 'Hell, what time is it?' Don's watch had stopped, mine was in Chamonix. We had a quick brew of tea and, leaving our bivouac equipment behind, rappelled down to the glacier, the climb up to our eyrie having been severe. We set out for the Capucin at a cracking pace; Don had attempted the climb before and knew its approaches well. We guessed the time as ten o'clock; it was a beautiful day, but over the horizon hung ominous clouds.

At the base of the Grand Capucin I could only gasp in admiration at its east face. It was hard to believe that the mass of rock at which I was staring was merely a tower on the huge sides of Mont Blanc du Tacul. I know of no rock face in the Alps more beautiful than the Capucin's eastern rampart; an unbroken sweep of firm red granite, it finishes in huge overhangs which form a summit cowl 1,500 feet above its base.

We kicked steps up a couloir bounding the face on its south side, and this easy approach gave access to a series of ledges leading into the middle of the face. We roped up at the beginning of the serious difficulties, a pitch known as the Grade-VI Slab. Don quickly crossed this obstacle, barrier to a series of fissures and grooves which weave through a succession of overhangs. I followed at a more human pace and joined him at the foot of a crack out of which protruded a line of closely spaced pitons. Apart from the first section, most of the climbing on the face is artificial; my experience of that style of climbing was strictly limited. I had pointed this out to my companion, to receive the same reply as on other occasions when I drew attention to my inexperience, 'Good climb to learn on then!'

Don bombed up the cracks and grooves which followed; he didn't use etriers but simply pulled on the pitons already in place. I followed, carrying our rucksack containing food and spare clothes, and though I was not as quick in climbing we made rapid progress. A party passed under the face; we shouted, they shouted back; they were British. 'What time is it?' we enquired.

'One o'clock.'

'We'll have to move faster if we are to get up today,' announced Don, and off he went up the next section, the series of overhangs. 'Etriers from now on,' he decided, swarming over a roof. When it was my turn to follow I got the ropes and myself into a tangle, and arrived to join him at a one-foot stance. 'Start thinking about what you're bloody well doing!' he admonished.

We climbed the 130-foot wall, the supposed crux, moving together once Don had run out a fair length of rope and clipped into enough pitons to make us bombproof. We could nevertheless appreciate the labour and difficulty of this section when Bonatti and Ghigo made the first ascent in 1951. This had taken four days, but with each repetition it had become easier with many pitons left in place until, at the time of our ascent, it simply involved clipping and unclipping karabiners and stepping upwards. The situations made up for the dreariness of this method; swinging in space beneath successive stepped overhangs kept one constantly interested, wondering where the route would take one next.

Among the overhangs, tempers flared. Don had reached the third Bonatti bivouac, and as I was feeling tired I asked him to haul up the rucksack. I tied it on to a hauling line; as Don began to pull it swung wildly across the face and jammed under an overhang. There was no way to free it but for me to climb across and dislodge the pack. This manoeuvre provided the hardest free climbing on the ascent; hanging from a hand jam and balancing on a thumbnail hold, I reached gingerly across and moved the rucksack off its obstruction. Don was holding me firmly on the rope but also had the sack-hauling rope held loosely in his forward hand. I gave him no warning about freeing the sack, thinking he held the attaching line firmly. The pack shot down thirty feet before Don stopped it, burning his hands in braking its fall. The air was blue! Many were the insults hurled as I climbed up to join him, the commonest that I was 'a bloody drink of water', but I took enough time reaching his stance for him to cool down and it did serve the purpose of urging me to greater effort.

Earlier in the day the heat of the sun had been a problem; you could have fried an egg on the 130-foot wall. Now the goddess of change decided we have seen enough of the sun and clouds in huge banks drifted over and blotted it out. Thunder rolled as a storm raced in from Italy. We dashed up the last artificial pitches, then stowed away our equipment and soloed the last rope-length to the summit.

My first Alpine route was accomplished, but there was no time to sit and discuss it in lengthy detail. 'Must have made good time,' Don decided, but neither of us could say if we had spent six or twelve hours on the ascent; it didn't much matter as cloud enveloped us and it began to rain. A series of rappels led immediately off the summit. I was so keen to get off that on the second rappel I nearly pushed Don off the mountain; I went down so fast, hastened by the storm, that I landed on top of him as he clung to a tiny stance. This time the air was purple! We reached a dirty loose couloir on the north side of the Capucin and as we descended this the storm broke in earnest. I thought we had been moving fast but Don insisted on more speed. 'Let's get out of here, we're moving like a couple of ta-tas!' And he sped down the loose rocks with me hard at his heels. By the time we reached the Brèche du Carabinier the rain had turned to driving snow, obliterating our vision almost completely. We roped up to continue the descent from the Brèche to the Géant glacier by way of a wide couloir; luckily Don had brought his hammer axe, so I was let down the snow a rope-length at a time, then he followed in my tracks, using the hammer spike to brake with. At one point the couloir was bare ice, but Don said, 'You could fall down this lot and get away with it.' Stepping on to the ice I did just that, to be stopped in fifteen feet by deep soft snow and Don with his hammer well belayed. We jumped a half-seen bergschrund and I breathed a sigh of relief when I stepped on to the glacier. But our most difficult task was still to come – finding the rock buttress on which we had left our bivouac equipment seemed a hopeless undertaking.

Don, belayed by me, climbed up and down rock walls at the edge of the glacier. It gradually became dark and the snowfall built up into a steady, all-pervading force. I had given up hope and sat holding the rope in a hole in the snow, prepared to spend the night there. Suddenly Don gave a triumphant cry: 'I've found it!' He had located the crack which led up to our bivouac. How he climbed up there in the dark and snowy conditions I don't know, but I wasn't ashamed to have a tight rope to join him. Soon we were sitting inside a large polythene bag, with a primus roaring and a hot drink prepared. Despite being wet through I slept the night away, and awoke next morning almost buried alive by snow.

We set off down, with snow still falling, through the dreariest, white-and-grey world of my experience. We dripped through the Géant icefall, slid down a Mer de Glace bared by pouring rain into a skating rink, and arrived in Chamonix for late breakfast. Almost simultaneously the two Joes got back to our tents. They had spent a dangerous time bivouacking in the Drus couloir and been forced to turn back by heavy stone falls and snowfall.

You cannot accomplish much in ten days' holiday unless the weather is good, and it was decidedly bad. I had only time for one more climb, a short frolic on the Aiguilles with Beardie, before I had to start for home. I had not achieved a great deal in my first Alpine season, but it had been educative and even a rich slice of life.

After this visit to the Mont Blanc range I could not resettle to work. I found life in a modern industrial society shallow and meaningless. I completed my studies in the winter of 1958–1959 and determined from then on to seek a different life, attempting to travel and to experience other cultures and modes of living, but always my direction has been towards mountains. How to escape was my problem. It is not easy to give up a profession or turn one's back on material prospects by changing a career in mid stream. Luckily for me, as it turned out, the man I worked for was an unpleasant, autocratic hark back to the days of harsh employers, and seemed to me out of touch with modern industrial relations.

In June 1959, Tom Stobart, the 1953 Everest expedition cine-photographer, was filming in the Dolomites. He needed climbers to act as assistants, porters and even doubles for the film stars in climbing sequences. The finished result was to be named *Hazard*, an industrial safety propaganda film, and of its type a large production. Joe Brown and Don Roscoe went out to help make the film and Stobart asked them if any more of the Rock and Ice group could travel to Italy to give a hand. There was work for as many helpers as could afford the journey at their own expense. Just at this time I had an argument with my boss; I could stomach his manner and attitude no longer and walked out of the firm never to return. I had taken a far-reaching decision, which embarked me on a new course in life. I contacted Eric Beard, Eric Metcalf (Matey) and Brian Fuller (Fred the Ted) and two days later the four of us set out for the Dolomites in my small van, with the promise of a month of film work ahead.

At Cortina we easily found Stobart, his film stars and crews, including Joe Brown and Don Roscoe; everyone seemed to know of their whereabouts. When we arrived the weather was abominable, but within a day a high-pressure system appeared and throughout the month we had good weather, often complaining about the oppressive heat as we worked in blazing sunshine. Climbing sequences were filmed throughout the Cortina region – Tofana, Tre Cime, Cinque Torri – and we soon learned that cine work is no rest cure. We acted as guides to the camera crews, led them up rock faces to good camera positions, portered heavy film equipment, built platforms for camera and sound recorders, and carried up to film locations thirty prepared dinners each day from the local refuges. Among the more bizarre items we carried around were a twenty-foot ladder and sacks of straw to put underneath in case of a fall; these were essential to get some of the stars above ground level! There were plenty of serious moments but also a lot of laughs, especially when we doubled for the stars.

At every opportunity we snatched a climb. Early in the month Beardie and I set out for our first grade-VI climb on Dolomite rock. On this route, high above the ground, there was a ceiling that involved swinging out on a piton to reach big holds on the lip of the overhang. Leading, I examined the piton carefully before swinging out over space; it was an eighteen-inch ice piton driven upside down into a perfect crack, as firm as could be desired. I reached a belay stance and began to bring up Beardie who managed easily till he got to the roof with the piton swing; he rested below this while I gave him instructions, then he too launched into space. He appeared over the lip but hung there on his arms, then suddenly let go and fell under the roof again. I heard a gurgling, choking sound as I held him on the rope but almost immediately he came back over the lip. 'Pull!' he shouted, and I heaved with all my might; one rope was tight to his waist, the other disappeared under the roof. The sun was unbearably hot and sweat poured off me as I pulled; Beardie also heaved away on his arms but to no avail and again he fell back under the lip, to dangle in space. I began to realise the seriousness of the situation: Beardie was near to exhaustion and was being suffocated by the ropes round his waist. He started to sob, 'The rope's jammed, it keeps pulling me off.'

'Are you sure you've unclipped both ropes from the piton?' I shouted in near panic.

'Both ropes? No, I only unclipped one. I thought that's how double ropes worked.'

With a last flailing effort he managed to get back on to the rock lip, and by letting out slack on the rope running through the piton and heaving on the rope direct to his waist I managed to get him landed on a small ledge for a rest. 'No wonder you couldn't get up, Beardie, pulling against that ice peg, it would hold the Cime Grande. You'd never pull it out!'

We eventually extricated ourselves, but I agreed with Beardie's comment that he hadn't a mechanical mind like Dolomite climbers seemed to have!

At the end of a month the film was successfully completed and everyone packed up and returned to Britain except Beardie, Matey, Fred the Ted and myself. We decided to drive to Mont Blanc via the Bregaglia, that superb granite range in eastern Switzerland; there we made a brief halt for the famous Piz Badile which gave us an enjoyable climb amidst wild rock scenery. Then on to Chamonix and a story of feverish activity by many British parties. Mortimer, Don Whillans and other friends were there, the *Walker Spur* had been climbed several times, and conditions were the best for years. We hastened to get up into the mountains.

Beardie and I set out for the *Route Major* on the Brenva face of Mont Blanc, and among other partnerships Mortimer teamed up with Matey for the Brown-Whillans route on the west face of the Blaitière. We packed our sacks and departed with high hopes of having hit off the long-awaited perfect weather. But Beardie and I had barely reached the head of the Mer de Glace when it became obvious that the weather was changing; clouds were rolling in from the south, thick, fleecy and dark. We about-turned and reached Montenvers and Chalet Austria in heavy rain, trying to be philosophical.

Next morning it was fine, but we decided to give the weather another day to settle; the *Route Major* is a high-altitude one and goes to the summit of Mont Blanc. In the afternoon we climbed the Menegaux route on the Aiguille de l'M. We were leaving early the following morning when another British climber arrived from Chamonix with the news that distress signals had been seen the night before on the Blaitière west face: Morty and Matey must be in some sort of trouble. Whillans was forming a rescue team of Alpine Climbing Group members on the campsite, but meanwhile he had sent the messenger up to Chalet Austria to ask any ACG members there to set out in advance to prospect the face for signs of our friends.

Beardie, Ian McNaught-Davis and I left immediately and raced along the path to the Plan de l'Aiguille, then climbed up under the west face of the Blaitière. The weather was deteriorating rapidly as we wandered along the foot of the face, searching for signs of life. We met the head of the rescue service from Chamonix, coordinating a search of the mountain by guides with two-way wireless, on the edge of the glacier. Mac, who is fluent in French, elicited from him that no sign of any climbers in difficulty had so far been discovered, although distress signals had been seen many times the previous evening by workmen at the Plan de l'Aiguille *téléphérique* station. We traversed round to examine the normal descent route, plodding up the Nantillons glacier until we were underneath the Spencer couloir. We saw nothing here, and in pouring rain decided to go down; as we were passing the foot of the north ridge of the Blaitière, a stone whirred down and thudded into the glacier close by. Following its fall line up into the rain and mist, we discerned a movement; a tiny black dot was moving through space, someone was rappelling down.

We started up to meet the lone climber, but were nonplussed when our hailing shouts were answered in what sounded like French; we climbed down again, thinking it must be one of the Chamonix guides searching the mountain. When the descending climber was within a few hundred feet of the glacier, we were relieved to recognise Mortimer, still shouting the one French word he knew, 'Secours!', thinking us to be French climbers.

Mortimer and Matey had climbed the most difficult sections of the face, but near the summit, while leading an awkward layback crack, Matey had unaccountably come off. Well belayed, Mortimer had managed to hold his long fall, but Matey had hurt his legs badly and was unable to walk or climb; he also kept lapsing into unconsciousness. Luckily there was a ledge below Matey, and Morty lowered him on to this and then climbed down to join him. They spent an uncomfortable night there, Matey in agony in his more lucid moments. Morty had signalled their distress until their torch failed, but was not sure if anyone had seen the signals. In the morning he waited to see if a rescue party would appear, but in the bad weather the guides, though they had passed close by, had not been seen or heard by Mortimer; tired of waiting he made Matey as comfortable as possible and started down to find help.

We crossed the Blaitière glacier, reporting to the French rescue party who declared it would now be morning before they could reach our injured friend. On the way down we met Whillans with a strong party of ACG members which included Dr Graeme Nicol; it was obviously common sense to get medical aid up the mountain as swiftly as possible, and they disappeared into the mist with careful instructions from Mortimer where they would find Matey.

There is sometimes criticism by visiting climbers of rescue services in the Alps, but no one could criticise the speed and efficiency of the French who turned out at first light to bring down the injured British climber. Whillans and the other ACG members had reached Matey the previous night but, hurt as he was, could not move him far. They had rendered first aid and made him comfortable, but they needed the help of the fully equipped Chamonix rescue service to get him off the mountain. The guides have to be seen at this work for their speed to be appreciated; by dinner time they had Matey out of his predicament and safely into a hospital bed in Chamonix.

Only when Matey was down in the valley did the ugly situation of a visiting climber, injured in the Alps, become apparent to me. I was in charge of his affairs and was staggered by the bills and financial claims. To be in hospital in France is an exorbitant business, but in retrospect it was the inefficiency of the doctors that was most distressing. After he had been in hospital a week, they diagnosed Matey as suffering only from sprains and abrasions, and pronounced him fit to leave. This amazed us for he couldn't stand on his legs. Eventually I contacted the British consul in Geneva, and drove Matey to Switzerland and put him on an aeroplane for London. The consul was not as helpful as I had hoped; despite promises, no ambulance was available to transport the injured climber from the plane to hospital. Luckily an acquaintance lived near the airport, one of the stars of the film, *Hazard*. He came immediately to the rescue and arranged for examination by a specialist; the crippled Matey had to undergo several operations and spent almost a year in and out of hospitals before recovering from his injuries.

There has been much controversy in the past few years about rescues in the Alps. From my experience, Eric Metcalf's case is fairly typical. The fault does not lie solely with visiting climbers; it lies with the government and people of the Alpine countries. It is fair to assert that climbers should be insured against the possibility of accident; this seems sound common sense. Matey was insured and a member of the French Alpine Club which pays part of the cost of rescue expenses. There is a limit to the insurance cover one can afford or even purchase, for alpine mountaineering is a risky business and accidents happen to the competent as well as the incompetent. Matey spent a year paying off all his debts when he started work again; some of the charges levied upon him were excessive, to say the least. In my view the governments of Alpine countries, especially France and Switzerland, should provide free rescue services to anyone injured in their mountains. There has grown up a myth that climbers are a nuisance; in fact, the cost of rescues is not worth considering when balanced against the amount of foreign exchange brought into the Alpine countries by mountain tourism. The Iron Curtain countries, America, Britain and other climbing nations have free rescue services, manned for climbers by climbers; surely continental countries should do the same.

On my return to Chamonix from Geneva, the weather was still bad and the campsite overflowing with weather-bound climbers. I loaded up my van and Beardie, Steve Read and I journeyed back to the Dolomites to visit the Civetta. Amongst Dolomite peaks the Civetta is for me the most impressive; a complete range, it has everything that is best in Dolomite scenery and climbing, and is so extensive that there can be winter on its 4,000-foot northern precipices while at the lower and southern end it is high summer.

We had no information about the area when we arrived in Alleghe, the town under the northern side of the range. There were no English guidebooks and we understood little Italian. Following a track which appeared to take us directly up to the frowning precipices, we set forth late on the evening of our arrival, overflowing with mountain keenness. But we had underestimated the distance, and after walking through a thick forest we lost our way in rapidly failing daylight. We blundered through undergrowth and small trees, staggering under immense loads comprising tents, paraffin, climbing equipment and food for a week, carrying in turn a polythene bucket full of potatoes. Eventually it became impossible to move safely on the rough ground and we had to bivouac on the spot. Next day, instead of retracing our steps, we determinedly pushed on and by evening we were putting up our tents at the foot of the Civetta's north faces. On the way we had ascended scree slopes, cliffs and even trees. My most vivid recollection of this fiasco is of balancing in a steep groove, grasping the bucket of potatoes handed up to me by Beardie similarly placed. I passed it on to Steve Read and climbed beyond him to have the bucket handed to me once more: all this in the middle of a 300-foot cliff.

The weather at the Civetta was little better than at Chamonix; during three days of rain and snow the faces above us became whiter and whiter. On the fourth day we abandoned that wintry scene and walked down to the Vazzoler refuge at the lower end of the range, which was bathed in sun through any small break in the cloud. The climbing hereabouts is superb, especially on those dream towers, Torre Venezia and Trieste. After some short scrambles, Steve and I succeeded in making the first British ascent of the *Tissi* route on the Venezia's south face. We set out knowing little of what to expect but anticipating a difficult expedition, as the route contained grade-VI climbing. Instead, we found no serious problems on one of the most beautiful ascents I have experienced, on good quality rock throughout. The finest pitches of the climb are also the crux, in the form of a typical Dolomite traverse set above overhangs, perched on the edge of all things but well protected with pitons. After the traverse, a line of chimneys completes the 1,500-foot face. Up these we laughed, racing two friendly Italian climbers who beat us to the summit when we lost the way on the last easy section. They made up for this by producing a large bottle of vino, and we celebrated according to local custom.

My theories about Dolomite rock were confirmed by this ascent: ochreous-coloured rock is dangerously loose, yellow rock is loose, and grey or black rock runs the gamut from firm to absolutely solid. The Venezia south face is grey and black, and is such an enjoyable climb that I have repeated it on subsequent holidays. The view from the summit is mighty, especially towards the white-flecked Torre Trieste, the hardest mountain in the Alps with no easy way to or from its summit.

At the end of our stay at the Civetta I had spent ten weeks in the mountains and because of money difficulties decided it was time to go home. This had been an unforgettable holiday; for the first time, I had been free to go where I liked and do as I pleased, without the worry of fitting my activities into a timetable set by someone else. I was uneasy all the same about the future; I still paid too much heed to older people whose typical comment was 'It's all right for you to do as you please, but what would happen if everybody stopped working when they liked? Society would collapse.' I could not then see through this facile argument and found the forces of conventionality hard to ignore. In any case, despite my disenchantment with modern industrial life, I was passionately interested in printing techniques and methods. On return from the Dolomites I got a job with a Derby firm who specialised in photogravure printing. Although this meant only two weeks' holiday the following summer, I was compensated by my new work which involved, in part, fine art reproduction – limited editions of the highest standard, reproducing by the gravure method prints of master works. I found this stimulating: the attempt to reproduce, as near facsimile as possible, a painting such as Salvador Dali's 'Christ of St John of the Cross' has technical intricacies which are absorbing, and on successful completion, satisfying.

In 1960 I resolved to return to the Dolomites, even for only a fortnight. Joe Brown was also keen to go back after his experiences of the previous summer, and we decided to team up. The end of July found us at the Tre Cime once more, camping in a quagmire, after a nearly non-stop drive from England. The weather was shocking. After we had done one or two short climbs, including the *Yellow Edge* on the Cima Piccola, the wintry conditions made it seem likely that the season would be outstandingly bad.

Joe had been in indifferent health for nearly two years, in fact since his accident in 1958 when he fractured a leg. He had developed stomach ulcers and was on a diet of milk, cheese and chicken broth. We had to drive miles every day, either before or after climbing, to purchase his supply of milk. The other two items we had brought from England, with the cheeses smelling horribly after a fortnight. By the end of the holiday I had put on six pounds, but hated Ovaltine and chicken broth for months afterwards.

To climb with Joe in an area like the Dolomites is a rich experience; he hates early rising, a sentiment which I echo, and our starting times were always late. In fact, we usually met continental parties returning as we walked up to the foot of the rock. I don't think I have ever climbed as fast as we did that year; Joe, mindful of his health, had to avoid bivouacs and stick carefully to his diet. We left the tent one morning shortly before ten o'clock, to return for his four o'clock milk-Ovaltine only minutes late, having climbed the north face of the Cime Grande; for some unaccountable reason we traversed out of the easy finishing chimneys and climbed one of the steepest, loosest and most exposed pieces of rock in my experience. This passed without comment at the time – Baron Brown was only worried about his milk schedule!

We left the Tre Cime with a following of British climbers and moved to the Tofana group; Joe always seems to attract a retinue – a kind of pied piper of the climbing world. We went up to the Dibona hut with our thoughts fixed on the Pilastro di Rozes by its south-east face. The Pilastro is only a small spur compared to the huge bulk of its parent Tofana, but it is 1,700 feet, nevertheless, with a belt of introductory slabs followed by overhangs and, finally, a line of chimneys. Since the first ascent in 1944 it has become a classic, one that both Joe and I had an ambition to complete; we had each attempted the climb with other partners, and had both been forced to retreat.

Luckily at the hut we found that the relief guardian was a man who had worked with us on *Hazard* in 1959. Our noisy party enjoyed a happy stay in his best rooms at specially reduced rates, which somewhat offset the atrocious weather. Conditions were so bad that we almost gave up hope of our climb, but stayed on feeling it must improve sooner or later.

We were woken up late one morning by two young Germans. Miraculously it was fine at last; they couldn't understand us lying in bed, didn't we want to climb after all? Snatching a glass of milk we left the hut in a hurry, and reached the foot of the climb stiff through inactivity. The first section of the route is 700 feet of grey rock at slab angle; followed by another British pair, Les Brown and Trevor Jones, we climbed this in a diagonal line sloping from right to left, starting at the very toe of the buttress.

Climbing with Joe Brown has its drawbacks; his speed, ease and command give one an inferiority complex, and I have always found myself suffering from lack of confidence in my own ability when with him. With a few exceptions, it is wasteful for anyone to lead when partnering him on a difficult Alpine rock climb, he moves so fast. In the Alps, because of possible weather changes, speed is safety; the faster a party moves, the shorter time it is actually at risk.

The weather had not really settled and we guessed the improvement would only be temporary. We reached the top of the belt of slabs and became absorbed in a series of roof overhangs; on one section there are two ceilings, one above the other, and from the tip of the second roof I looked down between my body and the rock to the base of the slabs we had climbed, hundreds of vertical feet below. No rock I have ever climbed gives such a feeling of cliff hanging as the Dolomites provide. It was a relief to get above the roofs and reach the first of the chimney pitches, a relief which was short lived when I gazed up at the monstrous leaning fissure. It had been clearly visible from the door of the hut, and our friend the guardian had warned us not to fall off here; two climbers had recently done so, and had died of strangulation through swinging in space at the end of their rope, unable to get back on to the rock again. It made me nervous to think of this and I broached the subject to Joe as he set out to climb the pitch; poker-faced he observed 'Mmm, yes, and they were both seconding!'

He was above the chimney and decided to haul up our rucksack before I had time to reflect further. I tied the sack to the hauling line, and gulped on letting it go to see it swing fifty feet out into space. Trevor Jones, climbing an overhang far below, was equally impressed, and was so frightened by the spectacle that he nearly gave up the climb. The chimney, like many such problems, was not nearly so bad as it appeared, but it is a unique pitch for all that, with its huge slant from right to left. One has the sensation of climbing a large roof as one back-and-foots out to the chimney's edge; the exposure is extreme but the climbing not actually severe. Above this obstacle the major difficulties are over; cracks and chimneys lead straightforwardly upwards.

Our weather predictions had been correct and once more the horizon was swamped by thick black clouds. The air was humming with discharging electricity; we didn't need further notice of impending storm. We raced up the easy summit rocks and then ran across the Pilastro's crown and on to the descent route. This was the easiest of ways off and twenty minutes later we arrived at the refuge, sweating but happy, just as the heavens opened. Les Brown and Trevor Jones were caught in the onslaught but dealt competently with the upper sections of the climb, to arrive back at the hut at nightfall, soaking but, like us, full of enthusiasm for the climb. Joe and I had not taken note of our climbing time but according to the guardian we had set some kind of record so the vino flowed. We hardly needed an excuse for a celebration, we were so happy at our success.

In spite of the weather we moved south to the Civetta, determined to do one of its major climbs, and camped at the side of the Coldai lake in conditions reminiscent of Scotland in November. The holiday was racing past, so on an indifferent day we set out to climb the north-west face of the Torre di Valgrande by the *Carlesso* route, a direct way up a typical Dolomite tower. This climb, though relatively short compared to major Civetta routes, and on a secondary summit of the mountain, is nevertheless a famous ascent of 2,000 feet, considered to be of a high order of difficulty.

We made our usual late start at nine o'clock and walked up to the foot of the climb. The first thousand feet of the *Carlesso* are easy, so we decided to solo to save time. It was cold and wet, with water running everywhere, and my enthusiasm was at a low ebb as I plodded along behind Joe, heading for the bottom of an obvious corner which is the start of the difficult climbing. As we moved up, I was awed by glimpses through the mist of the most stupendous walls in the Dolomites on our right.

We were surprised to find Steve Read and Les Brown a short way up the first difficult part. They had set out before dawn from our campsite to attempt the long and arduous *Solleder* route on the main Civetta summit but the inclement weather had made them change their minds and deflected them to their present course. This we didn't welcome; climbing behind another party in the Dolomites is dangerous because of the stones almost certain to be dislodged.

We waited till Les and Steve had gained some height, then roped up and set off in their wake. Joe had climbed the second difficult pitch and was just reaching a stance when the inevitable stone fall came whirring. One of the stones hit him squarely on the head just as he tied on to a piton; he let out a cry and slumped on to the ropes but soon recovered enough to bring me up to him. He was an alarming sight, blood oozed from under the peak of a flat cap he was wearing, his face was deathly white and he looked badly shaken. When we removed his cap, blood ran in all directions from a deep scalp wound. Joe has thick black hair and this had saved him from more serious damage, and it also helped to staunch the flow. It apparently takes more than a tap on the head to stop the Baron; he pronounced himself fit and set out once more, blood-bespattered but refusing to surrender the lead.

I couldn't understand the frantic pace from then on and began to think the head injury had affected Joe's judgement. At one stage we were both climbing together on difficult ground, Joe had run out the full 150 feet of rope between us but kept right on and I couldn't contact him. He was climbing free, I was starting on artificial climbing. I had to leap from piton to piton to keep up with his movements. It began to rain in torrents so we traversed off the correct line of ascent in a gully bed and went up steep walls at its side, as the route had become a mammoth waterfall. Suddenly, even above the drumming rain, we heard the roar of stone fall; missiles bombarded the rock exactly where we should have been climbing. There is no disputing the element of chance in alpine climbing, and few alpinists, however skilful, would deny that they owe their survival partly to luck.

I now definitely decided that the blow on the head had affected Joe; he was off like a hare before I even had time to remark on the stone fall when I joined him at the next stance. What seemed minutes later, bashing through the rain we arrived breathless at the summit. I gasped 'What's the rush?' as I joined Joe on the crest of the Valgrande. He didn't reply but pulled his watch from his anorak pocket, looked at it quizzically and subsided in giggles. My doubts about his mental state were intensified and I was relieved to hear the explanation. Lower down the climb he had looked at his watch and must have read it upside down. He had thought the time to be 6.45 p.m. when actually it was 1.15, and had decided we had to go flat out to avoid a bivouac. It was only 1.40 p.m. on the summit, and after a short abseil from just below the top on the south side we reached easy ground and got back to our tents by the lake in time for a late lunch of Ovaltine!

We had endured enough bad Dolomite weather and, with our holidays almost over, became convinced that the sun was shining on Mont Blanc. In a hurry we packed and the evening of the Valgrande climb found us en route for Chamonix. There the long faces of the crowds in the wet streets and the queues around the barometer at the French Alpine Club bureau told the story – conditions were at least as bad as in the Dolomites. The snowline was below Montenvers and all mountain activity was at a standstill.

We met two Scots climbers on the campsite, Robin Smith and Dougal Haston; they suggested that Joe and I should join them for an attempt on the unclimbed south face of the Aiguille du Fou, and in spite of the gloom we set out. Although Joe and I were fit and acclimatised after our Dolomite climbs, Robin was fitter. The walk to the Envers des Aiguilles hut under the Fou was furious in pace, and though the rest of us hung on grimly the powerful Scot one-upped us by singing the way up the final track to the hut. Surprisingly the mists drew back with the coming of evening and revealed the summits.

Bolstered by the hope of improving weather the Scots had us out of bed at the ghastly hour of 3 a.m., and wandering up the glacier to the foot of the face by 4 a.m. I felt sick and flopped away at the back. Dawn found us nearly under the Fou but once again the weather was up to its tricks and mists swirled down. The first spots of rain were enough for me; I about-turned and shot back to the hut and a warm bunk, leaving the others, of sterner material, to continue their upward path. I was cheered to wake at eight o'clock to rain pattering on the roof and the others returning to the refuge drenched to the skin. A return to Chamonix was the only answer, and for Joe and me the holidays were over. We spent a miserable time on the flooded campsite before we could set out to drive home. The roads were damaged and water lay every-where, and it was without regret that we left Mont Blanc to those with the time and money to wait for better days.

Back at home, I felt some satisfaction from our efforts; if you have only a short holiday, then several major climbs is success in a bad year. But I was unhappy about our unequal partnership; with a companion as good as Joe Brown, I was relegated to being little more than a moving belay. I decided that in future my Alpine climbing would best be undertaken with someone of similar ability to my own; only in an equal partnership on a rope do both climbers fully enjoy themselves. I judged that my apprenticeship was over, but nonetheless I shall never forget Joe's speed during that holiday; it was worth witnessing – some-thing to recall with admiration many seasons hence.

4   The Himalaya – Kulu, 1961

'This earth is the honey of all things.'
(Upanishads)

The Himalayan chain swings in a 1,500-mile arc through Asia, a geographic freak containing the highest mountains of the world, and the ultimate possibility in mountain experience by man on this planet. During the 1950s the ascent was achieved of the highest summits of the range: Everest, K2, Kangchenjunga, feats made possible by the slow build-up of knowledge about Himalayan climbing through previous decades, and signifying that technical development had reached the stage where the giants could be climbed by their easiest approaches. Despite the popular assumption of the finality of high-altitude mountaineering with the gaining of these summits, this was actually only a preface to the future story of climbing in this, the greatest range on earth. The best is yet to come if the yardstick is quality of ascent rather than altitude.

The Himalaya are made up of dozens of ranges with thousands of peaks, most of which have never been attempted and some of which are far more difficult than any single peak yet climbed in the massif; if one thinks of the endless permutations of possible ways to summits in the Alps, it becomes obvious that the Himalaya will provide goals for generations of climbers yet to be born.

These mountains are not solely for the extreme climber nor the professional explorer; there are unfrequented valleys, untrodden passes, easy but worthy unclimbed peaks, besides summits which demand of their suitors the highest technical ability. Every mountain lover should make it his ambition to visit the Himalaya, for there can be found whatever is sought amongst mountains. At present, he will need to be a person of wide interests fully to enjoy the experience; the out-and-out extremist bound up in the conquest of the vertical and little else may find the Himalaya disappointing. There are long approaches, many regions are still unexplored, few reliable maps exist, and much time is usually spent in travelling under primitive conditions, often with little real mountaineering in alpine terms at journey's end. The climber interested only in the technicalities of climbing had perhaps best turn elsewhere, or wait another twenty years until improved communications allow him a swift approach, possibly an airdrop into advance base camp. Any mountaineer interested in travel, in experiencing a new world and in adapting to different standards and conditions will find a visit to the Himalaya unforgettable, one that a journey to mountains in any other part of the world may not equal.

My own interest in visiting the Himalaya began when I moved to Derby in 1959; there I found that a group of local climbers, mostly members of the Oread Club, were trying to form an expedition to climb in the Kulu Himalaya and they invited me to join their party. I had dreamt about visiting ranges outside Europe since I was a boy but it had always seemed impossible for financial reasons. By 1959 Britain had changed vastly since 1947 when I began to climb, and new opportunities had come into being for the youth of the country. The possibility of grants from such sources as the Mount Everest Foundation meant that expeditions were no longer mainly the preserve of the wealthy or established explorer; any group with initiative could form itself into a Himalayan expedition. This had become apparent to the Derby party and myself. Fortunately, we had the aid of persons with previous expedition experience, but unfortunately our advisers favoured the large expedition pattern; we must have been one of the largest and weightiest parties to arrive among the lesser Himalayan peaks.

Kulu contains within its boundaries no really high summits by Himalayan standards, the maximum altitude of the range being just under 22,000 feet. Precipitation in the area is greater than in some other Himalayan ranges, and the permanent snowline is around 12,000 feet. 'Kulu' is the name of a town and a valley and is loosely applied to a group of mountain regions; at the time of the British Raj it was part of the Kangra district in the Punjab, but it is now accorded to the state of Himachal Pradesh, bordering on Ladakh, Lahoul and Spiti, and thus Tibet, and so only possible for limited access.

Through the valley, beautiful beyond words, rushes the Beas, one of the great rivers of the Punjab (Land of Five Rivers); its people are of a sturdy mountain breed, happy amidst their orchards, rice paddies, sheep and goat pastures, forests and mountains, and rich compared to the inhabitants of India's plains. A road runs up to and through the valley and from Manali, at the road's end, the approach to the mountains is relatively short.

The Derby climbers had chosen to visit Kulu because of ease of access; Bob Pettigrew, the leader, had been there once before, and he reported no shortage of good unclimbed peaks, some of apparent difficulty but not too high for a party with no real high-altitude experience. Bob's own Himalayan experience was limited; in retrospect we were innocents abroad, and our ideas as to what equipment was needed for a low-altitude area such as Kulu were vastly mistaken. At that date few climbers with our background had organised a Himalayan expedition; this was my first experience of what is involved in planning and organisation, and when I agreed to join the venture the problems were swiftly made clear to me.

I was in a difficult position over applying for leave of absence from my firm; I could hardly expect them readily to give me permission to join the expedition so soon after I had started to work for them. I vacillated, waiting to make sure that our plans would come to fruition, and unfortunately my managing director heard from another source of the proposed undertaking and my participation in it. I was duly summoned and given a dressing down; I had been undiplomatic to say the least, but luckily the scheme had become a patriotic county venture. Many influential Derbyshire personalities had pledged support, and finally my boss agreed to my going on condition I relinquished my post with the firm and returned to a different one when I got back. I could understand that my replacement would not take kindly to running my section for three months while I was in the Himalaya, then stand down on my return. I had to take it or leave it, but it was a pity for I enjoyed the work I was doing; in fact, this was the only occasion when I have enjoyed working for anyone but myself. However, after a week of indecisiveness, I decided to go to Kulu and hang the consequences!

For two years we plotted to get the necessary support for our expedition, and slowly we built up a mass of supplies. Anything donated free we accepted; we had masses of Christmas puddings and tins of rich fruit cake, and at one point, when we were offered a one-ton camp generator, we seriously and lengthily discussed the possibility of lugging this to base camp before refusing the outsize offer. We held meeting after meeting, some of which lasted most of the night, and organised fundraising function after function. For the poverty-stricken party it was essential to raise money to make the trip possible.

Some of our efforts were highly successful, but one which was not was the expedition dance. Just before the end of what would have been a financially rewarding evening, the gaiety erupted into a teddy boy versus climber free-for-all. Local roughnecks who wished us well supported our dance; through no fault of theirs, one of the climbers mistook their goodwill and hit the leader of the group between the eyes with his fist. It was impossible to stop a row after this. The Teddy boys never had a chance; outnumbered by many-to-one they were flung unceremoniously through the doors of the dance hall. Not surprisingly, they then lost their goodwill spirit and smashed the doors to pieces in a counter-attack. When our accounts were finalised, we had taken £25 at the box office, but the bills for repairs to property cost us £33. At least everyone, Teddy boys included, agreed that it was a memorable evening!

Eventually our efforts were successful and the party was ready to start, laden with literally tons of baggage. We boasted eight members, most of us with little idea of what to expect in the never-never land of the Himalaya, but all with a dream of trails and camps and fellow-feeling, setting forth in our turn to find that reality was something different and much more – a compound of the ultimate and infinite beset by the difficulties of human relationships.

Six of us caught a boat at Liverpool at the beginning of May 1961 – Bob Petti-grew, Ray Handley, Derrick Burgess, Trevor Panther, Steve Read and myself. The other two, Nick Smythe and Jack Ashcroft, were to meet the party later.

Life at sea was a revelation; I had never known such luxury, travelling by a first-class passenger ship, waited on hand and foot, overfed and overdrunk, with party games by day and night. We threw ourselves a hundred per cent into shipboard activities, in fact we made a hit, winning a reputation as a bunch of live wires. By the time we reached the Indian Ocean, I had forgotten the purpose of our enterprise and decided I could make a career out of Liverpool to Bombay voyages. They could have turned the ship around and I would cheerfully have gone back, ready for another voyage.

India impressed me as no country or experience has ever done. It was partly the contrast between the luxurious ship life and the harsh realities of the sub-continent, but also that widening contacts were awakening in me a regard for world problems, an interest in politics and other spheres of living besides mountaineering and self interest. I was appalled by the degree of poverty spread so openly before us; in other parts of the world there is human degra-dation and squalor, but nowhere is it so manifest, so paraded as in India. Here it was, plain to see, the India of all reports: human beings starving, the sacred cow, the rigid caste system, men truly believing by their millions in a religion, no mere church visit of a Sunday but a living, vibrant all-persuasive force, but the biggest shock of all was the thousands of people lying homeless and destitute in the streets of Bombay. I wandered those streets, disgusted by the filth and the poverty, outraged by what I saw. I was a typical young inhabitant of the western world and it has taken me several years and several visits to come to terms with and understand a little of the life force, the culture and the paradoxical contrasts that make up India. One thing that it did on this first visit was radically to change my own opinions and outlook on life.

We boarded a train and for two days and nights slowly trundled northwards; only then did I begin to appreciate the scale of the country. Every station had its kaleidoscope of Indian life, the homeless, the perpetual travellers, the beggars, the filthy urchins and the fantastic Sadhus. Who were these almost-naked men and what urge drove them to wander in this ascetic fashion? I gazed in awe through the carriage window and resolved to find out.

At the railhead of Pathankot, several miles north of Delhi on the outer rim of the Punjab plain, we were met by our Sikh liaison officer, Captain Balgit Singh, seconded to us from the Indian Army. This was a surprise; we had not realised that a large expedition demanded such an appointment by the gov-ernment. Balgit, a tall and elegant figure in his uniform, introduced himself, and joined in the task of reloading our tons of equipment on to a hired lorry and bus. He must have thought us a puny lot when we had to leave the final heavy work of loading to hired coolies. The heat and dust of the plains and the unaccustomed and unappetising food had drained us of any energy we once possessed. I felt better when, as we were rolling through the parched country-side, the first real foothills of the Himalaya appeared on the horizon.

The morning of the second day from Pathankot found us going through the Beas gorge with its 1,000-foot rock walls covered with tropical vegetation, loose and unstable, on the motor road cut so unbelievably in the early 1920s. We emerged into the Valley of the Gods and drove on towards Manali at its head, through orchards and rice paddies; the roadside teemed with human life, and the cheerful inhabitants smiled and waved a greeting. How different from the sullen masses lying in the Bombay streets! Downriver from Manali, our packing cases were unloaded and broken open and tents put up on a com-fortable site at Nagar Bridge at about 5,000 feet; thence we would cross the Beas for our march into the mountains.

We made nearly every possible mistake during this expedition. We had little idea of what foods we could safely eat nor of where we could have overnight stops. We engaged six Ladakhi high-altitude porters of whom four were raw indeed and nearly useless as mountaineers. But of the other two, Sonam Wangyal, later to become a true friend, was a climber of ability and by far the best porter I have met in the mountains, and Jigmet was a good cook; the rest were only good at eating. Our next mistake was to use ponies to carry our supplies instead of valley porters. This had seemed a good idea as a pony can carry over 120 pounds while the local porters will not carry more than seventy, but once we came to deep snow the advantages of manpower became appar-ent. We took on fifty-seven ponies and eleven pony-men, and the night before we left the valley our camp was like a travelling circus.

We set forth on 2 June in true expedition manner; in the absence of a reli-able map of the region, we had a famous shikari (hunter) as our guide to base camp. Renu Ram was a man of seventeen wives and many bear skins, posses-sor of a lordly bearing and an ancient rifle, boots with Lawrie's mark on them and a bush hat bedecked with peacock feathers. Marching at the head of our column, he gave a certain dignity to our otherwise ragged and straggling band. At first we walked by well-trodden paths through pine forests, ascending Chakki Nulla, an open and well-inhabited valley, towards the Chanderkhani Pass at 11,617 feet. Some of the party got lost on the first half-day of our march, and we had to halt the whole caravan while hillsides were searched. The miss-ing persons, when found, insisted that they had known their whereabouts exactly and it was the main column which had been lost! No further progress could be made that day.

Next morning, shortly before noon, we were stopped short of the pass by deep snow, still lying from the previous winter. The ponies couldn't climb the steep snow slope, despite determined efforts on our part, which included giving one a top rope and pulling while Derrick Burgess pushed from behind. This method was abandoned when the pony slipped its halter and glissaded backwards down the slope, landing on top of Derrick who managed to keep hold of its tail. We had no alternative but to offload the animals' burdens on to the backs of specially hired local hill men who carried the baggage to the other side of the pass while the ponies were blindfolded and led across. It was an expensive hold-up in time and money, but at least it allowed us to savour the grandeur of the pass and the view down into the Malana valley to the next stages of our march.

The steep, rocky descent of many thousand feet into the Malana Nulla provided another severe test for our pack animals. Not far from where we reached the valley bottom is Malana village, whose people have a curious and interesting history. At some time in the distant past their forefathers must have chosen this site of extreme solitude to found a religious community, following strictly the rites of the high-caste Hindu. They have little interchange with the outside world; for centuries they have been in isolation, keeping themselves to themselves. Over the years their language has altered sufficiently for it to have real differences from that of other peoples in the area and they have difficulty in making themselves understood. We found them unfriendly and inhospitable. They set their dogs on one of our Ladakhi porters, regarding him and us as unclean and untouchable.

We marched slowly up the Malana Nulla for two days, through forests of blue pine, deodar, spruce and fir and sparser plantations of maple, walnut and chestnut. The first evening in the valley Renu killed a roosting tree partridge with a single shot, which earned our respect for his marksmanship. Later that same night we discovered ourselves invaded by burrowing black ticks, obviously picked up from the Malana shepherds and their sheep and goats who had used the clearing before us. Here my first efforts as the expedition doctor made an impression, a burning cigarette being the successful antidote.

On 7 June we climbed above the tree line, but not before we had lost one of our party again, this time a loaded pony. At last we were close to our objectives, and as we went up a steep grass spur our range of vision widened with each step. Across the valley were the impressive rock peaks of Ali Ratni Tibba and the Manikaran Spires, straight ahead snowy summits brooded over the Malana glacier and above us, on our side of the valley, there were huge crags, nesting ground of eagles and other birds of prey.

Wearily we plodded to the site chosen for base, beside a large boulder perched amidst snow-covered alps at 12,000 feet, known to the shepherds as Umrao Thach, and overshadowed by the huge bulk of Ali Ratni Tibba (18,013 feet). With relief we unloaded the ponies for the last time, paid off their drivers and bade farewell to that noisy crew, with pleas to return before the monsoon to transport our equipment back to the valleys. Even without the animals, there were so many of us that we felt none of the isolation associated with the Himalaya.

From our base we could look directly down on to the snout of the Malana glacier, for we were camping high on the hillside above the tumbled mass of this our first obstacle. Our objectives were threefold: to climb Indrasan, a difficult and complex peak of 20,410 feet; to explore and attempt to climb either Ali Ratni Tibba or its neighbours, the Manikaran Spires; to survey and eventually prepare a map of a large section of the Kulu-Bara Shigri divide to the west of our base. Indrasan was our major ambition, but it was obvious that before attempting it we must gain experience of Himalayan conditions and make an easy ascent to acclimatise. For this we elected to go for Deo Tibba, a snow peak of 19,688 feet with a long history, already climbed four times, well charted and explored. Most important was the fact that the summit cones of Indrasan and Deo Tibba both rise from the same plateau, and the same camps would suffice for an attempt on either peak. The topography of these two mountains is remarkable: below them is a three-tier progression of steep ground broken by huge shelves, the first above the main flow of the Malana glacier, the next above its icefall, the final shelf under the peaks themselves. Surprisingly, although Deo Tibba had been ascended several times by this route, Indrasan had always been dismissed as too difficult.

Prominent among explorers of the two peaks have been General Bruce and his guide, Otto Fuhrer, de Van Graaff, Charles Evans, Eileen Gregory (Healey) and several others; Deo Tibba has attracted climbers almost from the beginning of Himalayan exploration and since its first ascent in 1952 by Jan de Van Graaff and his wife, Clare, it has become the most popular peak in the whole Himalaya.

The altitude affected Trevor Panther and myself severely; we knew nothing of acclimatisation problems and I was acutely worried. I did not realise that people acclimatise at different rates, some swiftly, some perhaps very slowly, and that sometimes the slower acclimatiser adjusts best in the end. Those who are affected severely must be prepared to allow themselves time to recover and understand that if they force the pace they run a serious risk of physiological breakdown.

I was ill by the time we reached base and could take little part in the work of establishing a first camp on the glacier; I was forced to take it easy. Trevor Panther, normally a man of immense physical strength, collapsed at 13,000 feet while trying to carry a load up the glacier, eventually getting back to base with the help of a porter. He looked a very sick man, complained of severe chest pains and had difficulty in breathing. I advised him to descend to a lower altitude for a few days and have a complete rest, but he was understandably reluctant to go down at the beginning of the expedition. He lay in a tent, ashen white and gasping for breath; I plied him with sleeping tablets at regular intervals and he slowly appeared to be getting better. My own condition improved suddenly after the first few days at base, almost as if I had been carrying a large pack and had put it down; I began to carry loads up the glacier and help prospect our line of advance. Returning to camp one afternoon, we were amazed to find that Trevor had packed up and started back to Manali. From there he went straight on to Bombay and caught the first ship to England.

There was ill feeling among the rest of us over this; at the time I was flabbergasted, but further experience has taught me the debilitating effects of altitude sickness. It can undermine the most determined of climbers, and I can imagine how Trevor must have felt mentally and physically, suffering alone at base camp.

Another early casualty was Balgit Singh, who twisted a knee on the glacier and was base camp chief from then on. One of the Ladakhi porters of ancient vintage was also sick and became another base camp dweller; the time came when we had more bodies at base than on the mountain. At least my post of 'Doc Sahib' was justified; I was kept busy dealing with ailments as varied as athlete's foot and Himalayan lassitude.

Luckily our dwindling strength was reinforced by Jack Ashcroft and Nick Smythe, the remaining members of our party, who also helped to demolish the mounds of food we had brought.

The ascent of the Malana glacier was easy and our first camp was placed in the middle of the flow, on the lowest shelf. By the time this camp was established and stocked, the load carrying had at last made me acclimatised and fit; thereafter I took over the lead with Derrick Burgess, for whom acclimatisation never seemed necessary.

Derrick and I found our way through broken ground on the lower edge of the icefall, to place a camp on the second shelf with the aid of Wangyal. We now found the way blocked by an immense line of barrier cliffs descending from the third plateau under Deo Tibba and Indrasan.

The way up this barrier was the key to our attempt on Indrasan, and several alternatives climbed by previous parties presented themselves. On the western edge of the second shelf was Watershed Ridge; in the centre of the barrier was Piton Ridge, running to a point on the edge of the third shelf known as Punta San Marco and first climbed by three Italian prisoners of war on parole leave; at the side of Piton Ridge was a huge couloir, 2,000 feet in length and used by de Van Graaff on the first ascent of Deo Tibba; finally, the upper icefall of the Malana glacier flowed directly off the eastern edge of the third shelf.

The icefall looked repulsive and the various ridges difficult for load carrying; the couloir seemed the most straightforward, if perhaps most subject to objective dangers. It started with a wide base and gradually narrowed and steepened, to exit directly on to the third shelf. It looked the original grind, but we could only find out by making an ascent. Wangyal had already shown himself to be that phenomenon, the born climber; the other porters could not be trusted on difficult ground, but our cheerful companion was obviously up to anything we might attempt and willingly agreed to try the couloir with us.

On 13 June, Derrick, Wangyal and I crossed the second shelf and started up the couloir at first light; struggling through abysmal snow we followed its bed. This was my first experience of bad Himalayan conditions, of sinking thigh-deep into sugary snow. Near the top of the gully we almost turned back when the sixty-five-degree exit slope gave every indication of being ripe for avalanche; however, we managed to traverse across to a rock buttress and, firmly belayed from this, I kicked and struggled my way up the couloir's head, turning the summit cornices by climbing a steep wall of snow on rock set at seventy-five degrees, sinking chest-deep for the last thirty feet. I flopped on to the plateau above the couloir absolutely exhausted and Derrick on joining me admitted for the first time to being fatigued, but Wangyal strolled up to join us as composed and fresh as when he started, his toothy grin radiating pleasure at the proposed site of our next camp.

We certainly had a striking viewpoint and position, on a vast sloping table perhaps three miles wide. Opposite us to the north was Indrasan, a huge battleship of a mountain, its west ridge forming one sweep of the formation and its east ridge the other. Bounding the shelf on the west was Deo Tibba, a large snow mound, and on its eastern flank was the jumbled mass of the Malana icefall. We had taken nine hours to climb the couloir, carrying only light loads, and it was obvious we must find some less-strenuous route for the heavily laden men establishing our third camp.

Leaving behind an erected four-man Hillary tent, a fuel container and the climbing equipment we had brought with us, we began the descent of the couloir. Halfway down we noticed what might be an answer to the problem; it appeared possible to cross Piton Ridge and enter our gully halfway up. There was an obvious notch at the crossing point and if it proved possible to place a camp on the far side, this would be the way to tackle the ascent.

Derrick and I were so tired by this climb that the task of investigating a new approach was taken over by Bob Pettigrew and Ray Handley. Bob had been on the third shelf during his previous visit to Kulu, and had climbed there by the Watershed Ridge, descending by de Van Graaff's couloir. He was surprised by the difference in conditions from those of 1958, when the couloir had been mainly a scree run.

Bob and Ray set out next morning with another of the Ladakhi porters, Ang Chook, one of the most bloodthirsty-looking characters I have ever met; he was more Tibetan than Ladakhi and he appalled me at base at the end of the expedition by calmly sawing off a live sheep's head with an ordinary table knife. Derrick and I watched the party reach the couloir safely by the new approach, then, after a signal from Bob, we began to ferry equipment and tents from our original site to re-establish a second camp directly under the notch. There we found, as we had hoped, a perfect place for tents, sheltered by ridges in a snow bowl. On the short trip, the indefatigable Wangyal gave an exhibition of his load-carrying ability – 120 pounds a time is no exaggeration.

That evening the party did not return from the couloir to our new camp as planned: something must have gone amiss. At dawn next day Derrick, Wangyal and I set out to look for them. We climbed the couloir at speed, this time on perfect crampon snow, and were surprised as we reached the top to see the missing men cheerfully climbing over the cornice. They had spent the night in the tent we had put up on the third shelf and to keep warm had lit a stove and kept it burning all night, using most of the paraffin we had so laboriously carried up there. We greeted them with stunned silence, nursing black thoughts, but by the time we regained Camp II we were able to admit to being glad to find them unharmed.

On 18 June Derrick, Wangyal and I occupied our Camp III at 18,000 feet, established with the aid of the other expedition members who carried a load and then returned to Camp II. Next morning we slowly crossed the plateau, walking downhill through deep snow to place the smallest tent I have yet occupied under the foot of the west ridge of Indrasan, at an estimated height of 16,000 feet. The three of us crammed into the tent and, after a restless night, on 20 June we easily climbed Deo Tibba – the fifth ascent. From the summit we realised that Indrasan was every bit as difficult an ascent as we had anticipated; above our tiny tent it reared up 4,000 feet in vertical height, with steep rock buttresses and high-angled snow slopes. If we had been more experienced, we should have recognised immediately that our proposed attempt by the west ridge was a bad mistake. To climb it as we intended, in alpine fashion, was impracticable, simply because the immense length of the ridge, at that height, was too great for an unsupported party, especially as we did not mean to make a calculated series of bivouacs on the way up. The clear, high-altitude light, plus our inexperience, led us to underestimate the difficulties and the distance involved.

Cloud began to drift slowly over the sun as we carefully avoided the immense crevasses seaming the snowy fields of Deo Tibba. We arrived back at our little tent early, and sat undecided whether to return across the plateau to Camp III, ready to ferry supplies the following day, or to make a swift reconnaissance of Indrasan next morning and then begin ferrying operations. As we discussed the alternatives, flurries of snow, no uncommon sight at Himalayan noon, began to fall and decided us to stay put. There followed the worst night I have spent in a tent. It soon became obvious that this was no ordinary snowfall but a major break in the weather. Lying nearly on top of one another in a tent made for one man, the three of us struggled to get breathing space. Despite the cold outside I thought I should suffocate from the heat inside; the snow buried the tent and pressed down on us on all sides. At last we gave up trying to sleep and sat, huddled and cross-legged, awaiting the dawn.

The grey filtering light brought us no relief from the whirling snow and we decided to retreat uphill, across the plateau to Camp III. We emerged into a complete white-out and couldn't tell if we moved uphill or down. Soon we were lost and sinking thigh-deep in the fresh powder snow. We got out a compass and tied on to the rope at seventy-five-feet intervals, Derrick at the back, myself in front and Wangyal in the middle ready to hold me if I walked over the edge of the plateau or into a crevasse. We couldn't see anything but we had to find Camp III and plodded on like blind men. We had a moment of terror when the nearby ice cliffs on Deo Tibba sent down a massive avalanche. All three of us ran panic-stricken in different directions, falling to the ground entangled and dragged by the rope, to flail helplessly while the rumbling threatened us. We were to find later that we had never been closer than a few hundred feet to the nearest debris.

Derrick's compass route finding was good, and we crossed the plateau safely. Finding the tent buried under the snow was another matter; it was a desperate trio who stumbled on the Punta San Marco in the early evening and from its position guessed where we should find the camp. We were soon installed in the comparative luxury of the four-man tent, but not before we had dug deep for it.

For five days we sat it out in unceasing snow; the tent had to be dug out time after time, Wangyal insisting this was his task although from the first he was keen to retreat; we in our ignorance simply sat or slept, feeling that no storm can last forever. On the third day, when our fuel gave out, Wangyal and I had to cross the plateau again, find and dig out the small tent under Indrasan and bring back the paraffin we had carried over there. Surprisingly, this didn't prove difficult; the tent was prominently marked, and by compass bearings calculated before we started we were back in a few hours.

Sitting it out began to seem a bad idea; food was running low – but could we retreat? The thought of the avalanche-prone couloir held us back for a further day, spent silently watching the snow as it buried the tent every few hours. Suddenly, with prompting from Wangyal, we made up our minds to start down; as we put on our equipment the energetic Ladakhi, who had been dressed and ready to descend for days, dug us out and made a path to the top of the couloir.

It was an unusual descent; we rode down the upper sections on sliding masses of snow, which for some reason never properly avalanched. In a matter of minutes we reached the traverse across to the notch and Camp II; here the true fight began. We punched, kicked and crawled our way laboriously to the gap, conscious that any minute the whole slope and us with it should, by any known rules, avalanche off. With a final all-out effort we reached the gap and swooped down on the unsuspecting occupants of Camp II. We were made to feel as if back from the dead by the warmth of their welcome. Later that night found us still full of mutual goodwill as we polished off a bottle of medicinal brandy.

Next day the snow was still falling, and we gave the cursed mountains best and set off for base, first through deep snow, then slush, then deluging rain. An hour later, out came the sun for the first time for over a week, and thereafter we enjoyed two glorious days sunbathing, teaching the Ladakhis to play cricket, and eating. Base had been transformed into a flower garden in our absence; the snow had melted on the surrounding alps which were now radiant with colour. No more beautiful heath can ever have witnessed a test match; after a short period of tutelage we played the porters in an England versus Ladakh match – six a side, with a ball made of cloth, ice axes for wickets, and a bat shaped from a piece of packing case. Shame to confess, they beat us!

Four days later, in the early evening of 29 June, I found myself leading a rope of Ray Handley and Steve Read up de Van Graaff's couloir to Camp III again; there we joined Derrick, Bob Pettigrew and the porters who had gone ahead. All the Europeans were now acclimatised and fit, but somehow we never managed to function efficiently as a team; a Himalayan veteran could have helped us enormously and saved much needless work but, as with all things, high-mountain experience is hard won.

We had our share of bad luck in the form of a strange illness that afflicted one of the porters, Chosfel, who complained of severe head pains and was repeatedly sick. Clearly he would have to be escorted down, but none of the party was keen to miss the attempt on Indrasan. After a bad night nursing Chosfel, action became necessary; Wangyal volunteered to shepherd the sick man down and regretfully we agreed. This was a grave error, as we realised when we knew the real nature of Chosfel's illness. Wangyal, almost carrying his fellow porter, cheerfully waved farewell and disappeared down the couloir.

The rest of us carried immense loads across the shelf to the forlorn, collapsed tent under the west ridge of Indrasan. The plan was for Derrick and me to attempt Indrasan while the others made another ascent of Deo Tibba.

At five the next morning we left our tents and parted company, Derrick and I pleased at last to be making an attempt on the expedition's major objective. A rock spur took us to the crest of the west ridge, happy to find good red granite. From the crest, our view was spectacular; we could see the Solang Weisshorn to the north, an impressive peak of superb contours, watch our friends winding their way through the crevasses on Deo Tibba and, behind them to the east, gaze at a myriad summits along the edge of the Bara Shigri glacier. After study-ing our ridge, we looked at each other speechless; it seemed to go on forever, pinnacle after pinnacle, snow ridge after snow ridge, interspersed by rock steps seamed with icy gullies. We still hadn't grasped the scale, and judging it by Alpine standards decided that with a bivouac we might reach the summit.

Midday found us struggling over a series of gendarmes. At an imposing pin-nacle with no easy way round it, I banged in a piton and belayed at its foot, then Derrick climbed across and joined me. Thoughtfully he examined the obstacle, stepped boldly on to its face, climbed upwards by a series of delicate mantelshelves, then stuck on small holds below the top. A leaf piton in a hairline crack provided a solution; a swift pull and swing and he was belayed at the top. I found this section difficult and considered it Very Severe by British standards. 'This is hopeless,' I said as I clung to the pinnacle. 'We'll need ten bivouacs at this rate.' We were only a quarter way along the ridge and it was already afternoon.

Derrick was still brightly optimistic and climbing well. 'Let's go a bit further,' he insisted. 'At least we may prepare the way for another attempt.' We clambered down into a gap, then ascended another large gendarme from which the only way down was to abseil into a notch. 'Hell, if we go down that, we'll have to bivouac for sure,' Derrick decided. Neither of us wanted to bivouac at so early a stage on the ridge; silently we about-turned and carefully descended the way we had come. Late in the afternoon we had to report our lack of success to the others, long returned from Deo Tibba. They volunteered to go and look at the east ridge of the mountain and we decided to continue on our attempted route next day.

Off with the dawn again, this time we reached our furthest point of advance before 8 a.m. Both of us felt on form and confident of pushing the ascent to the summit. We abseiled down into the gap, now mildly innocuous in the morning sunlight. But soon our progress was down to a snail's pace as obstacle after obstacle barred our way. By lunchtime we had to acknowledge the bitter truth: we had grossly underestimated the length and difficulty of the ridge. However, we were determined to see how far we could get and doggedly kept on. Several times we were forced to abandon the ridge for its faces, the iciness of the north face proving more stable than the insecure layers of soft snow on steep rock on the south. One of these gave us a fright when we were forced into climbing an almost vertical step, cutting holds into a thin layer of wet snow-ice clinging to the rock. It was a shock, after climbing or avoiding forty pinnacles in a half-mile of ridge, to find we were still not within striking distance of the barrier tower which we had seen from Deo Tibba, prominently guarding the summit.

We finally reached an overhanging corner under the tower, into which we traversed. Its formation was rather like the Amen Corner of Gimmer Crag, but smoother, and we needed artificial aids. By the time this was behind us, with a fine lead by Derrick, hanging out over the north face on well-spaced pitons, we had to resign ourselves either to several bivouacs in order to reach the summit and come down again, or to immediate retreat. We sat arguing for a while; what fools we were to think that such a long ridge offered the easiest way to climb the mountain. We felt inadequate, discouraged with ourselves, our party, our lack of experience. Derrick is a determined and successful climber of great ability, and will not retreat until it is absolutely necessary.

I felt we had shot our bolt and said so, and in the end he had to agree. Once more we turned about; a long and boring descent ended in relief as we reached camp in the evening light.

The others reported the east ridge to look highly improbable, but Steve Read was keen to try and he, backed up by Bob and Ray, set out next morning while Derrick and I rested. They were back in the late afternoon, having managed to climb only 200 feet of the ridge. Steve had been extended, leading thus far, and was forced to resort to artificial aids, with each pitch taking hours. We had to agree that we just weren't a strong or experienced enough party to climb Indrasan along the ridges; it obviously presented problems of difficulty comparable to any summit then reached in the Himalaya.

On a further reconnaissance next day Derrick and I became convinced that the obvious route up the mountain was by the south face, comparing favourably with some of the major Alpine face climbs. There was a good way to start, by a ramp; then an ascent by a hanging glacier, reminiscent of the north face of the Aiguille Blanche de Peuterey, led directly to the summit. The mountain was climbed by this route in 1962 by a Japanese party, who unfortunately had an emergency bivouac, with resultant frostbite necessitating amputations.

Sorrowfully we decided to abandon our attempt on the mountain; our supplies had run out and to reorganise for further attempts would mean dropping the rest of our objectives. Understandably, climbing Indrasan did not appeal to some of the others as much as exploration and surveying. Derrick and I, now philosophic, could cheerfully agree that we had experienced two of our best mountain days.

Leading down the couloir I had a narrow escape. While I was crossing an obvious avalanche groove a shout from Jigmet, holding my rope on the edge of the chute, made me look up. A large boulder was sliding straight at me. I dived to one side and the stone whistled past; I slid after it but stopped myself with my axe. I had just regained my feet when more stones came whirring, and this time I had no warning. I glimpsed or sensed one coming at me and in reflex action deflected it with my axe like a cricket ball, which knocked the axe out of my hand and unbalanced me; I shot off down the slope, head first, completely out of control. Jerked to a stop by the rope, I pulled myself the right way up and scrabbled my way out of the chute to safe ground, where I could stop and thank my anchor man for saving me. The rest of the party crossed quickly, while I climbed into a small crevasse to retrieve my ice axe.

At Camp II we were surprised to find Wangyal and Chosfel; the sick man had moved so slowly down the couloir that he and Wangyal were forced to bivouac and only reached the tents late on the second day, since when Wangyal had been doing his best to nurse Chosfel, with no real idea as to his illness. I took over, and as Chosfel was shivering we moved him to a large tent and put him inside two sleeping bags. He still trembled violently and his pulse was irregular although his temperature was almost normal, and Wangyal and I lit two Primus stoves in the tent. While I was in my own tent getting some medical supplies, Wangyal shouted for help. He was struggling with Chosfel who had crawled out of his sleeping bags, stuck his feet in the flames of the stoves and was screaming with pain. Only then did I realise that his illness wasn't physical but mental.

I covered his feet with burn dressings, extinguished the stoves and with Wangyal's aid managed to get him back into the sleeping bags, where he lay in a stupor. I stayed with him till suppertime, when he was apparently sound asleep. Another shout from Wangyal brought me rushing back. Chosfel had got hold of a glass sauce-bottle, broken its top off and with a jagged edge had slashed his own neck. I nearly fainted as blood gushed from the wound, and working to staunch the flow I was sick, but eventually the bleeding stopped. Wangyal, the ever reliable, moved into the tent to watch the patient through the night. We managed to give Chosfel a strong sedative and the hours passed without further trouble.

Next morning everyone was awake early and after breakfast every scrap of equipment and food that could be carried was made up into loads. The Ladakhis had ninety pounds each and we carried seventy or more. Chosfel seemed better and capable of descending in spite of his injuries. So we started down, with Wangyal, Chosfel and me in the rear of the column, Wangyal leading, ready to help Chosfel, and myself well back as anchor man.

At one point we had to traverse diagonally down an ice cliff from a platform at its top; the passage was marked with red flags, and we were moving down it together. Suddenly with a piercing scream Chosfel ran straight towards the edge of the drop, obviously intending to jump over it. Taken by surprise, I was almost dragged after him but got my axe rammed into the snow and his rope whipped round it as he reached the edge. The rope came taut as he leaped but luckily the axe held and Chosfel was stopped in mid-air like a jack-in-the-box, to shoot backwards and land on snow-ice at the platform's edge. I held him tight on the lip like a hooked fish till Wangyal climbed back and then we dragged him inch by inch away from the edge. He lay whimpering on the snow while Wangyal – the only time I saw him lose his temper – threatened and scolded him as a parent might an erring child. This appeared to calm him down but he was evidently in a suicidal frame of mind. I abandoned my pack in order better to be able to watch and hold him, and after a breather we set off once more, Wangyal on a long lead rope, with Chosfel and myself tied barely fifteen feet apart.

The others had disappeared, unaware of our troubles. As we caught up with them, Chosfel, in full view of an amazed audience, gave another piercing scream and tried to jump over a small barrier cliff between us and the party below.

This time I was ready and yanked him back to terra firma on which he landed with a crack, snarling and spitting. He leapt to his feet and, yelling like a wounded animal, came straight at me, brandishing his ice axe. I was terrified, for he was squat and powerful. With the desperation of fear, I rugby-tackled him at the last moment, diving at his knees and bringing him winded to earth. We rolled over and over amidst the crevasses, fighting for possession of his axe. Chosfel got on top of me, a knee in my throat, and the axe was slowly being wrenched out of my grasp as I choked. Suddenly he was snatched off me like a baby and I heard a resounding smash as Wangyal hit him in the throat with his fist. He crumpled sobbing in the snow as I lay gasping. Wangyal came over and helped me to my feet, then without a word walked back, kicked the unfortunate Chosfel to his feet and frog-marched him down the last steep slopes to the flat glacier bed.

Chosfel made one final weak attempt to do himself an injury by trying to jump into an open crevasse but Wangyal and I were too quick for him. The rest of the party were struck dumb by the performance; our cameraman, Ray Handley, was so amazed that he had failed to film any of it – a pity, as it would have made a sensational sequence.

I had to go back for my pack and my day was crowned when I fell into a crevasse, wedged by the shoulders, feet kicking clear. I don't know if Chosfel's example was contagious, but I hung there, unroped, giggling to myself: this was really the last straw! I was still laughing when Bob Pettigrew and Steve Read, who had waited for me, came and lifted me out.

Our psychotic Ladakhi was in the porters' tent when I got down to base, lying peacefully on a sleeping bag, but later he began to scream again. I made him take two sleeping tablets which had no effect, then another two, still to no avail, and later, in desperation, two more – three times the normal dose. Ten minutes after, he passed out and slept for thirty hours, waking calm but weak and sick. As soon as he had recovered sufficiently, we dispatched him to the valley, pensioned off from our enterprise. According to the local secretary of the Himalayan Club, he had never been on an expedition before and was known in Kulu as an unstable character.

The days of the expedition were numbered and the monsoon was nearly due. On 9 July the party split into two groups, one to complete the survey and exploration programme on the Kulu-Bara Shigri divide, for which Jack Ashcroft, our surveyor, and his assistant, Nick Smythe, had been doing the preliminary work, the other to reconnoitre Ali Ratni Tibba and the Manikaran Spires. I was not then over-keen on exploration so I joined Ray Handley for an attempt on the fabulous rock peaks that beckoned from the opposite side of the valley.

We insisted on having Wangyal with us; I personally had become attached to the dark-skinned, toothy little man. He appeared slight but his looks belied his strength; he was the best load carrier, and the only porter I have met in the Himalaya who seemed to climb because he liked it. He had fire in his soul; his flashing smile plus his enthusiasm and climbing enterprise made him a boon to any party. We also took Zangbo, the youngest of the Ladakhis, whom Wangyal was training as his apprentice and to whom he delegated all the menial tasks such as washing up and lighting stoves.

The four of us left base late in the afternoon to follow a branch of the Malana glacier into a vast cwm behind Ali Ratni Tibba where we pitched camp on hard snow at around 14,000 feet, directly below a small but steep icefall which we guessed would lead us directly to our objectives.

Next morning Ray and I set out to attempt the passage of the icefall, which, although short, looked difficult. As we moved up to its base we were aware of being watched; above the icefall a herd of chamois was inquisitively eyeing us. While we stood pondering on our route, the chamois suddenly took flight and bolted across the snow slopes out of sight, to reappear in a rushing mass down the side of a rock spur, traverse below us on the glacier and race past our tents. Their swift reappearance meant that there must be an easier way than the route we were contemplating, hidden from view on the other side of the spur. And in fact all we had to do was to pick up the chamois tracks and follow them up easy slopes to a saddle level with the top of the icefall. From there more easy snow slopes led to the faces of Ali Ratni Tibba and the Manikaran Spires. The highest of the spires attracted us but looked a difficult climb and as we had already wasted several hours of daylight, we decided to come back next day for an attempt. Closer at hand was another pinnacle of the Manikaran group, and after we had kicked steps methodically up a wide couloir a rock scramble led us to its summit at 17,391 feet.

The descent was pure joy; once off the rock it was possible to glissade every foot of the way back to camp. Standing and sitting, we whooped down the slopes to surprise Wangyal and Zangbo by getting back before they expected us; we found them perched on a boulder in the middle of the glacier, singing merrily. My first thought was for the bottle of brandy carried in the medical supplies for illness or celebration. But no! On opening the medicine chest, to Wangyal's hilarious delight, I was looking at a full bottle, corked, of what appeared to be brandy. It was a few days before I discovered that what I was staring at was cold tea: when this happened Wangyal was nowhere to be found!

At dawn next morning we and the Ladakhis left our camp to make straight for the highest of the Manikaran Spires. The weather at this period was fine in the mornings but by noon thick cloud usually developed and soon after snow was almost guaranteed. The monsoon could not be far away, so we hastened to make sure of at least one major first ascent. We gained height rapidly and at 7.30 a.m. reached a deep snow groove which led upwards for several hundred feet to the final steep wall of the spire, from this angle very reminiscent of the

Aiguille du Géant. We roped up; Wangyal insisted on coming too and Zangbo had little choice but to follow his master who was cheerfully prepared to lead a second rope. We front-pointed with our crampons up the groove, axe spikes plunged to the adze at each step.

This was enjoyable after our previous frustrations; the peak was the right size and altitude to climb in a single day, alpine fashion. Up and up we went; laughingly Wangyal tried to overtake but his rope-mate slowed him down. We reached rock and scrambled up easy granite to the steep final wall. The rock was grey here, but like the red granite of Indrasan, as firm as could be wished. Shortly before midday we got to a platform about eighty feet below the summit; here we changed to a single rope of four. Barring our way was a slightly impending wall; belayed by Ray, I traversed across the foot of this to reach a bounding chimney on the Malana side, which I climbed for several feet till it narrowed to a crack and forced me on to the wall itself. The last part was exposed and severe but well protected by running belays, and fittingly the final move was a mantelshelf on to the summit.

This was as fine a balcony as one could wish for; an almost knife-edged ridge sported an obelisk or tooth that had shown prominently from the base of the spire. This was the true summit, on which I now balanced and to which the others came up one by one as I took in their ropes. We sat with our feet dangling over the edge, happy as four climbers will be anywhere in the world after climbing a virgin peak. Our height was 17,696 feet. We watched the clouds rolling towards us from the south and gazed reverently at the bulk of Indrasan, dominating us from the north. It is not a beautiful mountain with its long spreading ridges, but we could at last appreciate just what we had rubbed our noses against! Wangyal was delighted with himself; he had led well and could have made the ascent without our aid. Zangbo was raw, but it was evident that he had complete trust in his senior partner.

Ray and I decided it was best to rope down to the platform eighty feet below, and draping the rope round the summit and down the face we quickly regained the shelf. There we stood waiting for the Ladakhis who were hesitating and talking excitedly. 'Perhaps they don't know how to abseil,' Ray suggested. We were about to start up again when Wangyal launched himself into space, hanging by his arms on the rope, and then proceeded calmly to descend hand over hand, singing and laughing at the Sahib monkey antics. Zangbo was not so enthusiastic and we stood by anxiously, ready to field him as he wearily grappled his way down to our stance.

Early evening found us trudging through thick mist to our camp. We now had to decide whether to attempt the impressive rock tower of Ali Ratni Tibba; we had seen that it was climbable but we had the problem of the monsoon, and anyway Ray and I felt the need of another rope to back us up. Wangyal was clearly up to the attempt but Zangbo was too raw for such an exacting climb. A break in the weather settled the issue and we packed up next morning in steady drizzle, regretfully abandoning Ali Ratni Tibba[1] to another party, and got back to our base in heavy rain.

A few days later the exploration team stomped back into base; they had covered a lot of ground, and Jack Ashcroft had completed the work necessary for his map-making. Derrick Burgess, Bob Pettigrew and Jack had made the second ascent of White Sail Peak, 21,148 feet, from the East Tos Glacier, discovered and climbed a new pass and enjoyed a thoroughly successful trip. It was clear that for Derrick this journey had been the high spot of the expedition; travelling light for days in high mountains had made more impression on him than any of his Alpine ascents, however notable. I could have kicked myself for missing the trip. It is all too easy to be blinded by one's technical climbing ambitions and miss the best the mountains offer.

The onset of the monsoon had truly overtaken us; day after day rain poured down. Once again we had shown our lack of knowledge by letting ourselves be caught in the mountains by the rainy season. The march out was abominable; we trudged through torrents of rain, soaked to the skin, negotiating swollen streams, building bridges, backpacking when the horses couldn't get through with their loads. Our march-in pony-man had let us down by refusing to return for us, and we had to rely on Punjabi plainsmen with horses. They had never been in the mountains before but while they were in Manali delivering goods they had been talked into coming up to get us out. They blamed the weather and their consequent miseries on us, staged strikes, threatened to leave us, demanded more money and even sank into tears of despondency when their horses fell or were nearly swept away by rushing rivers. The anticipated delights of Manali whittled our numbers down and down as members of the expedition left us to go ahead and prepare the town for our arrival. It was like the retreat from Moscow. We finally reached Manali when the heaviest rains were over, almost at the end of July, and the next day was sunny.

As we recrossed the Chanderkhani Pass, there had been a sudden break in the clouds, revealing an unbelievable iceberg of a mountain, floating, it seemed, without a base. I stood transfixed, trying to make up my mind if it was really a mountain or part of the clouds. Wangyal noticed my questioning gaze. 'Mukar Beh, Sahib,' he said. When I discovered that it was unclimbed, I secretly vowed to return.

---

1. First ascent May 1969, by Mr and Mrs F. Harper, C. Radcliffe, D. Nicol.

5 Alpine Nights and Days

'Out on the pitiless nordwand, where the bivouac sites are few,
Alone with a stone for a pillow, and an uninterrupted view.'
(From a song by Tom Patey)

Back from the Himalaya in September, 1961, I returned to the printing industry, but soon became bored and dissatisfied with the job my firm allotted me.
After an interview with my managing director, who was surprisingly understanding, I resolved to leave in mid-1962 and spend the summer in the Alps.
I was hopelessly and irrationally bound up with mountains, and in any case
had little enthusiasm for the world of commerce. This was my final turnabout;
hereafter I elected to try to earn a living in ways connected with travel and
mountaineering, and by casual work.

It was now possible by working and saving during the winter to hoard
enough money for three summer months in the Alps or further afield, instead
of scheming and dreaming about the mere fortnight of a few years earlier, and
this was becoming commonplace amongst keen British climbers. Such adven-
turers had to take potluck with jobs on their return, but their lengthy holidays
gave them the chance to become intimately acquainted with high mountains
and the time to await good conditions for difficult ascents. This had a tremendous influence on British alpinism and in the early 1960s the number of
Britons tackling *grandes courses* expanded dramatically.

The great essential for a long holiday in the Alps is a companion on whom
one can rely, with whom one can remain on amicable terms, and whose climbing ability and ambitions are similar to one's own. I was fortunate in meeting
Dez Hadlum while I was living in the Derby area, and I climbed with him for
several years. Dez was an apprentice pattern maker in Nottingham when I first
met him, but as soon as he completed his training he gave notice; this suited
my plans for 1962, and we joined forces for the summer. Quiet and unassum-
ing, Dez is one of those rare beings with whom it is difficult to quarrel. He is a
powerful climber, medium in height and built like a tank; his speed is impressive and his physical strength allied to stamina beyond his years made him the
ideal Alpine partner. He had already had two Alpine holidays during which he
had achieved some difficult ascents.

Setting out at the beginning of June, we made an Alpine roundabout, a sort of modern equivalent of the 'Grand Tour'. We started in the Kaisergebirge, travelled on to the Dolomites, crossed to Chamonix and Mont Blanc; baulked by bad weather we returned to the Dolomites and finished in the Wetter-steingebirge north of Innsbruck. The year of 1962 was an exceptional season, with weeks of fine weather and only occasional bad periods. We went back to several of the places I had been to before, to reap the harvest of earlier explor-atory visits. Many of our best ascents, such as the north face of the Cime Ovest di Lavaredo, the *Solleder* and *Andrich* routes on Monte Civetta, the south-east wall of the Fleischbank, and the frontier ridge of Mont Maudit were made in good times and without incidents. Such climbs soon fade in the mind; it is only when one is extended or plans go awry that makes for vivid recall, and we did experience our share of such adventures.

Our major mishap occurred in the Civetta range, when we made the first British ascent of the *Solda* route on the Torre di Babele. This grade-V-superior rock-climb on the south ridge of a typical Dolomite tower contains some fine pitches but unfortunately some loose rock. We successfully overcame the tech-nical difficulties and arrived on the Pulpit di Babele, a shelf several hundred feet below the summit of the tower. We were following a description of the climb from the Italian guidebook as no English version had then appeared. Our command of Italian was slight, but we gleaned that the guidebook recom-mended a descent from the Pulpit by an easy way down. However, I was keen to climb to the summit of the tower itself. Unroped we set forth and soon found out why the rest of the route was not advised: the rock was like mouldy cheese and crumbled at the touch. The last sections on to the summit were the worst of all; it would have been dangerous to rope up, there was nothing firm enough for belays, but the angle was easy, following rock shelves piled with scree. We agreed at the top that we wouldn't for anything go down the way we had come up.

Studying the guidebook, Dez found a descent mentioned on the north-east face of the tower which apparently began with a 100-metre free abseil. 'It can't!' I said. 'It must be a mistake. Who carries 600 feet of rope around with them?'

We clambered on to the north-east face and sure enough there was an abseil piton with an old sling attached. We stared at each other for a moment. 'I'll go down and investigate,' Dez volunteered, fishing a sling out of his rucksack which he attached to the piton and through which we doubled our 300-foot rope. He threw it down, prepared an abseil seat, then leant out on the rope.

'Can you see anything?' I demanded from the safety of a ledge above.

'Nothing. It overhangs!' For a second he hesitated, then lowering himself over the lip he disappeared.

It seemed like hours as I waited on that ledge. I climbed down and yanked at the rope but the tension told me Dez was still hanging on it. I heard the faint sound of a hammer driving a piton into rock, then the rope slackened and sprang loose.

Peering out over the void, I couldn't see or hear my companion, so I in my turn prepared an abseil seat and started down. Once over the lip of the overhang, I found myself dangling in space, many feet out from the rock. Far below me Dez was clinging to the face, perched on a minute ledge in the middle of an overhanging wall. Down I slid almost to the end of the rope; hanging out over an immense drop I drew level with Dez and nearly lost control. 'What the hell am I to do from here?' I demanded hysterically.

'Swing in, I'll grab you, I've got a good peg for a belay. But don't let go of the rope or we'll be here forever.'

I began to swing backwards and forwards and surprisingly it was easy to reach Dez, but keeping hold of the very end of the rope once I landed was a different matter. I teetered on the ledge and Dez held me on while I pulled the rope down after me. 'Phew, that was exciting!' I gasped with relief as I tied into the belay piton.

'We're not down yet,' Dez declared.

We had crossed our rubicon and had to get down somehow. I hammered in another piton and between us we managed to rig a second double-roped descent. Again we couldn't see a landing place; the face overhung below us and we didn't know if the rope reached a ledge or merely dangled in space once more. Dez insisted on going down first and without apparent emotion pushed himself off. Luckily the rope reached a landing on the edge of a deep gully and with relief I heard him shout that all was well and to join him. 'Jesus!' I exclaimed at the end of this second 150-foot abseil. 'It *was* a 100-metre descent as the book said.'

We coiled the rope and hurried off down the gully; our antics had wasted much time and we wanted to get off the mountain before nightfall. Dez raced away from me as I jammed in a chimney, hampered by the rucksack I carried for the two of us. The sack stuck and to free it I heaved with all my might; it came away, pulling with it a minor avalanche which roared off down the rock face straight towards Dez. I watched horror-struck, he was bound to be knocked off his holds. He had just time to cover his head with an arm before one of the stones hit him while the others exploded round him and then ricocheted off into space.

I blinked; somehow he was still there. Then I heard a groan as he keeled on his holds, grabbed with his left hand and clung to the rock. I climbed down and joined him. His right arm hung limp; it was injured and this was my fault. Dez didn't reproach me, but pleaded we should get off as quickly as possible and, although the ground was hundreds of feet away, insisted we shouldn't call for help.

We tied on to the rope and I held him as he climbed and swung his way one-handed down the cliff. We must have lost the true descent route which was supposed to be easy after the abseil; to reach moderate ground we had to make a diagonal traverse of which one pitch was grade VI, and to get down at all, following Dez, I had to bang in a piton so that I had the rope to protect me. After this manoeuvre we were able to go straight down and a row of abandoned pitons and abseils landed us at the foot of the tower. In the last shades of evening we found a footpath to the Vazzoler refuge and stumbled towards it, guided by its lights.

The guardian led us into his kitchen and plied us with soup while we examined the damage; the arm was fractured quite badly. The guardian's wife lent Dez a sling and we set out for the nearest hospital at Agordo. The Italians proved more accommodating to injured climbers than some other Alpine countries and the next day found us back under the Civetta peaks, Dez with his arm set and encased in plaster from wrist to shoulder and only mere shillings the poorer.

The accident was a terrible blow to our plans and there was nothing we could do but leave the Dolomites and head for the snow and ice of the Western Alps, where we hoped we could still tackle pure ice climbs or easy mixed ascents. Over the Mont Blanc range the weather was superb and Chamonix thronged with British mountaineers.

Dez, though right-handed, thought he could manage an ice axe with his left hand only, but before making an attempt on our chosen climb, the Brenva face of Mont Blanc, we decided to make a trial ascent on the Forbes Arête of the Aiguille du Chardonnet. Although obviously handicapped, Dez got along without too much difficulty, his main problem being the weight of his plaster cast. I have never seen a limb plaster of such thickness; the Italians evidently believe in complete immobilisation and they were almost successful for Dez could barely lift the arm from his side.

The good weather continued and the southern flank of Mont Blanc would surely be in perfect condition, but we couldn't be over-ambitious and settled for the easiest of its climbs, the old Brenva route. In our typical lazy fashion we delayed our departure till lunchtime and paid the price by walking up the Mer de Glace in stifling heat. We intended to bivouac in the refuge on the Col de la Fourche of the Frontier ridge leading to Mont Maudit, before going down early next morning on to the Brenva glacier to start our proposed route up Mont Blanc.

In the Géant icefall we were surprised to meet a very old man coming down through the maze of crevasses, apparently accompanied by a guide carrying an immense pack. We were even more astonished to find the 'guide' to be our friend, Eric Beard. He had hitch-hiked to the Alps as far as Courmayeur whence he had decided to cross to Chamonix. At the Torino refuge he met the old man who, mistaking Beardie for a guide, asked to be taken across to the Requin hut, and typically Beardie was doing the ancient this service.

'Where are you going and what's wrong with Dez?' he demanded.

'On to the Brenva!'

'Can I come with you? I'll get my client down to the Requin and run back up.'

'OK,' we agreed.

An hour later the three of us were moving together up the Géant glacier, Beardie with his vast load from which he promised he could keep us well fed. We crossed the bergschrund and climbed on to the Fourche slope in the late afternoon sunshine. The slope is notorious for variable conditions, and in places the surface was bare ice, but at the worst of it we managed to traverse to a rock spur and get security with good belays.

We clambered along the ridge to the bivouac box. The view on to and across the Brenva face was stupendous. The sun was setting and vividly etched the outline features of Mont Blanc's immense southern flanks. We could see our route clearly: Col Moore, the ice ridges, the summit séracs and Mont Blanc's crown bathed in rich sunlight. Letting the eye glide over the Aiguille Noire, the Aiguille Blanche and the upper slopes of the Peuterey ridge to the secondary summit of the Monarch, Mont Blanc de Courmayeur, one could appreciate that there was the longest ascent route in the Alps.

Inside the bivouac box other climbers recumbent on the communal bunks greeted us. Originally intended for five persons, this tiny hut is for me the most wonderful in the Alps, both for its unparalleled views and its solitude, or alternatively its usually interesting company. This time we found four Spaniards who had driven from Barcelona to Chamonix the previous day; they were all prostrate with headaches and nausea, presumably from lack of acclimatisation. They were amazed at Beardie's rucksack and even more at the Primus stove, quart of paraffin, potatoes, carrots, stewed steak and so on which he produced from its depths. None of the Spartan living usually associated with Alpine ascents for Beardie; carrying a heavy rucksack was easier than doing without food for him, and meant little in terms of effort to a man who ran 945 miles in nineteen days for fun.

We sat and cooked for hours, and after dining so royally we slept late; the Spaniards were off before we arose. I hate getting up in the early hours of the morning but on the Brenva there is no choice. At three o'clock we were brewing tea and by four on our way, roping down to the Brenva glacier through an inky blackness.

By the first glimmer of daylight we crossed the slopes leading to Col Moore. Sunrise at the Col is one of the most satisfying experiences the Alps can provide; after the cold and bleakness the soft morning sunlight brings a heightening of perception that lives on in the mind's eye. In the valleys of Italy it is still dark, but high on the Brenva face the definition is acute and the creeping fingers of light roll away the shadows to reveal the monarch's treasures: the summit séracs, the pear-shaped buttress, the snow arêtes of the Route Major and the Eckpfeiler buttress are summoned one by one out of the darkness.

There was no sign of the Spaniards, although as we came down from the Fourche we had seen lights as they climbed Moore's buttress. This we climbed in their wake, Dez coping successfully, and moving together we reached the snow arêtes above it. Here one clambers over a minor peak and down to a small col; at the bottom of the gap we came on the men from Barcelona, two of whom sat groaning and sick. The altitude was affecting them severely but their leader, who spoke English, declared they would sooner try to finish the climb than retreat by the way they had come. They asked if we would now lead and we set forth across the famous ice ridge. Conditions were perfect and our crampons bit and crunched into the excellent snow-ice.

Thick cloud had built up in the valleys and even to the shoulder of the Aiguille Noire several thousand feet below us, but the sky above and the horizon were clear so we didn't worry; it would obviously stay fine. It was still quite early when we reached the end of the ice ridges but on the final steep slopes, where the true difficulties on the climb are found, we slowed to a snail's pace.

The 'old Brenva route', as it is affectionately known, has held its place since 1865 as one of the outstanding ascents in the Alps for its perfection of line and beauty and its literary and historical associations; it still remains difficult and the final slopes can in certain conditions be severe. One can find hundreds of feet of pure ice or the way barred by dangerous séracs, or perhaps, if lucky, an easy passage by hard snow direct to the summit of Mont Blanc.

We were unlucky and came upon ice a few hundred feet above the slopes leading up from the ice ridges. There was no alternative but to cut steps, and slowly we moved upwards a foot at a time. By now it was midday and the heat of the sun and its reflection from the snow made a furnace of our surroundings; our tongues began to swell, our lips to crack and our skin to fry. Then the slope eased and we drew level with the base of the final séracs. The slope steepened again but this was the last obstacle, once through the séracs the summit of Mont Blanc was not far away. I thought I saw a way by a twisting gully that seemed to turn back on itself and lead above the séracs on to the summit slopes. But part of the way was hidden; we could only give it a try.

I cramponed up the gully, cut a platform and brought Dez and Beardie up, then led off once more. At the top of the gully where it disappeared into the séracs, I found myself in a deep trough under those menacing obstructions and with no obvious exit. 'There must be a way,' I kept muttering to myself as I brought up the others; ten minutes later when the Spaniards arrived we were still looking for it. Two of them immediately collapsed on to the snow and lay vomiting and groaning. 'There's no way out,' I told their leader ruefully.

'We'll have to go back down the gully and look for another route.' This news when translated to the rest of his party was greeted with more moans and groans. The leader asked if we would help them and we could see things were getting a bit tense; the two sick men refused to move and go down again. The leader became so excited that I thought he would hit them, but eventually he got them to their feet. I pointed out that our party was not without scars; Dez was suffering agony from his arm and Beardie, on his first climb of the season, although fit was also beginning to suffer from altitude sickness at over 14,000 feet. The best we could offer was to cut bucket steps for the rest of the ascent.

Going down the gully was exciting. I was at the back of our party and had almost reached my companions at a small stance on the ice when the first Spaniard started down and suddenly, with a startled cry, slipped. He was well held but he did let go of his ice axe which plummeted like a dart straight at me, balanced on crampon points but pick well into the slope. I automatically stuck up my spare hand as a defence and lo! the axe landed neatly on my upstretched palm, almost knocking me off the mountain with its force. This brought an appreciative 'Ole!' from the Spaniards, but I didn't hang around; using the two axes I swiftly reached Beardie and Dez, then traversed out of the line of any more missiles. The offending Spaniard did apologise, and uttered a heartfelt 'Gracias' when we handed back his axe a few moments later.

We cut steps across the face towards the Route Major, then mercifully a way opened before us without further obstruction. There followed 700 feet of axe-work on rubbery ice, of the type so prevalent on that side of Mont Blanc; I hacked step after step and slowly our train of seven men gained height. The leader of the Spaniards was a tower of strength and somehow kept his sick friends moving; in places he literally pulled them upwards on tight ropes. Finally the slope eased back and at 3 p.m. we staggered on to open snow between the summit of Mont Blanc and the Col de la Brenva.

A leisurely descent followed by way of the Grands Mulets, and the following evening found me celebrating with the Spaniards in the National bar in Chamonix. They were impressed by what they considered my eccentric companions, one with a limb encased in plaster of Paris, the other producing Primus stove and paraffin and making tea in a large billycan whenever things became a bit difficult.

While I was celebrating with the Spaniards, Dez calmly sawed off his plaster cast with a penknife. He nearly fainted when he pulled it off; certainly he broke every rule of conventional treatment as it had only been in place a few weeks, but he insisted he would climb better with it off than on and I had to agree that he had a valid point.

After I got back from the Alps, driven home by storms and end-of-season blues, I took a job on a freelance basis with a printer in Derby. I could work what hours I liked; if it was fine I climbed, if it rained I worked.

In September I accepted an invitation by the committee of the Alpine Climbing Group to become its honorary secretary. Three years earlier I had been persuaded by friends to apply for membership of the group and was duly elected. Up to then I had always been anti-club, but the ACG is not a club in the usual sense, but rather a gathering of keen alpinists dedicated to improving standards, spreading information and bringing together people interested in a broad spectrum of advanced Alpine mountaineering. By 1962 it had achieved most of its original aims but was foundering on the rock of organisational problems and needed a fresh impetus. I myself felt the group ought now to serve a different purpose and should in future concentrate on the spreading of information and guidebook work. I proposed that the group should found its own printed bulletin, for general sale to all climbers, giving information and supplements to different Alpine districts. In the spring of 1963, after much hard work by many members of the group, this policy was launched and has gone from strength to strength each year.

Despite the accident to Dez, 1962 had proved a successful Alpine season for us and had whetted our appetite for many areas, some of them rarely visited by British climbers. So we decided to repeat the experiment in 1963. For the first part of the summer we made up a foursome with Ian Clough and Dougal Haston, the four of us travelling in my van. The weather was not as kind as in 1962, but once more we managed to do a lot of climbs. Out of our twenty or so ascents, my most vivid memories are again of the times when things went wrong.

Our first misadventure occurred in the Dolomites when we were attempting the grade-VI *Eisenstecken* route on the Rotwand of the Catinaccio group. This climb has some horribly loose rock and as Dez was bridging and jamming his way up a vertical pitch several hundred feet above the start, his foot lightly touched some large jammed blocks. With a grinding rumble they slid out of the crack and bounced down to the ledge on which I was standing about forty feet below before shooting into space. I hadn't time to dodge but stood immobile and helpless, trying to gauge their fall. The stones rained about me but luckily only one piece of rock hit me a glancing blow on the shoulder. I felt a stabbing pain and became dizzy. Dez climbed down quickly to see if I was all right; as he arrived on my ledge I announced dramatically that my shoulder blade was fractured. My arm hung limp and I was sick with pain and shock, so without further questioning Dez prepared an abseil and we began to descend. At least I could now appreciate what my companion must have suffered the year before, but I am afraid I didn't display his stoicism or fortitude, and I have never been more pleased to reach ground level. By this time the pain had subsided to a modest but persistent throb, so I eased off my anorak, sweater and shirt and was relieved to discover no apparent fracture, but my shoulder was badly bruised and contused and I guessed I would be *hors de combat* for a while. 'Let's call it evens,' Dez grinned with obvious relief.

Because it was successful, I cannot recall much about our ascent of the *Detassis* route of the north-east face of the Brenta Alta except that it was hard and used to be considered the hardest climb in the Brenta Dolomites, but I do remember vividly a rock climb of British dimensions, the *Voie Contamine* on the south face of the Aiguille du Midi, when we were at Chamonix. We only did this as a filler-in, as something to do while we waited for the right weather for bigger things; in fact it turned out to be almost too big!

We started out with six pitons in our sack and then found that the route had been de-pitoned. Dez led the first serious pitch, a roof, completely free and when I joined him, not without great difficulty, he thrust me at the long thin crack that followed. The first part proved too hard for me to climb free and too wide for most of our piton stock – four leaf pitons and two angles. The angles fitted the crack well but the leaf pitons had to be used in pairs, driven together into the crack and tied off. I used my pitons over and over again, then two-thirds of the way up the crack I ran out of everything and managed somehow in desperation to climb the upper part free. It was the hardest piece of climbing I have ever led, and one of the rare occasions when I succeeded in impressing my young partner who, after ascending the pitch, declared it 'hard'. He soon recovered, so much so that he led the finishing cracks free, standing in places on the few remaining wooden wedges which others must have used for artificial aid, and elsewhere jamming or laybacking his way up. This latter style of climbing is my Achilles heel and I needed several pulls to follow him to the top.

Another expedition I shall never forget was an attempt with Terry Burnell on the Route Major of the Brenva face while Dez was climbing the Bonatti Pillar of the Drus in a single day with Joe Brown.

At first all went well, except that thirteen bodies were crammed into the Fourche bivouac when we arrived and we had a few hours' rest on the doorstep before moving on. We descended to the Brenva glacier and crossed to Col Moore in the dark, then started up the side of Moore's buttress, ascending diagonally towards the crossing place of the Great Couloir to the ridges of the Route Major and the true commencement of the climb.

A French party at the Red Sentinel bivouac near the crossing point were getting ready to move over the couloir as we climbed; the first morning light reached us and we stopped to watch them. The leader stepped boldly out into the Great Couloir, reached its centre and the end of his rope and began to bring his second across. The third man remained belayed on our side of the couloir, watching his companions who, close together, were on a rib of snow between deep avalanche channels. Suddenly there was a thunderous roar; an avalanche which had split off under the summit of Mont Blanc was being funnelled into the Great Couloir and sweeping down on the French. The second man scampered the last few feet to his leader and the two clung together, buffeted by spindrift and obviously expecting to be swept away by the rolling seas of ice. We stood transfixed; there is something compelling in watching the difficulties of other people and, hypnotised, I followed the advancing ice.

At the very last moment the waves parted and hissed down the channels beside the exposed climbers. 'Gosh, that was close!' I exclaimed. 'What is an avalanche doing at five in the morning? A freak I suppose.' We had barely started climbing again when a crack like a pistol shot froze us: a second avalanche was sliding down the Great Couloir. The French leader had set out to complete the crossing and scuttled back across the ice to his companion and the safety of the rib. Again the avalanche divided and left the climbers unharmed. We began to have second thoughts about going on, especially as a minor avalanche gushed down beside us and another large one came down the Great Couloir. The two French climbers on their perch seemed safe enough, but one can never be certain with avalanches and wisely they started to retreat.

The sun was on us by this time, and we sat on a rock sticking out of the snow, discussing the situation and watching the party above us with thumping hearts. The second man had almost rejoined the third, who had never ventured from the bank of the couloir, when a small powder-snow avalanche engulfed him and knocked him down the slope. He was held by the other two and regained his feet to complete the crossing safely. Terry and I about-turned and began our retreat. 'I thought it was too warm last night,' Terry said. 'I was sweating in my duvet jacket outside the refuge door.' When we were on the Col Moore the biggest avalanche yet roared down the face and it was a relief to see, as we recrossed the Brenva glacier, that the three Frenchmen were safe and following us down.

'I don't favour going down the Géant side of the Fourche,' I confessed to Terry. 'The snow's in bad condition, the sun will be beating on it and it could come away and take us with it.' Across on the Frontier ridge, the Calotte of the Brenva was in deep shade and its snow looked good. I pointed to it. 'Shall we have a go that way?' It meant climbing the Brenva side of the Calotte and descending the far side to the Géant basin and the route back to Chamonix. Terry the Gnome, taciturn as usual, nodded his head in agreement.

It turned out a wise decision. We enjoyed perfect crampon snow on the Brenva side of the Calotte but on the Géant side it was bad. A rock rib took us down from the summit, but when this petered out we found ourselves on steep snow and ice in an abysmal state under the full glare of a hot sun. Eventually we reached the bottom, only to be confronted by the biggest bergschrund I have had to cross in the Alps; it might have been thirty feet.

I couldn't pluck up courage to jump and teetered hesitatingly on its edge before having to give it best. 'We've had it! I can't jump this, we'll have to climb up again and go down the Fourche slope after all.'

'No, we will not,' Terry said with a confident grin, and taking off his rucksack as we balanced in ice steps he produced the longest channel piton imaginable. 'I always carry this with me, it's a get-me-out-of-the-murky special!'

He banged the piton into the ice and by the effort this needed we knew it would be safe. The dive over the bergschrund was spectacular nevertheless, even off the safety of a rappel rope. We congratulated ourselves on being cunning, adjusted our sacks and set off down the glacier, heading for the *téléphérique* at the Aiguille du Midi.

Looking back, I noticed three figures at the top of the Fourche slope. 'Christ, they're off!' and down they came, bumping and sliding. Terry swung round and we watched the French for the last time, leap-frogging each other and trying to brake without avail. They cleared the bergschrund and shot into the Géant basin; a few seconds later one of them got up and dusted himself down – quite an escape to fall 800 feet and stand up unharmed. But the other two lay crumpled on the snow.

I have never known a swifter rescue. A party near the Torino hut saw the French fall; a rescue team were at the refuge having lunch and arrived at the gallop. Mercifully, neither of the victims was fatally hurt but both had multiple injuries, fractured legs and internal damage. The guides rendered first aid and, as reinforcements streamed from the Torino to help carry, we wearily turned our backs and plodded towards the *téléphérique* with a mixture of thankfulness and regret.

Indifferent weather at the end of August found Dez and myself camped under the Marmolada, waiting to attempt a major climb. But it snowed and snowed and when we awoke one morning to a white-out we packed and set off for home. But, miraculously, as we came over the Sella pass the sun came out and the clouds rolled away. As if from nowhere, hundreds of skiers appeared, the lifts began to run, and it was more like the winter sports season than a summer holiday. We convinced ourselves that this was the start of a fine spell, changed our plans and headed towards our old adversary, the Rotwand. This time our ambitions centred on the Buhlweg, a recent ascent with a high reputation. In the early evening we walked up to the Paolini hut, hoping that the blood-red sunset reflected off the walls of the Rosengarten above us meant a fine day on the morrow.

The Germans, Hasse and Brandler, had made the first ascent of the *Buhlweg* in 1958, but it had been named after the famous Austrian climber, Hermann Buhl, who had made the first attempt on it. Due to a misunderstanding the recently published English guidebook gave the impression that it was of a mixed free and artificial nature; we were sadly disillusioned to find it almost all piton work.

The refuge was full of climbers and hillwalkers and next morning we had barely started on the first pitch before a crowd gathered below. It always amazes me how little sleep continental climbers need; here it was, eight o'clock, and people who could still have been abed were happily watching us climb; they were even lively enough to serenade us with songs like 'La Montanara'. It wasn't even fine, and I certainly felt that eight o'clock on such a bleak, grey morning was best greeted horizontally on a bed. Finally, a snow squall drove the fans away and made us curse yet again the unreliability of the weather.

The Rotwand is beautiful to behold, 1,500 feet of vertical and overhanging rock, which at sunrise or sunset well justifies its name, the Red Wall. But the Buhlweg is not a delight to climb; we found that it simply consisted of clipping into and out of pitons. There were a few short sections of free climbing but they merely made one glad to get back to the inevitable pitons, for the rock was rotten. There is no other way to climb many of the Dolomite faces; some overhang so much that one certainly finds oneself in unique situations, swinging in etriers over space, but the novelty soon wears off and gives way to feelings of drudgery, unlike pure artificial climbing in other mountains of the world.

A combination of weather worries, being fed up with the climb, and our fitness made us hurry. We reached the summit in what seemed a reasonable time, then sped down the descent route through hail showers. We were greeted as conquering heroes at the hut; the lady guardian produced a free meal and handed us several thousand lire. This, it was explained, was a gift from the walkers and climbers at the hut because ours had been the fastest time so far for an ascent of the *Buhlweg*. We were astonished; British climbers rarely pay attention to times other than guidebook recommendations, but obviously within certain limits speed is safety in the Alps and does hint at competence. To rush from face to face trying to set records seems futile to me, but it is surprising how contagious it can become, especially if material rewards are offered; we are all capable of being competitive.

We swallowed our pride, pocketed the lire and ordered wine all round. Next day the snow definitely drove us home.

Much to my surprise I again found it easy to get casual work after a three-month Alpine season. I went back to live in Leeds and took on freelance work, preparing estimates for printing contracts and making typographical layouts, and I bolstered my earnings by giving lectures to climbers and the general public on mountaineering topics. This latter activity developed by accident: I was invited to give a talk, the audience liked it, I was invited to give another, and so on. This built up over the ensuing winters until in recent years I have lectured two or three times a week, which has provided me with a source of income for summer mountaineering.

The year 1964 was dominated for me by organising and taking part in the Gauri Sankar expedition, but in 1965 I returned to the Alps with Ian Howell. We gave a talk early in June at the Alpenverein Haus in Innsbruck about the attempt on Gauri Sankar and afterwards were taken to climb in the Kalkkögel district of the Stubai Alps by guides of the area. The Kalkkögel have the loosest rock of any mountains I have climbed, but they have been the training ground and homeland hills for generations of Innsbruck climbers and their products, Auckenthaler, Rebitsch, Buhl, Rainer, have become legendary in the mountain world. There is a saying amongst Austrian climbers that if you can climb safely in the Kalkkögel you can climb anywhere.

From the Adolf Pichler hut we made our first climb of the season, a grade-IV-superior on a flank of the Riepenwand, a huge rock face reminiscent of the Dolomites; our climb was a mere outlying wing of the face. We were terrified by the looseness of the rock and equally impressed by the metal plaques everywhere commemorating fallen climbers. We were thankful to get to the top; ledges had collapsed without warning, stones had fallen and holds had snapped as we pulled up on seemingly firm jug-handles.

Next day we tackled a grade-VI climb, the *Schmidhuber* route on the Kleine Ochsenwand. Ian reasoned that, being steeper rock, grade VIs should be firmer than the lower-grade climbs. This proved to be so for much of the route, until Ian was leading on a steep wall and the handhold on which he was pulling up snapped off without notice. Luckily, below him was a piton into which he had clipped a long sling and which he grabbed as he fell. Several hundred feet higher I was leading the last difficult pitch, bridging out in a bottomless chimney that overhung the scree far below. I stopped for a rest on a large foothold and was enthusing to Ian on the merits of the ascent when my shelf departed into space and I found myself suspended from the rope, held by a running belay from a wooden wedge I had discovered. This was too much! How gingerly we climbed after this incident, testing every handhold and foothold, creeping over the waste-strewn summit ledges.

After this we fled to the Kaisergebirge and its firm limestone, leaving behind grinning Kalkkögel experts who insisted that all we needed was practice on loose rock!

It was an atrocious season. In the Kaisergebirge rainstorms and cloudbursts were frequent, the rock faces were plastered, snow lay deep everywhere, the Inn valley was flooded, the roads impassable and the Tyrol declared a disaster area. Between wading through floods and trudging through snow we did get up some famous routes. One classic, the east face of the Fleischbank, provided us with an intention fulfilled; this had been an ambition of mine ever since I first read about Hans Dülfer who made the first ascent in 1912. Our admiration for that great cragsman grew with every foot of climbing, particularly when we arrived at the tension traverse; no wonder Austrian and German climbers refer to such rope manoeuvres as Dülfer traverses.

The terrible weather eventually drove us on, but everywhere we went it was the same story: rain, hail, snow and meeting other climbers who had nothing but sad tales of miserable conditions elsewhere. We visited the Schüsselkar in the Wettersteingebirge, north of Innsbruck, and climbed its renowned south face by the Auckenthaler crack; the descent in mist and rain told us that to go on to Mont Blanc as we had intended was a waste of time. Instead, the lure of the Dolomites pulled us south to Italy.

There the story repeated itself; every climb, every start we made, was haunted by bad weather. Then I remembered the San Martino group at the extreme south of the main Dolomite chain. 'I was down there a few years ago and climbed the Scarf arête of the Cima della Madonna. Conditions are bound to be good there,' I told Ian. 'And the Sass Maor's east face is as beautiful as any in the Dollies.' We had just climbed the south face of the Piz Ciavazes, and the snow and mist on the way down would have made any climber keen to go anywhere with a hope of sunshine.

Twenty-four hours later we stood gazing at the Sass Maor from the Val Pradidali. This eastern side of the mountain has as bold an aspect as any in the range yet is not often climbed for it lies in a comparatively remote and unpopular area of Dolomite peaks. The great Emil Solleder, one of the best rock climbers of all time, had first climbed the wall in 1926, but he had avoided the true challenge of the 3,500-foot face by traversing on to it halfway up by a line of easy slanting chimneys which lead diagonally into the centre from the south side. Inevitably a direct start was later added, by way of a prominent rib of compact grey rock. Looking across the Pradidali valley, I could follow the route up the whole height of the enormous bastion. Beginning with the rib, it runs through a zone of terraces interspersed with steep walls, a line of chimneys (Solleder's original route), a series of roofs – presumably overcome by the famous traversing pitches – then a series of corners and finally the finishing wall to the tip of the point that completes the giant dagger that is the Sass Maor.

'Well, what do you make of it?' I asked with a proprietary air.

'Absolutely spiffing!' replied Ian in his best dulcet public-school accent. Ian, a powerhouse, strode from hard Alpine ascent to ascent, hiding his determined drive behind a Greyfriars school approach which matched his background and natural good humour.

At sunset the sky was clear, without a trace of cloud on the horizon, and inevitably I lectured Ian on my sound judgement. Unfortunately I spoke too soon.

Seven o'clock next morning found us moving up the rock rib with the confidence born of success on other climbs, and when the route description almost at once proved wildly inaccurate we cheerfully picked our own way, admitting that the steep and compact rock was harder than we expected. As we had nearly always improved on guidebook times and as the forecast for this ascent was eight to ten hours, we carried no bivouac equipment. Our food supplies consisted of oranges and boiled sweets and we carried some water, also four pitons each, having been led to expect free climbing. Our piton allowance soon began to worry us as we discovered few in place, and the compact rock provided no natural running belays. I have rarely climbed with so little protection.

We made good progress, completely absorbed by the climbing, so absorbed in fact that we didn't notice the first black clouds boiling up on the horizon in spite of the clear sky at dawn. Suddenly, with a roar a large rockfall swept over the rib below us. 'Thank goodness we're not down there,' I muttered.

'I don't like the look of those clouds,' Ian rejoined. 'But we'd better go on. We couldn't go back down the rib if we wanted to, I don't fancy being under the next rockfall.'

We climbed up and up the never-ending rib, and slowly the clouds came up until tentacles of mist crawled over us and our mountain. Soon we couldn't see a hundred feet up or down and it got thicker all the time; the first distant rolls of thunder put us on edge. 'We're in for it this time!' I said as I started to climb a steep crack.

Forty feet up I stuck; I couldn't move out of the crack that ended in an overhanging bulge. At that instant the rain began; within minutes it was torrential and I was soaked and almost washed off the rock. I had to do something, and quickly; with a hand jam I reached up and under the bulge and a frenzied glance revealed a possible running belay, a thread round a jammed chockstone. How I struggled to thread that stone! It was my whole life, existence itself. When my hands became frozen I used my teeth, I jammed my knee against the bulge and almost fell. At my last gasp I got the sling threaded, clipped a karabiner in, pushed in my rope, and hung on it. The rain was beating on my head so hard I couldn't look upwards. 'Go down!' came a voice from within, and as if it were an unchallengeable command I cast off and climbed down to Ian, sheltering in the bottom of the crack where we huddled together.

'We must get up before it gets any worse,' Ian declared as we pulled our cagoules over our soaking bodies. 'I'll have a try.'

He changed places with me to climb up to the thread runner. It was no time for niceties; Ian clipped another loop into the sling and standing in this reached round the bulge, then swung out and over the top. The temperature was dropping and the rain turned to snow. Shivering, I climbed up to Ian on a small ledge beneath a vertical crack. Whoever gave the description for the English guide was an idiot, we uncharitably decided; it bore little resemblance to reality. I had to ask Ian to lead the crack; my hands were numb and I knew

I wouldn't be able to get up without taking time to warm them up. Our world had shrunk to a few feet of wet rock. It is hard to re-experience the anxiety of such moments, but I have never been so frightened in my life. Ian's determination was unflagging, and with teeth clenched he set off again without a word, to the accompaniment of reverberating thunder. He struggled with the crack for what seemed hours; it became colder and colder and he had to stop in a small cave near the top of the pitch, blowing on his hands to get some feeling into them for the last few feet of laybacking. With a desperate thrutch he succeeded in reaching a stance fifteen feet higher and then, as he took in my rope, the snow began to fall with blizzard fury.

I joined Ian with difficulty and found him on a little shelf with no possibility of shelter. 'Shall we sit it out here or press on?' I yelled through the gale.

'We must keep going,' Ian declared emphatically. My hands were dead and I feared frostbite. I have never been in a storm of such violence in the Alps and its ferocity completely undermined me psychologically. I was for bivouacking on that small platform but Ian moved off again to tackle the steep wall above our heads. I could see he was as worried as I was.

Two rope-lengths of desperate climbing with icy holds and occasional stones peppering us brought us to an even more serious situation. Night was almost upon us as Ian brought me up to join him, both of us suspended from indifferent pitons with no ledge or shelter from the storm. 'Oh God, what a place!' I moaned.

'I think there's a cave above and to our right if only we can reach it,' Ian said, pointing up through the snowy dusk. 'We must get out of this!'

I forced myself to lead and hesitantly climbed towards the promised haven. My hands were frozen and I was desperate, yet somehow in the darkness, at the end of the rope, my experience, luck and reserves got me up. But what a disappointment! Our refuge was a mere depression in the rock, like a saucer – perhaps a melt-hole, but certainly no cave. I hammered in a piton and brought Ian up; for better or worse this curved hollow was our shelter for the night.

I shall never forget that night. We had nothing to protect us, though we did manage to take our boots off and get our feet into rucksacks. Feeling returned to my hands and the subsequent hot aches kept me occupied mentally for quite a time. We rationed our boiled sweets to one an hour and I began to look forward to this treat as if it was the most important in my life. Stones whistled down the face, but under the lip of our depression we felt safe till this illusion was shattered when one hit me in the back with a resounding thud. 'It's nothing,' I reassured Ian, 'only a little one.' We were surprised next day to find it had cut through my clothes and drawn blood.

'I think we've had it!' whispered Ian in half-spoken thought, during a slight lull. 'Certainly if it doesn't stop snowing soon.'

'Let's sing,' I suggested, but we soon tired of howling into the wind.

The snow continued to pile up round us. I felt myself suspended in time and space, full of my own suffering, as if I was dreaming inside a never-ending nightmare. A jerk brought me to full awareness; I was hanging on the ropes that tied us on. Peering through iced eyelashes I glimpsed stars. 'Ian, Ian, we're OK! It's stopped snowing!' Ian too had been locked in his own world of misery, but greeted this critical news with a characteristic 'Super!' and handed me a boiled sweet to celebrate.

In the last hour before dawn the intense cold had us writhing as if trying to escape from probing needles. Cloud covered the stars again and first light was heralded by fine driven snow; what it revealed made my heart sink. The steep rock was so plastered with verglas and snow it looked hopeless and I was for sitting it out, but Ian was unwilling to stay put another second and struggled into his boots.

Somehow he inched his way upwards; slowly and interminably the rope jerked out. 'Come on!' It was so like winter climbing in Scotland that I had to keep telling myself this was the Dolomites in summer at a mere 8,000 feet. I took over the lead and immediately felt better. I could not have led the first rope length but now I felt that nothing could stop us. We must be somewhere near Solleder's traverse on to the face; if we could find that we should know where we were and have an easy descent to the valley. But peering through the mist we couldn't see anything to tell us our position.

Around lunchtime, I came upon a big ledge while leading, and at the same moment realised that it was getting warmer. The snow ceased dramatically, but thick mist still blotted everything out. 'This must be the junction with the original route,' Ian decided, and I agreed. We walked along the terrace to the south; it became wider, then disappeared into a deep chimney. A rusty piton told us that this was Solleder's route.

At once our tension dispersed; our worries were over and we unroped and sat happily on the edge of the chimney, knowing we had got away with it. A lot of rubbish has been written about the spirit and comradeship of the hills; mutual admiration often runs riot and we sometimes see ourselves and our friends as some kind of hero, but Ian and I looked at each other sheepishly and grinned. This was the real thing – we had been to the edge and escaped by a combination of teamwork and luck.

It was late in the evening before we were completely off the hook, after slithering down Solleder's chimneys and scrambling and climbing down a thousand feet of loose and broken ground. We crawled into a cowshed at the foot of the face, feeling by then as virtuous as gods. The direct start to the east face of the Sass Maor had provided us with enough adventure to keep us happy, and we lay resting in the shed while it rained and rained.

Three days later, on the first fine morning, we completed the ascent, using the Solleder start. The climbing was classic, especially the famous traversing pitches, but it was an anticlimax after our involvement with the direct start. This time the route description was accurate, and we even restored faith in ourselves by being several hours ahead of guidebook time. Drinking tea as evening shadows dramatised the face, I decided we could still count our ascent as a correct, orthodox climb even though we had been almost a week in completing it.

Famous words came to mind, Robin Smith's I believe, about one of his own quixotic adventures: 'Unpremeditated bivouacs before, during and after the climb.' They almost applied to our own escapade.

Alpine climbing has little to offer now in the way of exploration in the usual sense of the word; apart from minor variations the goldmine is exhausted. But the Alps remain the perfect playground and will attract the mountaineer and mountain lover when their very last secret is revealed. It will still be possible to discover something infinitely more important than a first ascent – as we found on the Sass Maor – a little of our own true nature.

6   Gauri Sankar, 23,440 feet

'Where the gods dwell is hidden wealth.'
(Nepali saying)

The highest mountains of the Himalaya, as in the European Alps, are not the hardest to climb. The ascents of Everest, K2 and Kangchenjunga posed acute problems of organisation, logistics and human endurance but made technical demands of a comparatively low standard. The most difficult mountains of the Himalaya are yet to be climbed, namely the very severe lesser peaks, most of which have never been attempted.

It is perhaps fortunate for the future of mountaineering that the best of these lesser mountains have so far been protected from assault by access and political difficulties. We have reached a stage in the development of climbing technique where little is impossible given sufficient time, fair weather and reasonable funds, yet one views recent developments in Himalayan mountaineering with apprehension. Everest was climbed in 1953 and since that date there has been a revolution in equipment and know-how, yet expeditions are still being planned on the same cumbrous scale. This is not progress; we should by now be attempting to do more with less; certainly the greatest satisfaction in Himalayan climbing is achieved when there is a minimum of numbers, of use of artificial aids, and of non-mountain objectives. We must acknowledge that climbing a mountain means little; how the summit is reached is what matters.

No party has yet been successful on one of the extreme lesser peaks, but it is clear that they could be subjugated by large expeditions with plenty of money. More worthwhile would be to limit expedition membership to a maximum of four persons, dispense with porters above base camp and manage on a shoe-string. To me this is the direction that all future Himalayan exploration should take, otherwise modern technology will make ascents irrelevant. Such mountains as Menlungste, Shivling, the Ogre and their peers could provide the most rewarding ascents in climbing history if the men who attempt them limit themselves to light, unsupported expeditions and do not throw unwarranted forces at these magnificent virgin summits of the world.

This may seem somewhat hypocritical in the light of the following story of an attempt on Gauri Sankar in 1964, but the resources of that expedition were definitely limited, perhaps the minimum then required, and I think much can be learnt from its experiences. Gauri Sankar is not as difficult a proposition as some of the unclimbed peaks, but it is safe to say that no mountain yet attempted is of the same order of difficulty.

The idea of trying to climb Gauri Sankar was solely my own; how six of us reached Nepal and our base camp in a cave at 7,800 feet in the Rong Shar gorge, ten minutes' walk from the Nepal-Tibet/China border, is a long and wearisome tale. Suffice it to say that the year of frustrating preparations, the lack of funds and the difficulty of getting the necessary support were typical of such ventures. But we finally achieved our goal and in the autumn of 1964 there we were, with three Sherpas, two mail runners and a liaison officer and, behind us, 10,000 miles of overland driving through the heat of deserts and monsoon rains and several weeks of marching across Nepal in the rainy season, our bodies covered with and debilitated by blood-sucking leeches – nine weeks of physical discomfort, poor food and financial troubles. Now, somewhere above us, nearly 16,000 feet in vertical height and many miles in distance, was the summit of Gauri Sankar at 23,440 feet.

This is one of the most famous of Himalayan peaks. For many years it was thought to be the highest summit in the world, and it is a holy mountain to Hindu and Buddhist alike: Gauri is another name for Parbati, goddess of love, and Sankar is her consort, Siva the destroyer. The mountain is visible from Kathmandu and is worshipped as the dwelling place of those two immortals. Thirty-six miles west of Everest, Gauri Sankar spreads over the Nepal-Tibet border like a giant umbrella, guarded on all sides by steep ridges and precipices, deep gorges and rock barriers. Several reconnaissances had been made before our own attempt, each concentrated on an approach from the north which apparently offered the only chink in the peak's armour; none had gained a real footing on the mountain, and each party declared it impossible to climb.

The completion of the Nepal-Tibet/China border agreement in 1961 had delineated Gauri Sankar as being two-thirds in Tibet, including the north side of the mountain, but leaving the western precipices in Nepal. The reconnaissances had taken place before this agreement; no one had been to the west side of the peak and at least, though our attempt was restricted to this aspect, we did have a chance to break virgin ground – without reliable maps and with little topographical information. Before leaving Kathmandu we had been strictly warned not to go into Tibet on any account, the border being sited at a bridge on the Tibetan side of the Rong Shar gorge. So we were left with no alternative; somehow we had to find and force a route from the west.

We had also been advised to be on the alert for Khamba bandits, a tribe of marauding Tibetans who live by plunder and whom even the Chinese have not managed to subdue. In 1959 a Japanese expedition reconnoitring the north side of Gauri Sankar had woken one morning to find their base surrounded by Tibetans armed with swords and rifles. By the time the Khambas departed the poor Japanese climbers were almost reduced to underclothes, and had to beat an undignified retreat. Our liaison officer, Hari Das, sub-inspector of police at Kathmandu, was not taking the threat of banditry lightly; singing to himself he worked hour after hour at sharpening his kukris in case of such an emergency.

The ground about the Rong Shar gorge under the western slopes of Gauri Sankar is incredible. The gorge itself is a place of high precipices covered with bamboo and creeper and of thundering waterfalls, and is the work of the mighty Bhote Kosi river on its journey to the Indian plains. We had expected a difficult climb but nothing like the reality. Never in the history of Himalayan mountaineering had a party been forced to place its base camp at such a low altitude as 7,800 feet – 17,900 feet on Everest! The coolies from Kathmandu had refused to come even to that lowly site, and to reach the cave from Lamobagar, a small Sherpa community and the last village on the Nepal side of the gorge, had required many relays of load-carrying by Sherpas, Tibetan refugees and ourselves, the passage being made no easier by our having to walk directly through a large waterfall.

The cave, actually a cavern beneath an immense boulder, was forced upon us as the only flat piece of land for miles. The hillsides around were so steep that it was mountaineering to move up or down, yet the main highway from Tibet through to Nepal was just above our shelter, a singletrack that deserved an alpine grading. During the monsoon the path became so slippery and dangerous that it was not normally used at that season.

The party sitting in the cave on 19 September 1964, having a rest day at last, was very much a Rock and Ice affair, with Don Whillans as climbing leader, Dez Hadlum, Terry Burnell and myself members of the reformed club, plus Ian 'Kludge' Clough and Ian Howell who were both close and long-standing friends of the rest of us. All six, as we stared out into heavy rain, were beginning to wonder if we should ever see Gauri Sankar, let alone climb it, if the monsoon continued so inexorably.

In Nepal, as in many Himalayan regions, there are two possible climbing seasons, before and after the monsoon, each with advantages and drawbacks; in spring the weather is warmer but there is more danger from avalanches, in autumn it is extremely cold at high altitudes but the avalanche menace is less. For a mountain over 25,000 feet I would prefer a spring attempt, under 25,000 feet autumn is perhaps best because of more stable weather. In any case we had elected to make our attempt after the monsoon.

One factor of an autumn expedition that must not be underestimated is that the approach march is usually made at the height of the rains when in Nepal the leeches are at their worst. These worms cannot be taken lightly;

they invade all privacy and are not easy to remove from tender parts of the anatomy. Some are so small they could crawl through the eye of a needle; others are as large as ordinary earthworms. One can burn them off with a smouldering cigarette but the wound continues to bleed, for they inject an anti-coagulant into the sore. If one pulls them off, the head usually remains beneath the skin and soon the sore festers, possibly even blood poisoning develops. When one sleeps on the march, the leeches continue to feed and a dozen feeding simultaneously on one limb is no record. On 19 September Don Whillans and Terry Burnell were both victims of blood poisoning from leech bites, and pumped full of penicillin.

Our equipment and food had stood the rigours of the march better than we had, and thanks to modern barrier-packaging techniques the incessant water had been kept at bay. Organising the expedition had been my problem and I was more than pleased that everything and everyone had arrived, if not in tip-top condition, at least in one piece at the base of the mountain. Our total budget was £3,500, and to get six men and three tons of equipment and food to the peak with some chance of success was, I hope I may say without immodesty, a feat in itself.

The most cheerful man amongst us was Hari, our liaison officer. 'You climb the mountain now, boys?' he chuckled.

'Unlikely!' I was forced to admit.

'Where is this mountain?' he demanded.

'Up there!' Whillans declared, jerking a finger towards the rain and mist.

Our Sherpas were obviously upset at the lowliness of base camp; they realised that we should require them to carry loads from there onwards and they didn't like it. Below the snow line, carrying is normally the work of coolies to whom the high-altitude Sherpa feels far superior and to do such work would be a blow to their pride. We explained that we too would carry heavy loads but they were plainly incredulous: no true Sahib carries heavy weights at low altitudes in the mountains. A few days later I think they felt we were not Sahibs at all! Initially the amount of load carrying which loomed ahead was frightening – three tons to be hauled out of the cave and over the mountainside – but soon we took the work for granted and never seemed to move anywhere without a pack.

Apart from its altitude the cave was ideal as a base, and we quickly made it comfortable. It provided dry quarters during the remainder of the monsoon and once the rains ceased we welcomed a never-ending stream of Tibetan and Nepali traders, travelling through the gorge on business missions. It turned out that the cave was the local 'Hotel Splendide' and had sheltered generations of travellers, and the Tibetans and Nepali still came to stay despite our presence. Hari managed to learn a smattering of Tibetan, and with the aid of the

Sherpas we too contrived to learn how these people live, about conditions in Tibet and the effect of the Chinese occupation.

In spite of the rain we started to explore our surroundings, and from the cave the gorge was traversed as far as the Tibetan border at the footbridge over the Bhote Kosi. Fortunately, a few hundred yards below the bridge, a narrow mouth-like opening led up on the east into a steep hanging valley. From the riverbank it appeared dark and mysterious and in the mist and drizzle one could not see very far, but it appealed to me as the setting for a scene from *The Lost World*. This valley was our only possibility; we had to cut a way up through its jungle in the hope that we would eventually emerge under the west ridge of Gauri Sankar.

Working in relays we attacked the jungle with flailing kukris, our camp hatchet, even ice axes; foot by foot a path was hacked out of the mass of bamboo thickets and hanging walls of creeper. I have never seen vegetation so dense or growing at such an angle. Every few feet we had to climb a rock buttress, some of them reminiscent of recent routes pioneered in Britain! These crags had to be equipped with fixed rope to make load carrying possible. Our progress was hindered by continuing rain, lack of vision and the occasional leech and it took a week of back-breaking effort to reach an altitude of lighter vegetation, shrubs and rhododendron.

In the valley was a large stream which, when it rained heavily, turned dramatically and quickly into a raging torrent. Our route entailed crossing the stream so we resolved to build an all-weather bridge, for the possibility of our retreat being cut off in case of accident or illness was real and serious.

Whillans was soon off his sickbed and into the fray, smashing hour after hour at the bamboo like an automaton. The problem of erecting the bridge was taken on by Don and myself and it proved one of the most exciting undertakings of the expedition. The only possible place for the crossing was immediately above a seventy-foot waterfall where a slip would have been fatal. First we cut down two large trees and lugged them to the water's edge, then, balancing on a greasy boulder in the middle of the rapids, Don used his physical prowess to lever the logs into position. The finished bridge was of an unusual construction, and broken into several sections with side ropes, holding lines and a safety rail to cling to on the way across.

Once the trail had been cut through the first and thickest section of jungle, it became obvious that the distance to the treeline and a site for an advanced base would be too great for laden men to cover in a single stage. So on the first flat place above the crossing we rigged a tarpaulin as a dump and began to carry our baggage there. Above this provisional haven the jungle gave way to rainforest with, mercifully, no more bamboo.

Wandering alone in the woods could be frightening; bears were common and it was easy to lose the way. As an aid to route finding we notched the trees to mark the trail. In places we had to climb crags again and even sometimes a tree, and over these obstacles we once more had to leave rope in place. Our humour was still good at this stage and the unconventional mountaineering caused much laughter and many suggestions for extending our experience by variations on the theme.

Eventually we reached the treeline and found a campsite in a rhododendron forest at, we guessed, 14,000 feet, and from the cave a full day's slog from dawn to dusk for a heavily laden man. In over a week's labour a route had been forced through some of the thickest jungle in the world, vegetation so dense that in its perpetual twilight it was impossible to tell if it was morning or evening. Throughout the week it had rained almost non-stop, and the cost had been high in blistered hands and gashes from bamboo, broken ice axes, kukris and knives, but over 6,000 feet in altitude had been gained.

Four of us moved to the site chosen for advanced base: Don, Kludge, Dez Hadlum and myself. For one night we bivouacked, then set to work and chopped down rhododendron and cleared earth throughout the next day until it was possible to erect tents and a cooking tarpaulin. As we were almost at the height of a normal base camp, we were glad to put up our largest tents, including one that looked as if it had been left behind from Agincourt.

All this time we hoped the valley we were climbing would lead straight to the foot of the west ridge of Gauri Sankar. Our only topographical guide was one aerial photograph of the whole western flank of the mountain, which was misleading because it was impossible to guess any scale. We gazed and gazed at it, but in the bad visibility it was of little help. So our plan was simply to get enough food and equipment up to the mountain proper and to begin serious climbing the moment the weather became favourable.

Once out of the rhododendron above advance base, bushes gave way to open moorland and we could at last see something of our environment. The four of us climbed this moorland to the world of mountains proper: scree, then a rock buttress, and finally a moraine snout that led to a small glacier and an idyllic campsite beside a small stream. We had brought up heavy loads and Don and Kludge moved into a tent here. The date was 2 October and we still had no inkling of our true whereabouts; there was no clear view and, before Dez and I went down, we all argued about our position on the mountain.

Next day we were rewarded with the first fine morning since we left Kathmandu. Don and Kludge quickly ascended the glacier above their camp and climbed to a col at its head, which they estimated to be 17,000 feet. They were amazed at what they saw as they bounded on to the ridge: they were on a mere spur of the mountain and gazing head-on at the huge south-west face of Gauri Sankar. Our calculations were all awry for there was no true west ridge, but they could see, many miles to the north, the sweep of a huge crest, the steep north-west ridge of the mountain. This was our only hope, but was it in Tibet?

Utterly dismayed, they climbed down as rain and mist returned and drew a veil over the scene; the monsoon was not yet through with us as we were to find to our cost. Dez and I arrived from advance base with further supplies to be greeted by this shattering news. Whillans, forthright as ever, declared 'We've had it, lad, not a bloody chance from here!'

Kludge was equally pessimistic. 'It's so far to the foot of the ridge,' he said. 'If only we could have approached from Tibet! It's an easy walk in from that side, coolies could have carried to 15,000 feet or higher.'

We sat and talked over the possibilities for hours; the big problem was the distance from our base to the foot of the north-west ridge, which we estimated as at least twenty-five miles. Our plan had originally allowed six weeks on the mountain, but we had already spent two weeks getting thus far and were still a long way from the foot of the mountain proper. We decided with the doggedness that defies reality to see just how far we could get. At least we now had some idea of our whereabouts; Don prepared a rough sketch and we even managed to pick out our approximate position on the aerial photograph. We couldn't have crossed into Tibet from the Rong Shar gorge without causing an incident but whether high on the slopes of Gauri Sankar we should be in that country or not we felt mattered little.

We now had to replan and reorganise. Don and Kludge would stay in the lead as our strongest climbing combination while the rest of us repositioned our supplies and acted as their support. Our principal worry was provisioning; logistics had been thrown haywire and we should need many more camps, dumps and time than originally allowed for. This was my responsibility and I went down to base in the Rong Shar to try and make fresh arrangements. We found it was possible to buy potatoes from the Tibetans, and using this additional food source liberally I estimated that if we lived on potatoes in the low camps and carried wood for cooking below the snowline we could last for a maximum of six weeks more.

Ian Howell was in charge of load ferrying and the two of us took over the task of keeping the supply lines flowing. This work was tedious in the extreme, the same slog day in, day out, but no expedition member moved uphill without carrying something forward. Don and Kludge out path finding were carrying seventy and eighty pounds each, Dez and Terry who were keeping them supplied did likewise, and the rest of us, including the Sherpas, never missed a day humping loads. By 7 October we got the last load to advance base; between us and the Sherpas we had moved our three tons of supplies up 6,000 feet of the roughest country in the world. If only we had known – the load carrying was just about to begin!

During the next week Don and Kludge found a way out of our approach valley by a 17,000-foot col; this led them down to a beautiful glacial lake at

16,000 feet in a setting reminiscent of a Lakeland tarn. From there they were forced to climb over another 17,500-foot col with a steep descent on the other side over large rock faces, one of which necessitated airy traversing and a climb down vertical chimneys. During this period the final days of the monsoon were on us; the rain lasted longer in 1964 than anyone could remember, and Don and Kludge had some uncomfortable bivouacs. Once they had cleared the rock buttress the way was open for a steep descent to the valley that led under the north-west ridge.

This ridge and the adjoining west face of Gauri Sankar are of impressive architecture. Nine thousand feet of precipice set at an incredible angle and swept by avalanches make this west flank a climbing proposition for generations hence; to gain a lodgement low down on the north-west ridge would obviously provide a climb worthy of the neighbouring challenge.

When Don returned to advance base and told us of the way ahead, it sounded gruelling merely in the telling. 'We need an American Everest expedition,' he reported. 'It's bloody miles away from here, and wait till you see the route – up and down, up and down. We'll need to rope up hundreds of feet between here and the ridge. It's a basket! We'll split up, Dez and Terry can come back with me, you and Ian can look after the supply problems.'

We decided to make a camp and dump beside the tarn to which Ian, the Sherpas and I would bring food and supplies, then Terry and Dez would carry over the second col and down the rock faces to the moraine under the north-west ridge. Meanwhile, Don and Kludge would try to climb and prepare a route up to the crest of the ridge. To be relegated to mere load carrying is galling on any expedition but it is unfortunately an essential part of the game; our team was functioning well and it would have been difficult to change the order of things.

On 8 October the rain finally ceased and slowly the clouds dispersed. The view, even at our low advance base, was breathtaking as peaks shimmered in a hazeless sky, crystal clear as in a dawn of rebirth.

The carry from advance base to the tarn camp was a marathon, first through rhododendron, then across the steep moorland for three hours to the scree, a huge shoot on the north side of our valley. This scree was terribly long and arduous: one foot up and one foot down, it took hours to climb loaded. From its head, which we referred to unromantically as the first col, I could at last see for myself something of Gauri Sankar; nothing I have seen anywhere appeared so unclimbable as the south-west bastions of the mountain. Truly, to look at such an aspect was to feel the presence of something divine.

Down steeply from the col and we were at last able to cast our wearisome loads by the side of the tarn. Eight hours is a long carry on any peak (it became the norm on Gauri Sankar) and to lose a thousand feet over the descent was annoying, but our mood was optimistic. Once we had got enough supplies to the tarn, we moved to the camp there and took over ferrying to the moraine, where the other four had established a well-stocked stronghold whence Don and Kludge began operations on the route to the crest of the ridge, with Dez and Terry now free to back them up.

The carry to moraine camp with its steep climbs and difficult descent was even harder than from advance base to the tarn. The traverse of the large rock buttress, which had cost Don and Kludge so much time fixing ropes, exposed to us the limitations of our Sherpas. The idea that has pervaded the mountain world that these men are skilled and practised mountaineers in the modern technical sense is erroneous. No one could be more loyal, trusting and willing than a typical Sherpa, but they have little knowledge of climbing techniques. Some are born climbers and, with several years' training such as the dedicated European mountaineers undertake, would doubtless become outstanding performers, but in terms of present-day climbing standards they are mainly novices. Expeditions that ignore this fact and take their porters into situations of high technical difficulty and danger, could in some cases be unintentionally guilty of manslaughter. Such is the trust and childlike simplicity of these fine people that they will follow their Sahibs anywhere, a virtue which may cost them their lives if expeditions, attempting technically difficult mountains in the years ahead, continue to look upon Sherpas as porters who are also capable of modern high-standard climbing.

At the end of the traverse of the rock face was a 250-foot descent followed by an overhanging chimney, all equipped with fixed rope. After the chimney was a short difficult descent where we simply could not afford to place more rope. Only Girmee, the best of our Sherpas, could manage these manoeuvres successfully; one of the others had to be helped across unloaded, and we decided it would be unwise for any but Girmee to climb on the mountain itself.

Once off the buttress the ground was straightforward; an easy descent led on to the moraine and we crossed this nearly to the snout of the glacier. In this chaotic world of boulder and crevasse was the moraine camp, which we called Camp II. It was an impressive place; hours had been spent levelling out the tent platforms and a terrace for sunbathing after work!

From here to our base was perhaps twenty miles; luckily we had brought some tins of red paint for route marking which proved a boon above the treeline and more artistic than cairn building – some of the signs, such as 'CAMP II – FIVE MINUTES', gave scope for talent and embellishment.

We had by this time taken almost four weeks to reach the foot of the mountain and the real climbing had just begun, but at least the weather was set fair, with only an occasional afternoon snow shower to cause discomfiture.

Immediately above the tents reared a 3,500-foot wall of rock, snow and ice on which the front men were having a hard time. Don and Kludge were bivouacking on a rock spur at the commencement of the real difficulties and Dez and Terry were keeping them supplied with food and equipment from the moraine. A note I received from Kludge explained the position and ended in his usual optimistic manner, 'It looks just like the Eiger!'

They slowly gained ground and eventually reached the crest of the north-west ridge; to make the route feasible for load carrying they had to put fixed rope up the last 2,000 feet of snow and ice. Our communication system was by passing notes back and forth; each one Ian and I received bore the same message: 'Bring over more rope!' It was obvious that we had not got enough of this commodity although we had brought from Britain 5,000 feet of fixing line and 1,500 feet of climbing rope. Checking on usage, I found that we had placed over a thousand feet down in the woods and on vegetation-covered rock faces.

After five days of continuous climbing, Don and Kludge had completed their work and the way to the ridge was open for laden men, but it had proved such a difficult ascent that it was actually named the 'Little Eiger'. Enthusiastic messages termed it photogenic, but I am afraid that carrying a load up that face was too near the limit of my endurance for me to be able to capture its more aesthetic qualities.

On the crest our pioneers met a new problem: the ridge was knife-edged with many barrier walls of ice and rock connected by double-corniced, high-angled arêtes. The possibility of climbing further appeared remote and it looked like defeat.

By a piece of good fortune the point where the Little Eiger reached the ridge was the only place where it was possible to get to a site for tents. An easy traverse from the crest by a huge blade of rock led to a flat snowfield, the only one on the whole ridge. Another camp was established there and Don and Kludge moved in, then took a well-earned rest day while the rest of us made the first load ferry up the Little Eiger.

Ian, Girmee and I had moved over to join Dez and Terry at moraine camp the night before and the five of us set out at first light to carry loads up to Don and Kludge. The first 1,500 feet were by scree and an easy rock buttress leading to the bivouac site. The fixed rope began at that point, traversing up and down for a few hundred feet to an obvious ascent line by steep snowfields, rock chimneys and ice gangways to the ridge itself. The loads tugging at our shoulders upset our balance and progress was slow. The Little Eiger seemed never ending; it was the most exhausting carry so far, eight hours of back-breaking toil with nowhere to rest. In places the angle of the snowfields attained sixty degrees and the rock steps in between made one curse and gasp, for on these vertical sections the pack frame tended to pull one off. The last rope lengths to the crest were the most difficult; the angle reached seventy degrees and at the blade of rock which marked easy ground I collapsed in a state of exhaustion and relief. The sun was on us throughout the climb, relentlessly dehydrating, and the eight hours had tested my endurance and stamina to the limit.

Recovering, I joined the others again and traversed across to the small bivouac tent on the snow shelf, outside which Don and Kludge were resting from their labours, sunbathing in full duvet outfits against the cold. What an impressive position this camp occupied! Directly above swept the awesome north-west ridge abutting on the equally impressive north face of the mountain which was bounded in its turn by the steep north ridge. But outdoing everything in beauty, ferocity and impregnability was Menlungste, immediately to the east. What a mountain! There for my money is the finest of all peaks, a Matterhorn, Ushba and Nanda Devi in one, remote, unattempted, unsullied, unequalled. To the east again was Cho Oyu, seventh highest mountain in the world, and peering over a shoulder of Menlungste was Everest itself, thirty-six miles away and more of a climber's mountain than I had dreamed.

This was the first time we had all been together for more than a week, and we sat and discussed the situation and its possibilities. Don and Kludge, backed by the rest, were sure that the continuation of the ridge was not worth trying; I was not so sure but completely outvoted. I am now convinced that I was right; if we had gone at the ridge with the determination with which we subsequently attempted the north face, I feel we should have been successful. So much precious time and effort were required to reach the alternative that I believe if we had devoted these to launching an immediate attempt on the ridge, despite its great technical problems it would have yielded.

From our position on the north of the mountain, the previously reconnoitred north ridge appeared the surest way of success despite the reports of previous expeditions to that side. It is amazing how soon times and opinions change; Mummery's old adage about the certain downgrading of climbs still holds true. Unfortunately this ridge was now far inside Tibet, and to reach it from our present position would have meant a traverse of the whole immense north face; we should then have almost completed the first girdle traverse of a mountain in Himalayan history!

Don and Kludge were keen to try to force a route directly up the north face, even though this meant our going down again from 19,000 feet to 17,800 feet. After study the proposed route did look feasible, though reminiscent of the north faces of the Aiguille du Plan and the Triolet in tandem, two of Mont Blanc's finest ice climbs. The others unanimously agreed to attempt this way, and feeling too weak to argue I also agreed that we should try the slender possibility.

Each day now the weather was getting noticeably colder; we were well into October and despite constant sun and fair weather a wind had begun to blow down from Tibet which cut like a knife. On the lower parts of the mountain we had been protected, particularly on the Little Eiger, but once on the northern slopes we were exposed to its chilly force, warning us that winter was not far away.

From Camp III on the north-west ridge the way to the foot of the north face was not easy; once more Gauri Sankar defended itself. After an initial traverse from the tent, Don and Kludge found their way barred by a steep rock face with bands of snow and ice set at high angles. Over the next few days they managed to force this route and climb down to the foot of the face while the rest of us concentrated on building up their Camp III by ferrying loads up the Little Eiger. Climbing in full duvet suits because of the wind, with Don in the lead and at the top of his form, traversing pitches of Alpine grade VI were overcome and roped and a safe all-weather route established.

The ground below the face was uniformly steep, with no possibility of placing a tent camp. Thenceforward the only way of producing living quarters was to dig snow holes or ice caves. These are the answer for the next era of Himalayan exploration; over the last few years there has been a refinement of snow-holing techniques and a development of equipment such as ultra-lightweight snow saws for cutting shelters.

We had brought from home a secret weapon for this situation, namely a 'hut'. It was made up from Dexion sections which bolted together, covered with canvas, but unfortunately our model, the brainchild of Whillans, was a prototype and made of too heavy materials. Carrying it, even in sections, was far too fatiguing, especially up the Little Eiger, and as its porter I cursed Whillans and his stupid little box every inch of the way and had to hand it over to Girmee for the last rope lengths to Camp III. Seventy-two pounds was a ridiculous weight, but once the boys had it in position inside an ice cave it proved a boon, providing comfortable living even under extreme conditions. Obviously the idea has future potential, and if developed with lightweight materials could supersede tents for mountain expeditions.

Don and Kludge, aided by Dez and Terry, placed and occupied the bivouac box, stamping through waist-deep powder snow to gain a lodgement on the first slopes of the north face. A difficulty of being on this face of the mountain was that the sun's power rarely reached it with any effect and the snow remained in dry form. When every available foot of rope, piece of equipment and box of food had been carried to Camp III via the Little Eiger, Ian Howell, Girmee and I climbed up to join Terry and Dez on the snowfield, a residence buffeted twenty-four hours a day by the wind of Tibet.

In the evening, swathed in duvet, I watched the sun set on Menlungste, carefully following the shadows as they lengthened for some sign of a weakness, a break in those formidable defences, but there was not one. It might be possible to put a camp right under the peak itself with none of our difficulties in approaching Gauri Sankar, but the mountain would remain as intrinsically difficult as any.

Time was running out for us, rope and other essentials were dwindling, each dawn was colder, each sunset clearer and more icy, the wind more relentless. Living in ice caves on the north face proved warmer and more comfortable than in the snowfield tents, the first caves in any case being at a considerably lower altitude. Our job at Camp III was once again that of mules, to help the front men and keep them supplied. Dez and Girmee moved out to join Don and Kludge on the face and the rest of us went across with them. I was beginning to feel the first signs of illness and had an inkling I should not be able to go on carrying or climbing much longer. Soon after starting out that day I had to abandon my load, but I was keen to see the north face situation for myself before I possibly had to retire from the attempt. The way to the ice caves was every bit as difficult as reported; Girmee, who had been to Everest, Ama Dablan, Gyachung Kang and many other Himalayan peaks, declared the climbing so far to be much harder than anything in his previous experience. Although such comparisons mean little and later need qualification, we were pleased to hear that Gauri Sankar was as special as we estimated.

From the ice caves under the face the only possible route was an almost direct ascent of the wall above till it was possible to break out on to the north ridge at around 22,500 feet; thereafter it looked easy, and we reckoned that if we could reach that point the peak could be climbed. Four thousand feet of steep ice and winter almost upon us … It looked a hell of a route and I judged Kludge the optimist of the year when he declared it 'not too bad'.

Back at the ridge camp I developed a sore throat and fever and began to sweat profusely. I could not earn my keep by carrying loads and would be consuming supplies that might be critical to our success, so I decided I must go down. Losing altitude is usually the only way to recuperate on a high mountain as the increased oxygen content assists the body's powers of recovery; at 19,000 feet one is not replenishing the body as much as one is depleting its reserves. Regretfully I prepared to descend alone.

Meanwhile, our storm troops were excelling themselves. Whillans, unequalled in such situations, produced the best performance of his life; hour after hour he cut steps, hammered in alloy stakes and affixed ropes. It was impossible to climb from the ice caves to the summit and back in a single day; the route had to be prepared and somewhere amongst those steep ice fields a further shelter had to be found. Backed up extremely well by Kludge, Don slowly made his way up the face; nothing in the past history of Himalayan climbing had been of the same order of difficulty. Alpine standards had at last arrived in the ultimate range, but I hasten to add not alpine methods. Fixed rope then appeared essential, a lifeline with the dual purpose of enabling heavy loads to be carried and of securing retreat. But here again time is changing our outlook; these methods are slow and laborious, fixed rope will soon be obsolete and Himalayan climbing will have passed another milestone.

Just before I left Camp III Dez arrived with an appeal for still more rope. A note from Kludge told of such good progress that he felt sure the top would be reached within the next few days. They had climbed so far up the face that it had become necessary to start cutting an ice cave for a further shelter, a jumping-off place for the summit. Over 2,500 feet of the face lay below them, a difficult ascent but apparently free of objective dangers, for no avalanches had fallen anywhere on the face during their presence. They had been undecided where to try and cut the cave on the sixty-degree slope. Don, moving about freely on the ice, had suddenly been startled when his axe broke through to reveal a hidden crevasse – our first piece of real luck in the whole expedition: this would serve as a shelter. They climbed down inside the slit in the ice and soon enlarged it enough to take a small tent. This was to be known as Camp V although we had actually placed eight camps, including our base.

I went down to moraine camp to find Dawa Tensing and Ang Tchering waiting, accompanied by one of our young mail runners, Pasang Namgyal, known to us as Yum-Yum for short. They were anxious about our fate and glad to see me appear on the glacier moraine. Yum-Yum, though only a boy, was a wonderful load carrier and had come from base with a sack of potatoes as well as the mail. Throughout the expedition he was either helping to ferry loads, running off with our mail to a Swiss mission many days away (he always halved the expected times for the journey), or working in the kitchen.

A letter from Hari, our liaison officer, reported that while we had been battling with the mountain he too had been having his personal Everest. One of the friendly Tibetan traders who kept us supplied with potatoes had arrived at base to warn him that the bandits who attacked the Japanese in 1959 were in the vicinity and planning to attack us. They had seen our camps on the mountain and an informant, a refugee Tibetan living in Lamobagar, told them of our intentions, spying while visiting our base. They were getting ready to plunder our tents and belongings as far up as moraine camp, so Hari immediately went down to Lamobagar and brought up the Royal Nepalese Army to defend our property.

Six soldiers from the army post in the village escorted Hari back to the cave in the Rong Shar, and who should they meet on their arrival but the Tibetan who was acting as lookout for the bandits. Hari sprang on him like a tiger and set about terrifying the poor man out of his wits with his kukris. He finally let the spy go, sending a message by him to the bandits that he was waiting for them to attack. He then turned base into a siege camp where he was joined by friendly traders armed with kukris while the six soldiers patrolled with rifles. Much to Hari's disappointment the bandits were frightened off and they never took up his challenge, but the episode played havoc with our potato supplies with all those extra mouths to feed and we had to start buying a sack a day! It was a pity in a way that the bandits didn't show up, for Don Whillans grappling hand to hand with a Khamba chieftain on the moraines of Gauri Sankar would have added immense lustre to my fund of Rock and Ice fables.

Up on the mountain our attempt was reaching its climax. Don and Kludge from the tent in the ice grotto planned to prepare the last section up to easy ground below the summit. Once this had been completed Dez and Girmee were to join them with another tent and help them to place a camp on the very summit slopes in case of emergency, or indeed if the final stages should prove harder than they appeared.

After several days of working on the upper part of the face the way was almost open and the moment to try for the summit had arrived at last. Dez and Girmee, carrying the tent and other supplies, left the ice caves of Camp IV and climbed up to the grotto called Camp V and on past this haven to join Don and Kludge, who were on the difficult section up to the north ridge junction and only a short distance from achieving their aim.

They came up with the leaders just as Don was traversing into a gully that exited on the ridge, barely 300 feet to go. 'Hell! It's pure ice,' he observed as he stared at a seventy-degree green wall which barred the way. There was no hurrying over this and Don had to resign himself to several more hours of laborious work. 'You'd better drop the loads and head down,' he told Dez, 'and we'll finish the job off.' Dez hesitated, but there was little to be gained by waiting around in the perishing cold and he and Girmee began to descend.

Don and Kludge stuck grimly to their task; progress was desperately slow and they used the last possible rope for fixing, a 150-foot climbing rope, on the first part of the gully. Apart from the rope they were climbing on, the rest of the expedition were moving around solo, relying completely on the prepared route. Chip, gasp, chip, gasp, Whillans cut his way up, but time flew by and the increasing cold became unbearable. A couple of hundred feet to go when Don said: 'Better come back tomorrow and finish it. We'll dump the tent as soon as we reach easy ground, then try for the summit. If necessary we can spend the night on the ridge before coming down. Let's go back!' he ended decisively, his voice rasping in the rarefied air of over 22,000 feet.

Suddenly without warning the whole slope shuddered and seemed to collapse. Above their heads, from the side of the gully in which they were standing in steps, ice broke away, to come hurtling down in an avalanche of large proportions. Don telling us about it afterwards said he had thought 'This is the end!' It happened so swiftly that neither he nor Kludge had time to react but luckily the ice runnel they were in sheltered them from the worst of the avalanche though it buried and battered them with its debris, almost choking Don and knocking Kludge off the slope and on to his axe belay, but leaving them both in position and unscathed.

They were shaken by the closeness of their escape and surprised to find themselves still alive. But where were Dez and Girmee? The carefully prepared route, the labour of days, had been swept away in a matter of seconds. 'Oh God! It must have taken them with it!' But once more fortune had been with us; a few minutes before the avalanche fell the two men had reached Camp IV and climbed into the ice cave to make some tea. They heard a sound like thunder and the ice around them reverberated, but the avalanche roared harmlessly overhead – another example of the worth of such shelters. Don and Kludge were more than relieved when Dez appeared in answer to their agonised shouts. Getting down the ice where the route had been damaged and ropes swept away was no joke; the angle was steeper than any ice field on the Eigerwand and it was late in the evening before they reached safety.

What a disappointment! At one moment, against all the odds, success had seemed certain; at the next, all was in jeopardy and only luck and skill had got them out with their lives. Without a fixed line and only one climbing rope they had little option but to retreat, and the next day found the whole party safely back at Camp III on the north-west ridge.

There they remained resting for a few days, unwilling to pack in completely with success so nearly in their grasp. They sat watching the north face for signs of more avalanches but nothing fell and they decided that their one must have been a freak. How stupid to give up with the summit so near, they thought; why not one last attempt? If they stripped rope off the Little Eiger they could repair the damaged route. Yes, they would have one last fling.

In retrospect, another attempt was against good sense; food was almost finished, everyone was tired after eight weeks of effort and they were harassed by the increasing cold which had become extreme as the days slipped by into November. However, a good carry of the remaining food by Ian, Terry and Dez put Don and Kludge back in the ice grotto of Camp V. As they moved up they repaired the route and placed rope removed from other parts of the climb. Don was going flat out this time as he chopped and cut his way to the grotto and beyond, backed up as ever by Kludge. Up and up they fought until once more they were within striking distance of the summit, almost at their previous high point.

'My feet are dead, Don,' Kludge gasped. 'I've got frostbite.'

'Hang on just a bit longer, we're almost there,' the hard man replied.

Then, crack! 'What was that?' Don paused in his endless cutting to listen. Silence; the axe began to swing again. Then another cracking sound and the whole slope began to tremble. 'Jesus, it's going to avalanche again! Down as fast as you can! It's all unstable after the other fall.'

In spite of his numb feet Kludge needed no urging, and they turned and fled.

The watchers at Camp IV could not understand the panic until they heard Don order them to get the hell out of it. The tone of his voice told them he was scared and that was enough, the whole party belted off the north face at the double. Providence had been with them again: as they sat resting at Camp III on the ridge, a momentous roar and a telltale white stream pouring down the north face confirmed how close they had once more been to disaster.

'What a mountain!' Don said later when he told me the story at base. 'It's a lady! The red light came on as if to say "one more step and you're dead". We took heed and she let us off the chopping block!'

Down on the moraine I got weaker every day; I had difficulty in keeping any food down and suffered from insomnia. The Sherpas did their best to look after me but I felt such a passenger by this time that I convinced myself if I didn't head back to base soon the rest of the party would have to carry me there.

Girmee had refused to go back to the north face for the second attempt and came down to moraine camp, where I could do nothing but sympathise with his decision. One must appreciate that Sherpas do not usually climb mountains for sport; with few exceptions it is for them only a lucrative way (by their standards) to make a living. I was sorry for him, he was obviously upset by having turned tail and I knew how tough Don was and his attitude to anyone who let him down. Girmee had done well on the mountain, one of the best performances ever by a Sherpa, and it was not his fault that an avalanche had foiled the attempt so near to its goal.

My own condition continued to deteriorate, and being expedition medic I decided I must take action. Leaving the Sherpas at moraine camp with strict instructions to wait for the others, I set out for base. The journey took me three days, and I finished in a fever, crawling through the Rong Shar gorge on all fours and yelling for Hari to come and help. It was night before I reached the vicinity of the cave and hours before our liaison officer would venture out to look for me. Once it is dark in the mountains of Nepal no one usually moves around and Hari was scared out of his wits by my shouts, believing me to be the fabled yeti or some other animal good at imitating a human cry. Over the next few days I lay at base, ill and in an agony of suspense about the rest of the party.

It was with heavy hearts that my teammates gave the mountain best; they had put up a terrific effort and shown the peak to be climbable, contrary to all opinion. Once retreat was sounded the evacuation was rapid. The Sherpas moved colossal weights and within days everything worth salvaging was down at base.

The boys strode into the cave still full of fire but one had only to look at their faces to see the strain they had been under. Ian Clough looked years older, his face lined and set, but the part he had played was one of outstanding feats and he was still full of energy. I began to feel much better physically but remained emotionally shattered. My own part in the saga had been most inglorious; it had been my idea to attempt Gauri Sankar and I had crumpled long before the end.

Everyone wanted to get away quickly for it was winter now, with freezing temperatures even at base; there was no food left except a sack of rice, and we swiftly packed, hired coolies and started back for Kathmandu. The return march in the cold, clear first days of winter was like the rest of the expedition, completely without any physical comfort: sub-zero temperatures at night, icy winds blowing on the high ridges we crossed each day, without food of our own and, with the onset of winter, finding it possible to buy only rice at the villages where we stopped along our route. I can still hear Whillans pleading with Ang Tchering, our cook, to try to get him 'just one egg'! We existed on rice, fried for breakfast and curried for the evening meal.

Throughout the march we could see Gauri Sankar and as we slogged into Kathmandu, weary, dejected, unwashed and ragged, fed up with ourselves and with each other, it gleamed high in the sky on the horizon, a reminder that time would heal the wounds. The famous Swiss climber Raymond Lambert met us there; he had himself led a reconnaissance to Gauri Sankar. 'You did not fail,' he told us. 'I said Gauri Sankar was impossible above 18,000 feet, but your party made over 22,000 feet. That was a great climb!'

That Gauri Sankar is climbable our attempts in 1964 proved. We learned much on that expedition though we made mistakes, but it was an epoch-making attempt and was carried out with the minimum of resources for the period. Big advances have been made even since then in equipment and technique and I believe the mountain could now be climbed with a really small party. Four men, climbing alpine style, living in ice caves, using the best modern equipment, dispensing with fixed rope and simply descending on long abseils: that is how   Gauri Sankar should now be climbed. I repeat what I said at the start of this chapter: the large expedition should be a thing of the past; any large party, equipped with the best money can buy and with plenty of resources, can be successful, but such climbs henceforth will be hollow victories.

Gauri Sankar climbed would lead to attempts on Menlungste and the other superb and difficult lesser peaks. These are the Everests of the future, and I hope they are climbed, not conquered! The tide must turn; the new generation of mountaineers will understand that alpine-style climbs in the Himalaya are the mode of the future. The tragedy of the latest crop of large, success-at-any-price expeditions is that they are gobbling up good objectives; once a mountain is climbed it can never be unclimbed, whatever methods have been used in making the ascent. Even our own attempt on Gauri Sankar, if it had been successful, would have robbed some small party of a great first ascent. Fortunately for them we found Sankar, the destroyer, firmly in command. A light expedition of the future may find Gauri, goddess of love, in control and ready to succumb to the right suitors.

Ian Clough was killed by an ice avalanche at the end of May, 1970, while descending to base after the first ascent of the south face of Annapurna I. His enthusiasm for climbing and mountains was unequalled; the worse the conditions and the weightier the task, the higher the barometer of his keenness mounted. On Gauri Sankar, it is fair to say that the high point reached in our attempt can in large part be attributed to Ian's unquenchable will to win.

7 The Rock and Ice – Present

'Like … but oh, how different.'
(William Wordsworth)

Towards the end of 1959, when I was living and working in Derby, I renewed my climbing association with Nat Allen, one of the outstanding personalities of the disbanded Rock and Ice Club. Nat, a stockily built figure, with flashing smile and ready wit, had by then married and set up house on the outskirts of the city. His wife, Pat, known to everyone as Tinsel, is an equally distinctive character, and their home soon became a meeting place and hospitable refuge for local and visiting climbers. Two winters earlier, Nat had injured his knee in a fall while attempting the first ascent of the *Point Five Gully* of Ben Nevis with Joe Brown and Nip Underwood, another Derby climber. The injury still troubled him but he was slowly regaining his form and fitness, climbing every weekend in the Peak District or North Wales, and was gradually doing routes of increasing severity.

We climbed together most weekends, and on midweek evenings often met and discussed past climbs and friendships. One can become surprisingly nostalgic over a glass of beer; I began to appreciate for the first time how much my associations with the Rock and Ice Club had meant to me. Nat too looked back on the halcyon days of the Rock and Ice with affection, and often expressed regret at its disbandment. We frequently met other former members, particularly Don Whillans, and one weekend, after a discussion between Nat, Don and myself, Nat decided he would resurrect the Rock and Ice and asked me to help with its reorganisation.

I had never been a 'club man' but the Rock and Ice had been something special to me, and thinking over the proposal I decided that if it was to be resurrected I wanted to participate. Many ex-members answered the rallying call – the Greenall brothers, Ray and Pete, Eric Price, Joe Brown, Vin Betts, Don Roscoe, Alan Taylor, Don Whillans, Fred Goff, Mortimer Smith among them – and there were several others, such as Charlie Vigano, Doug Verity, Steve Read, Harry Smith and Eric Beard, who like me had been long-standing associates of the club or its members and joined when it was reformed. It was again organised with a minimum of rules and regulations and the smallest possible subscription. Half a crown was the yearly fee (it is now five shillings), and the president was chosen each year at the annual club dinner by the simple procedure of pulling a name out of a hat containing the names of every member. An inaugural meet was held at Stanage when Nat Allen was invited to be honorary secretary and the first president out of the hat was Don Whillans.

It was plain from the first that the club would be somewhat different from its predecessor, if only because most members were that much older and over the years they had become widely scattered. But the ideal was that meets should be held once a month, and when a member found it possible to attend he could usually count on an enjoyable weekend. The club has grown more sociable over the years and the annual dinner has achieved such fame that it is a 'must' in the calendar for any climbing social butterfly. The reformed club was at least as rich in characters as its forebear and could boast a greater all-round range of talent, with runners, singers, canoeists, fishermen and sundry other performers among its members.

The club had an early setback when its brightest young climber, Mortimer, was badly injured in a motorcycle accident at Capel Curig. Although none of us fully realised it at the time, this put paid to his brilliant climbing career. Before he was twenty-one he had packed into his few years of climbing a host of notable ascents at home and abroad. New routes on Clogwyn Du'r Arddu, the west face of the Petit Dru and many other successes indicated what might have been. Two years later he reappeared in our ranks with one leg shorter than the other and hip permanently stiffened, but he walked on his own two feet and could still climb as well as most. His cheerfulness was unchanged, but his ability and ambition were now directed into other channels. Against our predictions Morty won his way to college, passed exam after exam and eventually qualified as a teacher and lecturer. He still climbs and one can always be sure of a good day on the rock in his company and hear the same gravel chuckle.

One of the first meets of the new Rock and Ice was a joint gathering with the Derby Mercury Cycling Club at Ilam Hall in Derbyshire, which took place on the nearest Saturday to bonfire night. The cyclists had challenged us to an evening of rough games, being under some form of delusion that climbers are fit, strong and physically tough because of the nature of their sport. They obviously expected unusual feats of agility and strength from us and, basking in this unexpectedly high assessment of our capabilities, we didn't attempt to correct the false impression. In any case this was soon made unnecessary by our being severely trounced in every event staged, and towards the end of the session, sporting multiple bruises and the odd black eye, we sought in desperation to restore our severely dinted prestige by introducing a round of 'wall squatting'. In this form of self-inflicted agony the masochistic individual sits with his back against a wall, without a chair, arms folded and knees lightly touching, and measures against the clock how long he can endure the posture.

This was a famed endurance test throughout the climbing world at that time; Bob Downes had been rumoured to be at least a ten-minute man, and our youngest member, Steve Read, was acknowledged champion, capable of fifteen minutes at his fittest. We put him forward with Beardie, an eleven-minute man, as our representatives and, confident of victory, threw down a challenge to the Mercury cyclists. The bike enthusiasts had not seen this antic before but quickly grasped the essentials, and Eric Thompson, the Olympic star, and Neil Burton, one of their younger aces, sat down beside our pair. Ten minutes elapsed and Beardie collapsed; fifteen and Steve fell on his backside; at twenty minutes Eric Thompson stood up declaring it 'a bit tiring' and after thirty-one minutes Neil walked away muttering something about it being 'pointless'. The verdict of the two wheel riders was that 'climbers must be hopelessly unfit'!

Later that evening the Mercury provided a pantomime which Nat's wife, Tinsel, a Mercury girl, had produced. The standard of this diversion truly surprised us; it was hilarious and the acting of certain members of the cast was of a high order.

To wind up the meet, a cross-country run was held on Sunday morning on a course through part of famous Dovedale. Although this had been a feature of the Mercury calendar for several years, the 1959 run was the first open one with an outside group taking part – the first of many memorable Dovedale Dashes.

Again the cyclists beat us hollow. Neil Burton overtook Beardie on the finishing straight and the rest of the climbers were somewhere in the rear, running in confusion and not sure of the route. I took a wrong turning and ran in the opposite direction altogether, adding an extra mile to the four-mile circuit!

When the 1960 outing was held the River Dove was in high flood and the rain fell in torrents, driven by a cutting wind. The route crosses the river by some stepping stones and these were submerged under at least a foot of swift-flowing water. To ensure the safety of the competitors, the race marshals had placed a climbing rope across the river, belayed from tree to tree, and one simply monkeyed over with only the lower half of the body in the water. The Rock and Ice were determined to avenge the drubbing of the previous year. As we raced up to the stepping stones Beardie was lying third, behind the Derbyshire schools champion in second place, with me in fifth place and our next counter a short way behind. As the schools champion reached the water's edge and grabbed for the rope, Beardie overtook him to seize the rope on the outside. The champion, of tender years and small in stature, bounced off the rope like a fish jumping the line and plunged into the torrent. Beardie, in true athlete's style, never looked back, swung across the river like an ape and tore off after the leader with barely a mile to go to the finish, while unknown to him the schoolboy was in danger of drowning, struggling against the current. Luckily his plight was noticed and several people jumped into the river to help.

The Derby climber, Hank Harrison, got the lad to the bank and I gave him a hand up on to terra firma. By the time we had sorted ourselves out many runners had passed us, but the boy was a tiger, and spitting water out of his lungs he muscled across the rope in pursuit, with me close behind.

We passed runner after runner, the lad taking me with him as he cut a path through the wind and rain. I felt guilty when I passed him in the drive of Ilam Hall, the two of us finishing fifth and sixth. It then became apparent why he had run so hard from the stepping stones, for he tore straight at Beardie who had won the race for the first time and was cheering home the other runners as they raced up the road. The boy obviously thought the incident at the stepping stones had been intentional, and Beardie was flabbergasted as the boy ran towards him, fists flailing and yelling abuse. It took three or four burly adults to restrain the angry youth but eventually he was persuaded that his near-drowning was by accident and not design and good humour was restored.

Over the years the Dovedale Dash weekend has gone from strength to strength. It features on the meets list of many climbing clubs, climbers coming from Scotland, London, North Wales to take part, as well as some of the major athletic teams; hundreds are drawn to Ilam Hall for the nearest weekend to bonfire night every year. The run is still organised and controlled by the Derby Mercury who try to ensure that the original spirit of the race is maintained – as a race for the super-fit athlete and the least fit of unfit climbers. These last are not really interested in who wins the race but in personal challenges to climbing acquaintances: 'I'll beat you, unfit as I am!' The event has attracted much newspaper publicity, and photographs have appeared in the popular press of well-known and respected mountaineers racing along in merely their underclothes (safety pin in fly for decency's sake!) beside athletic champions of renown.

It wasn't long before women wanted to take part, and there is now a prize for the first lady home, who often beats many of the hardened cragsmen. The gentle sex can be very competitive in the dash and many a muscular mountaineer has been knocked flying as one of the women entrants stormed past, speeding lightly over Dovedale's muddy reaches.

In tandem with the Dash were the pantomimes on the Saturday evening before the race. Tinsel proved herself a producer and actress of great talent, and each year the productions grew more lavish and spectacular, with musical accompaniments and integrated sound effects. The Derby Mercury always provided the chorus girls and many of the other performers, but climbers began to take a more active role in staging the shows. I wrote two of the early productions, during one of which occurred the funniest thing I have ever seen on any stage anywhere. In 1961 we had packed an audience of hundreds into the main room of Ilam Hall to see *William T'Hell*. As there were no scene changes, between the acts Beardie had the part of court jester whose job it was to tell a few jokes, sing the odd song and announce the next scene: 'Act One – the Baron's Castle'; 'Act Two – a Swiss Mountainside', and so on. He wore a jester's costume with long pantaloons, tunic and a dunce's cap with bells.

After he had announced the finale the chorus girls, eight buxom female cyclists, were supposed to dash on and rip off his long pantaloons, to reveal him in a pair of frilly knickers with 'I love Sabrina' stencilled across the front, Sabrina being the nickname of a particularly well-endowed female Mercury cyclist. But when the time came the chorus not only ripped off Beardie's pantaloons but the knickers as well, leaving him naked; they then ran off screaming as rehearsed. For a brief instant Beardie did not realise what had happened and mistook the audience's hysterical roar for amusement at the catchphrase supposedly revealed; when he realised his predicament he too ran screaming from the stage. I have never seen such mass hysteria, cast and audience helpless with uncontrollable laughter and the building reverberating with the roars. One or two of the spectators collapsed altogether and, sobbing, had to be passed overhead, from hand to hand, to the exits. It was about fifteen minutes before we could get on with the final curtain when for once – and although the crowd yelled for him non-stop – Beardie refused to face his fans!

Success followed success, with *Swine Lake, Davy Jones' Locker, Cleopatra* among them, but it became such a major undertaking to write, produce and promote the shows that they now only appear every few years. Months were being spent on making costumes, duplicating and learning scripts and other preparations, as well as ten weeks' hard rehearsal, and keen cyclists and climbers were losing too much outdoor time for the annual productions to continue.

For the first year or two the new Rock and Ice, like the old, did not encourage new members, but it became apparent that if we didn't change this attitude the club would sooner or later fade out once more. Nat Allen was a first-class honorary secretary, keeping the club as informal as ever, sending out newsletters which a less-spontaneous type of organisation would have found it hard to equal in wit and contents, but in every organisation there is a need for new blood once in a while and we began to feel it was time to put the club on a firmer base with a younger membership. We wanted the outlook and spirit of the Rock and Ice to remain the same, with each member well known to all other members, and firm friendships as the cement of the club, rather than formal rules. To maintain this ideal, it would have to remain small and intimate, and any newcomer must be or become known to the majority of existing members. We decided on a form of aspirant membership whereby anyone proposed had to serve a year before being admitted, attending all meets and getting to know well as many of the Rock and Ice as possible. Existing members who did not keep up their contact with the club would be retired, and any aspirant who didn't fulfil the requirements of meet attendance would not be made a member. Such rules, even though they are liberally interpreted, are perhaps regrettable, the Rock and Ice and clubs like it have thrived on an anarchistic basis, but the introduction of these measures has proved effective and its new recruits have carried the Rock and Ice forward, maintaining a light-hearted but efficient organisation.

One of the first new members was Dez Hadlum from Nottingham; climbing regularly with me he often came to meets and thus made friends with the Rock and Ice, and his climbing ability and willing nature made him an ideal recruit.

Another early entrant was Gordon 'Lightning' Smith. Dez and I met him late one winter's afternoon on a snow-covered Gardom's Edge in the Peak District. He was then a young schoolboy and when we came upon him he was stuck, solo, halfway up a crack choked with ice. He addressed me as 'Mister' and asked if we had a rope. I belayed above him and lowered the end of the full-weight one I carried; he tied on and climbed up to join me on top of the edge. His ear-to-ear grin was the largest I had ever seen and certainly didn't belie the difficulty of the climb he had just made, though he conceded 'That's a bit tough.' He informed us he was dossing in a nearby barn. 'Are yer going t'pub tonight?' he demanded. 'I'll buy yer a pint!' He ignored my enquiry as to his age, and we were amazed later that evening as he downed his sixth pint of beer in rapid succession – not bad for a schoolboy. 'Been drinking for years,' he cheerfully informed us. Dez and I were convinced that here was a 'must' for the club; Nat Allen was also quickly won over when we introduced our find, and the schoolboy proved over the next few Rock and Ice meets that he could not only out-walk but often out-climb us, and invariably drank two pints of beer to our one on Saturday evenings. We called him 'Speedy' because of this and 'Lightning' because he spoke so slowly.

The Greenalls, Ray and Pete, had a younger brother, Brian, who had started to climb. 'He's a typical Greenall,' Pete told us and when he came out to a meet we agreed.

As Nat said: 'What will the Rock and Ice do without a Greenall in the ranks? He's a natural follow-on.'

Dez and I met Terry (Gnome) Burnell and John (Midge) Midgeley in the Dolomites in 1962; they both came from near my home in Leeds and were keen to join the club. Midge soon showed promise as an organiser and the annual dinner is his forte, for which he has been accorded the title of honorary social secretary.

One of our discoveries of greatest promise was made a year or so later when Terry and I were climbing at Almscliff one evening. A youth wearing a large red woolly hat followed us up each climb and every boulder problem. Some of the other climbers there kept ribbing him: 'You look like Daniel Boone in that silly bloody hat!' He took little or no notice, even when Terry and I referred to him as Dan. As we were about to go home he came up shyly and asked if I would give him a lift and drop him for a bus to his home in Bradford. During a break in the conversation on the way he suddenly spoke out for the first time, saying slowly and deliberately. 'My name is not Daniel Boone, it's Jimmy Fullalove.' We burst out laughing; 'Daniel Boone' has stuck and so did Jimmy Fullalove in the Rock and Ice.

It seems to be a natural phenomenon that once a club has a regular continuity of new members applying it continues to tick over successfully. The original Rock and Ice was discouraging to this essential flow of fresh blood not because they were unfriendly or narrowly parochial but because they never recognised its necessity; when all the members of a group are young they never feel they will one day be older or become too scattered to make regular appearances.

In the new era, our recruits soon introduced other aspirants, such as Paul Grainger, Bill Marsh, Alex Webster, Dave Musgrove, Bob Knapton. But the law of natural wastage kept our numbers small and our total has never gone over thirty. Several of the older members have more or less 'retired', and even some of the new ones disappeared after a year or two. Perhaps the most unusual of these was Will McLoughlin, known to us as 'Little Mac'. We should have recognised the signs when he started bringing out a bible and religious texts and tracts at weekends instead of the usual sackful of karabiners, slings and climbing hardware. He is now a Jehovah's Witness and, I believe, is working in Norfolk as a missionary. I hope our loss is Christianity's gain!

To describe the club's activities at length would be boring and boastful, neither of which are typical of the essential nature of the Rock and Ice members. They are as footloose as ever, and the Himalaya, Patagonia, the Andes, the USA, North Africa, New Zealand, the Pamirs, Canada, Turkey, Norway and anywhere else where there are mountains have been their magnets. The Alps have remained a kind of home ground, and members have achieved most of the well-known routes from the Eiger Nordwand and the *Walker Spur* of the Grandes Jorasses to the extreme direttissimas of the Dolomites, as well as adding several first ascents of some importance. Typical of the club's unchanging attitude was the remark of one of its senior members after Jimmy Fullalove's fourteen-day Alpine holiday in 1969, when he climbed the Pear Buttress of Mont Blanc, the *Walker Spur* and the Eiger Nordwand: 'Once Dan Boone learns how to use an ice axe and crampons efficiently he may be able to climb something worthwhile, instead of only three routes a season!'

In Britain there has not been the same concentrated enthusiasm for Wales as in earlier days, in fact many of the younger members rarely go there. The loss of the traditional club base in Manchester, greater mobility and a widespread membership has resulted during the last decade in pioneering taking place from the Cornish sea cliffs to the north of Scotland. Club meets are as chaotic as ever, and it is still true that if two or more members find themselves in the same climbing area it can be considered a meet. We do have a meets list each year and occasionally there is a hundred per cent turnout, but with members living in or near far-flung mountains – North Wales, the Lake District, Scotland, Colorado and Vancouver – this can only be a very rare event, and meets are mainly attended by the younger enthusiasts without family ties who can be out climbing every weekend. The new cosmopolitan flavour of the Rock and Ice is emphasised by two members being Scots, one of whom is the present honorary secretary, Alex Webster, an Aberdonian living in Derbyshire.

Increased sociability has resulted in the annual dinner becoming the climax of the Rock and Ice year. It is surprising that such a small body, some of whose members live abroad, always has so many people wanting to attend that guests have to be rationed to one each, plus wives and girlfriends. Guests of honour are invited each year, and dinner is followed by speeches, dancing, rough games and cabaret. When Beardie was master of ceremonies the cabaret was entertainment of a high order. Certain items have become traditional, such as the Greenall brothers singing a trio or Joe Brown leading the whole gathering in a rendering of 'The Barrack-Room Opera – The Sergeant-Major', a twenty-minute concoction about a young soldier on trial for stealing a barrel of beer sung to tunes from Italian opera and Gilbert and Sullivan, which Joe had learnt when he was on National Service in the Far East. At one dinner early in the 1960s, Joe collapsed into uncontrollable laughter part way through the singing. He sings and laughs in a curious high-pitched falsetto and this had the effect of reducing his audience to a similar state of hilarity; the more he laughed the more the audience hooted back. To restore order, Mortimer, Ron Cummaford and I were called upon to bolster Joe in barber-shop-quartet style, in an attempt to finish the opera. When we started singing Joe stopped laughing and took over as lead singer again. All was well till near the end when he collapsed into hysterics once more. This time he appeared completely beyond himself. I had seen him laughing uncontrollably before, but never like that. He laughed and laughed and so did the audience; slowly he sank to the ground, giggling in high-pitched choking sobs, hugging his ribs and helplessly rolling from side to side.

'I'll have to hit him,' I said to Ron and Morty.

'Sooner you than me!'

I hesitated, but we were on a small platform and at any moment Joe would fall off, with quite a drop to the hall floor below. I bent down, grabbed hold of him and punched. In an instant he was up on his feet like a jack-in-the-box, lashing out in a reflex action. I grabbed at him again, caught hold of his coat as he came forward, and the pair of us fell backwards off the platform. His impetus carried Joe over my head like a judo throw and landed him on the back of some chairs, which damaged his ribs. Some of them were cracked and he had to be strapped up. 'That'll teach you to tussle with me!' I told him, and it certainly stopped him laughing for a while.

The rough games at the dinner were imported from battles with the Derby Mercury, 'the mat'[1] being a speciality which brings out the keenest competition each year. At some past dinners the games were a little too energetic and there was a period when we had to discover a new hostelry every year, but we now have an annual Yorkshire Dales fixture and as long as any damage caused by musical-chairs-rugby, passing the rope, or the mat is paid for, the landlord regards our antics with cheerful tolerance.

The Rock and Ice suffered the greatest single blow in its history in November, 1969, when Eric Beard was killed in an accident on the M6 motorway on his way back from the Lake District. Beardie had grown in stature over the years; open-hearted, cheerful, optimistic and fantastically fit, he had found his true self. He was good at making people laugh – a born entertainer – and brought happiness to others simply by his presence; in the last few years of his life he had developed into a great 'character'.

Because of his essentially simple nature he was able to get on terms with any child or group of youngsters. His own formal education had ended when he was fourteen, and partly because of this he felt deeply about deprived or handicapped children and spent much of his time and his athletic prowess on their behalf. He helped at a school for mentally handicapped children, and in the last few months of his life he had run from John o'Groats to Land's End, 945 miles including variations, and from Leeds to Downing Street almost non-stop, to try to raise money for children's charities. The week after he died he was to have made an attempt on the world twenty-four-hour track record, a sponsored run in aid of the Save the Children Fund.

He became an integral part of the winter Cairngorms where he taught young children to ski and instructed in climbing on a temporary basis. And two nights a week he ran his famous 'Beardie's Sing-Song'. Everyone knew him, with his honey butties and mugs of hot sweet tea – his training diet! It is odd to reflect now on a recent pronouncement by scientists to athletes that a high carbohydrate diet is best for long-distance runners – Beardie's was just that.

He was no mean climber. Besides the ascents mentioned in earlier chapters, he had climbed the Südost Verschneidung of the Fleischbank (grade VI), the north face of the Cima Grande, the Zmutt Ridge among others, yet he always gave the impression when talking about his own climbing of being a very

---

1. The mat: a circle of men, holding each other by hooked fingers only, try to pull each other on to a mat inside the circle. Anyone who touches the mat is out, and if the circle breaks between two men, they are both out. As numbers diminish, the mat is made smaller by folding it.

moderate performer. But let him be in a situation requiring speed or stamina over mixed or easy ground when he wanted or needed to push himself and he was without an equal in my experience, particularly in bad conditions or storm. Some of the best climbers in Britain today owe something of their survival to having been with Beardie in a crisis when it was not their skill which pulled them through, but his incredible stamina.

My wife and I, with our baby son, were at Land's End to greet him when he came jogging down the road at the end of his John o'Groats run. He was fresh, and could have run to America if the sea hadn't been in the way. As he came down the last half-mile, his long arms and legs, on a disproportionately small body with its barrel chest, moved effortlessly in unison, and he was singing at the top of his voice, just with the joy of being fit and alive. He had bivouacked each night on the way from Scotland; Dave Gilmour, the driver who had accompanied him in an open jeep, looked in far worse fettle.

I drove him to the 1969 Dovedale Dash on November 2nd, the last race we were to run in together. We enjoyed the outing immensely, and afterwards I dropped him on his way to Liverpool where he was going to prepare for his twenty-four-hour run. 'So long, pal,' he said, pulling a large monster's hand over his own and waving a typical comic farewell. 'See you.' I was never to see him again.

Completely unconventional, without money or possessions except for his tent, his climbing and skiing equipment and his running togs, Eric Beard was one of modern society's true dropouts. He gave what he had to give, and above all himself, to what he cared for most. He was no saint and had his faults and weaknesses like all men, but even when he went too far in his enthusiasms he was forgiven because he had the rare gift of making people laugh. And his mockery of the world's materialist outlook struck a chord in innumerable hearts. Hundreds of climbers, runners, skiers, hillwalkers and children attended his funeral and openly wept for his passing.

8   The Northern Bens in Winter

'A short cut axe – heavy 'sacks, a sheer of white – no respite,
The northern Bens in winter!'
(From a poem by the author)

Scottish winter climbing is often said by the not-so-discerning to provide Alpine conditions, intending a comparison with climbing in the Western Alps in summer. To the non-initiate this is misleading, for the northern Bens are not usually Alpine in that sense but more accurately Arctic, and because of this they offer the most demanding, fatiguing and variable mountaineering in the British Isles. This mountaineering has several special features: short days which demand speed; generally harsh weather; sudden changes in temperature severely affecting snow conditions; storms which no one, however competent, can survive if exposed to their fury on open ground and, in consequence, the probability of any mistake being serious. Finally, the scale and isolation of the mountains combine to give any winter ascent in Scotland a spice and attraction lacking in summer crag or cliff climbing and put such ascents in the realms of greater mountaineering.

The development of winter climbing north of the border has been mainly the product of the sturdy individualism and parochialism of the native Scots, with small enthusiastic groups in their local areas working out their own methods and climbing philosophies, solving the problems presented by the terrain. The Aberdeen climbers have tended to concentrate on Lochnagar, the Glaswegians in Glencoe, but slowly over the years techniques have been evolved which enjoy general acceptance and this has produced a school of Scottish winter climbing with traditions and standards of its own. From contact with Polish, Austrian, Czech and other foreign climbers, I feel one can justifiably say that the epic quality of Scottish winter climbing is on a par with that of any other mountain region.

My own acquaintance with Scotland in winter began in 1950 when 'Dad' Lyons and I spent a holiday in Glencoe. Armed with the then ubiquitous ex-War Department ice axes we kicked and scrambled our way up and amongst the Glencoe summits. Like most English climbers on a first visit, I had no true appreciation of the harsh qualities of the Scottish winter, but this lesson was soon learnt. In the late afternoon of Christmas Eve a snowstorm drove us off the summit ridges of Bidean nam Bian and down into the Lost Valley, thus forcing us to walk many more miles than we had bargained for to regain our base at the Glencoe Youth Hostel. By the time we reached the end of the valley night had fallen and we were faced either with a further detour or an attempt to wade the River Coe, roaring in spate and fearsome in the blackness and falling snow, in order to reach the safety of the motor road. Then fifteen years old, I was tired out and soaked to the skin; my makeshift anorak, a cut-down raincoat, let water through its fabric like a sieve. Unwisely, we decided to cross the river, trying to feel our way from boulder to boulder, the icy water making me gasp at its bite. At one point I slipped and fell full-length, luckily where the water was not deep nor the current too strong, but when I eventually staggered to the opposite bank I was so numb with cold that 'Dad' had to help me to climb up and out of the water.

In those days we hadn't heard of the exposure syndrome, but I must have been close to becoming its victim as we slopped along the Glencoe road in a howling gale, almost falling through the doors of the youth hostel. A brawny Scot took one look at me and declared 'Och, ye look like ye've been for a swim!'

The following Easter found me with several of the Bradford Lads on Ben Nevis. This first visit, though not blessed with good conditions or notable for routes climbed, nonetheless impressed on me the difference between the Ben and any other peak in Britain. Its huge northern precipices, boasting climbs of 2,000 feet, draped in their winter raiment of ice and snow, with sweeping ridges, bulging ice gullies and verglassed rocks, filled me with an awe and respect which have remained with me ever since. The most enjoyable outing of our holiday was a traverse of the Devil's Ridge amongst the neighbouring Mamore summits which, though not technically difficult, provided one of those Scottish hill days which live forever in the memory and left me yearning to return. From then on, until the death of Alf Beanland in 1958, the yearly pilgrimage to Ben Nevis was a must. We might stop off on the road north to climb on the Cobbler at Arrochar or to traverse the Aonach Eagach, the northern rampart of Glencoe, but the 'Big Bad Ben', as it was known to us, was not to be denied. Slowly I learnt the topography of the mountain and inevitably, it seems, because of the nature of winter climbing on it, I had my share of adventures and narrow squeaks.

An amusing incident occurred in the winter of 1951 while I was climbing the straightforward *Number Two Gully* on the Ben with Ernie Leach. He was a crampon enthusiast; he had learnt the technique in the Alps and correctly decided it would be applicable to Scottish winter climbing. At that date the Scots, with rare exceptions, maintained that Tricouni nails were best for the Ben and even frowned on the use of crampons. Ahead of us in *Number Two Gully* were two well-respected Scottish Mountaineering Club members in the inevitable Tricouni-nailed boots. Ernie soon gained on the pair in front, cramponing up the hard snow on his front points, leading out 120 feet of rope at a time, cutting a large stance, then tightrope walking me up to him in my nails. The gully steepened and the SMC men were forced into cutting steps while Ernie stomped past them with a courteous Yorkshire 'Ahh doo'.

The Scots were furious and their leader, brandishing his axe like a claymore, yelled at Ernie 'D'ye no ken crampons are taboo in Scotland?' while his second intoned 'Keep your cheating aids off our mountains!' This was my first real brush with Scottish parochialism, and so fearsome did the Scots look in their anger that when my turn came to follow I scurried past them, fearful of being pulled off the slope. I was soon to learn the other side of the Scottish character – the generous hospitality, the deep and sincere friendships, the utter reliability – but as a boy, on first acquaintance the Scots appeared wild men to me. Crampons were adopted by many of the Nevis clientele shortly after this episode and today no climber would be advised to set off for a winter's day on Scottish hills without his twelve-pointers.

In 1953 another winter ascent gave me the fright of my young life when, with Alf Beanland, I made the ascent of the Castle of Carn Dearg, the secondary summit of Ben Nevis. This buttress, comprised of a band of easy-angled slabs capped by a headwall, has a notorious propensity to avalanche. Although of a medium grade of difficulty, with the actual climbing problems concentrated in the final chimneys which thread a way up the summit rocks, the lower slabs, innocuous in appearance, are in fact dangerous as the collecting ground and source of many avalanches. Alf and I had walked up from Glen Nevis and, despite an early start, found ourselves well into a bitterly cold grey morning before we reached a sloping shelf leading on to the toe of the Castle.

From our reading we knew of the vicious side to the Castle's nature. Linnell and Kirkus, two of the greatest of English climbers, had been avalanched off its sides, Linnell had been killed and Kirkus injured. So we approached the climb with extra caution, telling ourselves we would retreat if the snow was in bad condition. Alf, wearing Tricounis, led off and was soon ready for me to follow. As we gained height we met trouble; after climbing on firm snow for the first rope length we came on to powder lying directly on the rock. The actual climbing was not bad but there was an absence of security with nothing to which we could attach good belays. The downward-sloping slabs were trapping us and Alfie had to lead over rock deep in powder snow with no hope of my holding him if he fell, unable as I was to belay to anything but an axe stuck in the snow as a psychological attachment. After two more rope lengths we held a council of war and decided to give it best and either go down or traverse off into the South Castle Gully on our left.

I started to descend, but at once the snow began to slide away from under my feet, a warning that conditions were ripe for avalanche. This unnerved me and I insisted on climbing back to Alfie, who then made an attempt to traverse off into the gully so enticingly close. It began to snow, the wind was rising and, as Alf balanced his way over the slabs in deep powder snow, the mass on which he stood suddenly jolted and slid down six inches, making us both gasp; my leader immediately and rapidly moved back to the stance on which I was merely standing with nothing in the way of belay.

'We'll have to go up,' Alfie declared, and off he led once more. Fresh snow began to pour down the headwall and on to the slabs on which we perched and every minute the avalanche danger increased. Alfie calmly led up through the choking spindrift, kicking his nails deep into the snow, somehow gaining safe lodgement on the rock underneath. At moments we were completely cut off from one another, the screeching wind whipped the falling snow into a blinding, hateful torment, and our only knowledge of each other's presence was through the rope, snaking out of frozen hand, clumsily gripped, but still our bond of faith despite its uselessness as a safeguard. Rope length followed rope length till at last we stood together, teeth chattering, clothes frozen like armour, fingers and toes bereft of feeling, under the final steep wall of the Castle, firmly tied to a chockstone and safely above the dangerous slabs.

Powder snow continued to pour down on us, and in worsening blizzard conditions Alfie traversed back and forth along the foot of the headwall, look-ing for the finishing chimneys. We knew these to be somewhere on the left edge of the buttress, facing the rock, but in the storm it was impossible to tell if the cracks we finally followed were the correct route. I belayed at the foot of a narrow fissure and Alfie led off, his Tricounis biting the rock covered with verglas, definitely an advantage here. Once he had gained a few feet he was out of my vision, for the snow pouring over me made it almost impossible to look up and I had little idea of the struggle taking place above my head. Suddenly I heard a wild rushing sound below my feet, the whole slope was moving, cas-cading into avalanche; if we had been ten minutes later, we should have been caught in the upper reaches of the slide, but under the headwall we were safe.

The rope tugged at my waist, telling me that Alfie was ready for me to follow. The crack opened to a chimney, bulging in ice where the leader had neatly cut nicks for hands and feet. I cleared out their covering of snow and moved up against the force of the spindrift and downdraught which was almost suffo-cating; it tore through the patches on my windproof trousers, inside my ex-War Department anorak, down my neck through the opening of my wool balaclava and into my socks via the open tops of my boots. By the time I reached Alfie I was near exhaustion and the cold seemed more biting than ever. 'I'm shattered!' I gasped. 'Did you hear the avalanche?'

Alfie, his asthmatic chest and thin frame shaking with cold, was nevertheless calm and in control. He nodded. 'Not far to go now,' he shouted encouragingly above the wind and, after a quick changeover of belays, moved off again.

We followed some easier chimneys but still the falling snow made the going difficult, and suddenly we realised that the gloom was not just the storm – it was getting dark! Alfie moved up as swiftly as he could, pulling the rope between us as tight as possible each time he reached a belay, and I followed; no niceties but a desperate scrabble to get up and off, quick and alive! We traversed some rock slippery with ice and realised we stood more or less on top of the Castle. But our troubles were not over; Ben Nevis in a storm is serious by any route up or down, true to the 'venomous' meaning of its name.

We took up the rope into hand coils and moved on together; only the boiled sweets I forced into my mouth kept me going as I stumbled along a foot behind Alfie, he too floundering through the storm but, as ever, bang on course. His sense of direction was uncanny and he led me out by open slopes on to the plateau of Carn Dearg, then directly to the tourist route leading back to Glen Nevis. Luckily, in many places the track was blown clear and elsewhere the fresh snow made it possible to slide down the Red Burn. Falling and reeling, by now in pitch dark, we reached the easier part of the descent route, the bogs and the long plod to the valley. As we crossed the footbridge over the Nevis I thanked my lucky stars that I was with a mountaineer of the calibre of Alf Beanland.

At Easter, 1954, I was back on the Ben, this time camping with the Rock and Ice in the Allt a'Mhuilinn, the glen running directly under the mountain's northern faces. I shared a tent with Ray Greenall and Joe Brown, pitched on snow a foot deep when we arrived, but a sudden rise in temperature and a rapid thaw left us stranded in a quagmire. The tent was at best rudimentary and we spent the rest of the holiday in wet clothes and wet sleeping bags, baling out water that oozed through our makeshift groundsheet. By the time we returned to Manchester our bodies had wrinkles all over them like prunes, and Joe, influenced by his recent army service, declared after careful inspection that we had developed trench feet!

Our first day was unsuccessful, when Joe decided we ought to inspect the then virgin *Zero Gully*. Early in the morning we climbed straightforward slopes to the base of the climb, dodging a bombardment of falling ice out of the gully itself. At the foot of the first ice pitch Ray and I installed ourselves deep inside a bergschrund-type opening, well belayed, while Joe prepared to lead the pitch. He put his head out of our sheltering cave, found nothing was falling, launched forth and began cutting steps. The rope moved stealthily out until suddenly a noise like a Bren gun popping followed by screaming missiles told us, deep in our crevasse, that all was not quiet on the Zero front. The rope sagged and grating Tricounis gave the signal that Joe was retreating. 'Whoops!' Into our shelter he dived as a larger missile whizzed past its opening. 'The ice is in bad condition!' he informed us, chuckling. 'We'll have to retreat.' An hour later we were still in the cave, waiting for the ice to stop avalanching. As the morning progressed it became worse, stirring Joe into activity. 'We can't stop in this hole forever,' he announced. 'Coil the ropes and we'll jump for it!'

'Jump for it?' Ray and I echoed.

'Yes, jump out of here, slide down and brake with your axe before those small cliffs in Observatory Gully.'

'We'd better unrope!' So we untied and coiled the ropes, but Ray and I nervously cowered deeper as more falling ice blocks thundered by.

Joe climbed to the edge of the hole, looked up once more to see if anything was coming, explained, tongue in cheek, that the idea was 'to go down the same speed as the ice' and nonchalantly leaped out into space. He landed several feet further down, then careered down the slope at an oblique angle in a perfect standing glissade at a speed I have only seen equalled by falling bodies, covering perhaps 500 feet in seconds. He crowned this performance with a swift roll over, face up and to the slope, and with a deftly executed braking movement stopped himself a short way above the barrier crags, got up and ran out of the path of falling debris.

Ray and I followed his actions wide-eyed. 'You next,' I suggested.

'You're kidding! You go.'

I crept to the lip of the bergschrund but a large ice block screamed past and I scuttled back to the fielding bosom of Ray. Faintly we could hear Joe yelling, 'Come on, you ninnies!' Out to the lip I crept once more, looked up the bulging ice of Zero, looked down to Joe impatiently waiting. *'Jump!'* he shouted, and with rather too much impetus I sprang far out as a falling icicle burst about me. I hit the slope with a bone-shaking jar, then shot into space once more in a complete somersault so that when I landed again I slid rapidly down the snow head first. I had kept hold of my axe but try as I might I couldn't get myself the right way up. I got on to my side but still head first and as I swooped down like a swallow, I became conscious of two things – the line of cliffs directly in my path and Joe running across to try to cut me off before I shot over them. Somehow, on easier-angled ground but still moving at high speed, I managed to right myself at last, then in a panic, lying on the axe and pressing with all my might I stopped my flight almost dead. My shoulder and arm were nearly torn out of joint, but I got to my feet in time to greet a panting Brown with a grin.

After this performance, no name-calling or cajoling would persuade Ray to imitate my antics. Finally, he stepped boldly on to the slope, facing it, and slowly and methodically kicked his way down. Falling ice exploded all round him but he resolutely ignored this and when a minor particle hit him he shrugged it off. Watching was more frightening than action, and it was with relief that we welcomed Ray to our safety, where he gave us a short lecture; 'Always be in control!' It was a happy threesome that headed back to the wet tent; what was that against the hot brews inside it?

Next day Joe teamed up with Don Whillans to make the first ascent of the *Sassenach* climb on Carn Dearg, Ray dug ditches to try to divert the stream that intermittently flowed through our tent, and I left in the late afternoon with Don Cowan for Tower Ridge. The speed with which we accomplished this climb, in perfect conditions, seemed miraculous to me then. Cowan, one of the silent background figures of the Rock and Ice, tall with fair curly hair and a marked South Yorkshire accent, was then perhaps the club's most experienced mountaineer. His forte was Alpine and Scottish winter climbing, and his speed and fluency on the Tower Ridge made me realise yet again what a wealth of talent the group contained. We soloed the *Douglas Boulder Direct*, the 700-foot introductory buttress of the ridge, and moved thereafter with rope coils. Normally I don't climb like that if I can avoid it – I would sooner solo or move more slowly and belay – but with Cowan I felt very safe. We overtook many parties and among them, as we set off across the *Eastern Traverse* which avoids the major obstacle of the ridge, the Great Tower, were two ropes, two men and a woman and two women.

We completed the traverse successfully, a wonderful airy situation to which I have returned many times, then climbed to the summit of the Great Tower. From there we descended slightly, crossed the tower gap with a swift look down *Glover's Chimney* and finally, almost at a run, climbed the upper slopes of the ridge to the summit of the Ben. The sun was shining, there was little wind, in fact the day gave a first feeling of spring. Two hours after leaving our tents, Tower Ridge behind us, we were glissading down Number Three Gully on perfect snow, unaware that one of the parties we had overtaken was in serious difficulty.

In the rope of two who climbed the *Eastern Traverse* after us, one of the women had fallen during their ascent of the Tower. Her companion had held her but she fell about forty feet and her head had hit the rock. The party[1] were not able to pull her up, and all they could do was to make good her anchor and go for help.

We had just settled in for the night when the call for help reached our tents, and putting on cold wet climbing clothes on top of warm wet underclothes was an effort. A Creagh Dhu party was camping close by, so half the Rock and Ice group set off with two of the Dhus to try to climb up to the side of Tower Ridge and reach the injured climber from Tower Gully while the other half climbed to the summit of the Ben and descended Tower Ridge to the scene of the accident. I was in the second party with Whillans, Brown, Slim Sorrell and Don Chapman, and despite everyone being tired and the night dark with the thick clouds which had come up at sunset we reached the summit plateau

---

1. The two ropes were Eileen Gregory (Healey) with Ernest Snow and Peter Bunney, and Betty Emery, who fell, with Anthea Russell.

without too much difficulty by the slopes of Carn Dearg.

Finding the top of Tower Ridge was no easy task in the darkness with a wind whipping snow into our eyes, even though I myself had been on it only a few hours earlier. In the end we tied our ropes together and, anchored by the rest of us, Joe found the finish of the ridge. He and Don Whillans, held from above, climbed down to the Tower Gap, then forming a rope of two somehow were able to reach the anchored rope on which the unfortunate woman was hanging, but their combined efforts couldn't raise her an inch. Eventually they were joined by Bob Hope of the Creagh Dhu, Don Cowan and Ray Greenall who managed to climb up and out of the Tower Gully to join them on their perch, a ledge cut out of the snow below the summit of the Great Tower.

Even with all five men pulling they still couldn't get the woman up the cliff face, so in the end, again held from above, Joe climbed down to her; by this time she was of course dead. Small wonder they couldn't move her, the body was jammed against the face and Joe had a difficult task to free it.

While this was going on, Slim, Don Chapman and I up on the summit plateau were in danger of becoming exposure victims. We had no means of communication with those below so, after cutting ice bollards and anchoring the ropes to these, we found refuge by tunnelling into the ruins of the observatory, buried but accessible under the snow. The night seemed endless; we had no food and the cold bit deeper and deeper as the hours slowly ticked by until we couldn't keep still for a moment. We were cheered by the arrival, shortly before dawn, of the RAF mountain rescue; their well-provisioned and equipped team sporting flasks of coffee, stoves and food.

At first light we descended Tower Ridge and shortly afterwards the four men of the Rock and Ice and the Creagh Dhu stalwart appeared with the body. Events moved rapidly after that, including a brief 'incident' when an RAF officer appeared, took overall command and proceeded to give Whillans his instructions and a dressing-down. He was in charge and would suffer no insubordination! Don soon let him know that he was no member of HM Forces nor ever likely to be. But we were all glad to hand over to the RAF boys who quickly and efficiently completed the task of getting it down.

A sequel was the typically inaccurate press reportage. Nat Allen and Ron Moseley, who were on the Rock and Ice meet, took no part in the operation for the simple reason that they didn't get back from climbing till after the rescue parties had set out. They spent the night in their sleeping bags and only heard the news when we returned to camp next morning at about 8.30 a.m. Yet somehow Nat appeared in some of the papers as the hero of the piece, while the people involved were barely mentioned.

Slowly over the years Ben Nevis has become for me a familiar though always respected mountain. Many of my climbs there were made in textbook fashion but with memories no less vivid for that: of fine situations, the swing of the axe, the crampon's bite, aching calf muscles, knifing wind and biting cold, the blizzard's roar, the incredible feeling of calm on the few windless days, the alternation of snail's pace and speed which is so much a part of winter climbing. And most of all, the panoramic views from the summit on clear days, unsurpassed for beauty on mountains anywhere. The names alone – *Cresta*, the *North-East Ridge*, *Observatory Ridge*, *Glover's Chimney*, *Italian Climb*, *Comb Gully* – bring back climbs and companions sharply etched in recollection.

Some Nevis climbs I have repeated several times, *Gardyloo Gully* for example, a classic climb always interesting despite its lowly grading, which gave me a frightening experience when I climbed it with a Merchant Navy officer home on leave after a long Pacific voyage. Four of us set out one bitterly cold March morning in the mid-fifties, foolishly wearing Vibrams and without crampons. The snow was as hard as concrete, and slowly we cut and kicked our way up to the foot of the massive chockstone spanning the gully, the main feature of the route. In a normal winter one climbs behind it by a tunnel-like aperture leading on to steep snow slopes and the summit cornice, but that day the chockstone was completely buried and the only way to get up was on its outer walls and the retaining side of the gully by a steep ice pitch of about sixty feet.

John Ramsden was leading the first rope and I was leading the second, tied to the sailor whose lack of training and the effect on him of the cold wind made us painfully slow. Ram and his partner quickly forged ahead and by the time I started up they had disappeared from sight. I balanced up the ice on neat steps sloping inwards so that even a Vibram sole couldn't slip off, a fine piece of handiwork, and above the chockstone I could trot up the snow slopes by the bucket steps of the first team. I ran out all the rope and on a large prepared stance I took an indirect belay round my ice axe deep in the slope above me.

All seemed well with the sailor for the first thirty feet or so, then suddenly there was a sharp tug on the rope which dragged me off my platform and on to my axe belay – he had fallen off the ice. Mercifully, the axe held but I could do nothing except cling grimly to the rope, as my partner seemed to make no effort to get back on to the climb. Just as my hands were about to give out the rope slackened; he was on the steps again and I hauled myself back to the stance. When he came into sight, his face was as white as flour, his eyes were glazed and he slumped forward. 'I'm going to faint!' he gasped. I pulled the rope taut just in time to hold him as he passed out.

Holding his eleven stone from a waist belay for what seemed a long time, I was struggling for breath. Ram appeared at the top of the gully, worried by our non-appearance. 'What's happening?'

'Help, Ram, for Christ's sake!' But I could not make him understand.

Slowly my partner recovered consciousness, then began to vomit into the snow. At last, with a tremendous effort on his part and maximum pulling from me, he got to the stance where he sat on his haunches, obviously close to another collapse. 'I'm sorry,' he stuttered with chattering teeth. 'I've been used to temperatures of 100 plus. Today's the coldest I've ever known.' I had to agree about the cold; my own teeth were moving so rapidly up and down that Ram couldn't understand my incoherent shouts.

I tied the sailor firmly to his axe, then moved up the ladder of steps prepared by Ram; as soon as I was within clear shouting distance I begged him to drop me a rope over the cornice. Ram and I were used to climbing with each other and normally would have retreated sooner than ask for a top rope, but he guessed from my voice that I was in earnest and a few seconds later a rope end snaked down the slope.

How gladly I attached myself to that security! Ram is over six foot and immensely strong; tied to him I felt much happier. 'Take it tight! Tight! Tighter!' I shouted, then pulled hard as the sick man struggled up to me. Tying him to his axe once more, I climbed up to and over the cornice, an impressive formation that had needed much cutting; from the summit plateau the three of us guided our unfortunate companion to safety. He was shaking uncontrollably with cold and fatigue so we started down at once. Surprisingly, he was able to move downwards at a fair pace, but it was a great relief when we had him safe in the valley.

In March 1963, four of us – Eric Beard, Terry Burnell, Dougal Haston and myself – were staying in the CIC hut, the property of the Scottish Mountaineering Club, in Allt a'Mhuilinn. The wind was vociferous in the way only a Scottish wind can be, sobbing, roaring, screeching, sighing, dying. We were perplexed about what to do with our day as we sat in underclothes, sweating round the pot-bellied stove, a monster of heat. We had maintained the temperature in the hut at over ninety degrees, despite the inclement weather outside, and had made real attempts to equal the record that was said to be over the hundred mark. But in spite of constant attention, pot belly had never attained this figure for us. The CIC hut was in my opinion the finest climbing hut in the country, including its decor of creosoted wooden boards and ill-lit corners. It had atmosphere, with its small interior and half-dozen bunks; arriving alone, late at night, one could see in imagination the ghosts of old masters preparing for the morrow's climb, before the image was dispersed by lighted lamp and candle. Alas! The pot-bellied stove is no more and the CIC has been modernised.

The evening before, we had staged an eating contest in which Beardie had won a famous victory by polishing off seventeen pancakes covered with raspberry jam left behind in a large tin by an RAF mountain-rescue course. Still heavy with food we idled, the Sassenachs leaving decision about the day's climbs to Dougal, judging that the Scots know their own mountains best.

Despite his huge intake of calories only a few hours ago, Beardie was at work preparing a stock of honey butties, 'for emergencies' as he liked to say.

'I think Tower Ridge will be OK for you and Gnome, Beardie,' Dougal said, 'in spite of the wind. I have a wee route on *Number Three Gully Buttress* for Dennis and myself to have a peek at.' Tower Ridge was Beardie's ambition in Scotland; each day for almost a week he had been declaring he would climb it but each day he had been talked by agile tongues into other plans. He had climbed *Number Two Gully Buttress*, a route on the Trident and had led a rope up the *Italian Climb*, but these meant little to him in spite of their severity; Tower Ridge, he kept telling us, was his Everest. At last he had his way and half an hour later he and Terry left for the Ridge, with Beardie singing loudly as he stepped into the gale, carrying a rucksack bulging with spare clothes and his never-to-be-forgotten butties.

Dougal and I put on our crampons in the hut doorway and started for *Number Three Gully* against a fierce crosswind. At the foot of the gully we broke out to the left and climbed to the base of the gully buttress; above the wind's fine spindrift the sky was a cloudless blue, and the snow was in superb condition. On the side of the buttress runs the line of a summer rock climb, a Severe called *Gargoyle Wall*; this was our objective for, we hoped, the first winter ascent. The summer route goes up a steep rib and immediately on the right of this is a line of shallow chimneys containing a good build-up of ice and snow, the obvious way for a winter ascent. At the foot of these we were sheltered from the wind; when I complimented Dougal on his judgement, he replied 'Ach nae, Jimmy Marshall's often said that west-facing routes are usually free of wind. The Ben's prevailing winds are mainly north-easters.'

Using a single overweight rope, Dougal led off, the epitome of the modern Scottish winter climber with his heavy clothing, long gaiters and twelve-point crampons, a short axe in one hand, an ice dagger in the other. He cut an efficient ladder of holds up the first ice pitch, then moved on to rock, traversing slightly to the right to a small ledge where he placed a rock piton for a belay, by far the safest assurance for winter climbing other, of course, than a firm natural rock belay. The way up to him was more awkward than difficult; we changed places, he traversed back into the chimneys and soon his axe was cleaving air in a steady rhythm. Dougal was not then so well known as his later Alpine ascents were to make him, but it was by no sudden miracle that he attained the standard of the Eiger and Matterhorn north walls in winter; years of winter climbing in Scotland lay behind these successes, although his youthful looks and grace made him more like a Pre-Raphaelite poet than a winter hard man.

Carefully he worked his way up the chimney and the open groove that followed until the rope ran out, but no belay could he find, no crack for a piton, no ice suitable for an ice screw, so he rammed his short axe a few inches into snow and, with this psychological safeguard, straddled the groove and brought me up. Again the climbing proved less bad than it looked, but the lack of real security made it feel serious – a 'big route'. I stopped a few feet below Dougal, wedged myself as best I could and simply played out his rope round my body as he climbed, knowing that if he fell we would both go. Dougal went up the last section of the groove with methodical ease – a short ice pitch and he gained a chimney up which he bridged in his crampons. This finished on the very crest of the buttress, and an awkward landing on to a balcony deep in snow brought Dougal to a safe lodging. A moment later I left my awkward resting place with relief; wedging in the groove had given me pins and needles in the thighs.

There was a series of corners and snow arêtes above the balcony and here I took over the lead, glad to see that Dougal had a good belay. 'Ye can finish it off!' he said with a grin. 'It's mere snow bashing from here on.'

On the first snow ridge my position was impressive. To the left was Tower Ridge and the Great Tower on which I could see two little figures, Beardie and Gnome, on my right were the Trident buttresses and further away Carn Dearg with its galaxy of climbs gripped in winter's vice, and above my head, less than a rope length away, was the edge of the summit plateau with a light cornice looking like whipped cream and sunshine on the slopes; there was only one drawback – this final section was smothered in deep powder snow. I swam up the corners and chested my way along the short arêtes, taking a long time to reach the cornice, but this was easily turned in the direction of Tower Ridge by an unorthodox western-roll type of movement which landed me panting on the top in blinding sunlight. Dougal chuckled as he joined me and let out a traditional Edinburgh victory cry.

The view was incredible – Cairngorms, Mamores, Loch Eil, the glorious north-west; having drunk our fill of this heady draught we walked over to watch Beardie and Terry climb the last slopes of Tower Ridge. They bubbled with enthusiasm for their climb which they agreed was 'a plum'. Unroped, the four of us left the Ben, leisurely traversed the Carn Mor Dearg Arête and climbed to the top of Carn Mor Dearg whence a marvellous series of standing and sitting glissades brought us whooping and laughing to the door of the CIC hut and the end of a perfect day.

The more I knew of Scottish winter climbing the more I wanted to be north of the border in that season. When I returned from Gauri Sankar in the winter of 1964 I resolved to spend a year or eighteen months in Scotland travelling and climbing, and started of course with Ben Nevis. Coming straight from the Himalaya I found myself totally out of condition – anyone who thinks a Himalayan expedition puts one in good shape has never experienced its debilitating effects – but a week on Nevis with half a dozen climbs soon made a difference to my fitness. I then paid my first visit to Creag Meagaidh and the magnificent cliffs of Coire Ardair, but bad conditions only allowed an ascent of *Raeburn's Gully* before I turned east to the Cairngorms.

I had been there years before when I climbed an easy route and ascended Cairn Gorm by walking from Rothiemurchus, but by 1964 the scene had altered out of all recognition; the skiing potential of the region had changed it from one of the most remote mountain districts in Britain to the swinging centre of Scotland's winter sports. The road to the ski lifts, built high on to Cairn Gorm itself, now gives quick access into the mountains, and although some climbers may deplore the invasion of what had been their winter domain, one does not have to walk far to avoid the piste-bound downhill hordes.

I took on some guiding and climbing instruction and with clients learnt my way up and about the classic ascents of the region such as the *Vent* and *Savage Slit* of Coire an Lochain and *Jacob's Ladder* and *The Runnel* of Coire an t-Sneachda. The northern corries are little short of ideal for teaching or learning winter climbing techniques. The climbs are short enough to allow adequate instruction time in good conditions, usually there are good belay positions and all kinds of terrain present themselves, from easy snow slopes with safe run-outs to fine ice pitches such as those in the *Vent*. An ascent of *Savage Slit* proved far more than a training climb; it is a steep chimney or crack several hundred feet in length, with combined rock and ice pitches which I found near my limit as leader and up which I literally had to pull my second – who, I hasten to add, was responsible for our tackling the climb, it being one of his ambitions.

Towards the end of the winter Eric Langmuir, an old friend, invited me to visit Glenmore Lodge, the outdoor/mountain centre of the Scottish Council of Physical Recreation, of which he had recently been appointed principal. The invitation was to help with instruction on the survival course, then a new and unique type of course which rapidly became legend. To augment his permanent staff, Eric had assembled a group of temporary instructors of outstanding talent, especially on the climbing side, with Hamish MacInnes, Dave Bathgate, Jim McDowell and George McLeod among them. I gladly accepted the invitation, realising it would be an opportunity to learn more than I could teach.

For me this turned out to be the first of several such courses over the following years. We practised the latest winter climbing techniques, navigation, snow-holing and emergency bivouac methods, mountain rescue with two-way wireless coordination, first aid and so on. One of the most interesting days was when Hamish MacInnes gave a demonstration of the use of dogs for mountain rescue work, particularly in searching for victims buried by avalanche, he being the pioneer of their use in this country. The biggest avalanche danger in Scotland is from windslab, especially in the Cairngorms. We would simulate an accident by burying an instructor under the snow as volunteer victim before Hamish arrived with his dogs. I recall with gratitude how they found me when I was buried in one of these exercises and a blizzard suddenly reduced visibility almost to zero. My burial squad had left the scene, I had stupidly refused to take a two-way wireless under the snow with me, and I doubt whether without the dogs I should have been found again for quite some time!

Being under the snow is an eerie experience; you can breathe as long as fine powder snow hasn't choked your lungs, and you tell yourself that you will get yourself out the minute you don't like being there. But six inches of snow heaped on top of you, even as a practice, and you are imprisoned as immovably as if you were set in concrete. I was under the snow for twenty minutes during this exercise, I lost all sense of time and was sure I had been abandoned. The feeling of panic was real, and I almost choked. You know if people are walking about over you and can even hear their voices, but they can't hear you however loudly you shout. Even in a blizzard a dog can smell its quarry, and I have never been more of a dog-lover than the day Hamish's Alsatian dug me out in the roaring gale. A dog is by far the most efficient searcher for avalanche victims; it can find human beings buried almost twenty feet deep, locating them by the carbon dioxide exhaled as they breathe. The alternative method of search, by rescue workers probing suspected areas of burial with long rods, is slow and laborious in the extreme.

The Cairngorms are almost ideal for these courses, with their Arctic weather, high plateaux and enormous build-up of snow. Those who attend them vary in their experience; some are instructors from outdoor centres, others service personnel, some are teachers responsible for taking young people into the mountains. A wide range of fitness is encountered, but usually all agree that they will never forget their two weeks in the Cairngorms. Perhaps the highlight is when the skills learned during the first ten days or so are put into practice by spending the last three days and nights out on the mountains. During daylight climbs are attempted or peaks traversed and each night is spent in snow holes or bivouacs, with a different site each night. If the weather is of the usual February pattern, everyone is soon convinced that the only hope of survival is by seeking shelter under the snow. Outside the wind may be gale force (it usually is) and even the strongest would soon succumb, but once in a snow hole the temperature may be at freezing point but there is no wind chill. A sixty-mile-an-hour wind lowers the air temperature by many degrees and, as the unfortunate exposure victims on British hills have shown, temperatures well above freezing can still be dangerous if there is a strong wind, especially if it is also raining.

Occasionally things have gone wrong on a course. One night Joe Porter, Eric Langmuir and I, high in Coire Gorm of Braeriach, found ourselves unable to shelter under the snow because each of us had left the all-important snow saw and shovel to be carried by someone else. We only had ice axes to dig with and our attempted shelter kept collapsing. We had to spend the night in a coffin-like trench with a bivouac sack as roof; when I woke next morning there was no sign of the sack but no wind either, and I had several inches of snow on top of me!

During my first survival course I realised the importance to mountaineering of many of the techniques discussed and practised, for example, the use of saws for making ice caves and snow holes on difficult Himalayan climbs; the beginnings of scientific avalanche study in this country, very much through the enterprise of Eric Langmuir; the problems of recognising and dealing with exposure cases. The bringing together of so many experts proved fruitful, and several survival course discoveries are now in general use among climbers. One example is the deadman belay for snow and ice security suggested by George McLeod, an idea he adopted from his experience in the Antarctic; although today's commercial models are refined and better designed, they work on the same principle as the prototype made by George from a piece of plywood and a nylon sling.

The survival course is aptly named, but I suppose difficult to defend except in terms that make mountaineering sound institutionalised, the biggest danger, incidentally, to the future well-being of our sport. One of the most famous Scottish mountaineers, when he saw me on the Cairngorms, demanded 'What the hell are you doing rushing about like a patrol of overgrown girl scouts?'

'Learning to survive!' I could only meekly answer. But it is one of the few mountaineering instruction courses I would recommend anyone to attend, since it retains the element essential to me in all climbing – individual spontaneity.

After a whole winter among the magic delights of Lochnagar, Skye, Glencoe, I decided to live and work for a further spell in Scotland. I got a job in Glasgow and at the end of September 1965, moved to Edinburgh to live, looking forward to the winter season with keen anticipation. I was by then well attuned to Scottish attitudes and opinions; for instance, friends in Glasgow regarded my living in Edinburgh and associating with its climbers as unpardonable. 'Sassenachs are nae sae bad as the denizens of Auld Reekie!' they told me.

Edinburgh is, however, a mountaineer's city, within easy reach of the Highlands, and has produced a royal line of climbers – the Marshall brothers, Robin Smith, Dougal Haston and, more recently, the outstanding leaders of the Edinburgh Squirrels. Despite Glaswegian forecasts the Squirrels greeted me with open arms and I soon struck up a close friendship with one of their younger members, Alistair McKeith, known to us, and everyone else for that matter, as Bugs.

There is something infectious about Scottish nationalism. Every Scot I have known well is at heart truly nationalistic, and if one wishes to annoy one has only to criticise this attitude. But it is surprising how quickly the Sassenach living in Scotland is won over, becoming more 'Scotch' than the Scots. Some English climbers known to me, who have moved north, have donned the kilt and sporran; I didn't go that far but I did adopt the habit of plan and plot veiled in secrecy which is such an essential part of mountaineering in Scotland – the telephone call in the middle of the night to ask about conditions, the mad drive along icy roads and the long plod in the dark to reach an objective ahead of rivals, real or imaginary. There is room in Scotland for innumerable first ascents in winter but, as with climbing elsewhere, a little publicity makes one route seem more desirable than any other until it is climbed when another outstanding first-to-be takes its place.

To Bugs and myself the outstanding first ascent awaiting completion was the girdle traverse of Creag Meagaidh. The cliffs of Coire Ardair on this mountain immediately north of Loch Laggan are second only to Ben Nevis in scale and grandeur; a mile and half in extent, they provide some of the finest climbs in the country, with buttresses of over 1,500 feet. Across this intricate face is a natural traversing line which follows a horizontal fault for about 8,500 feet, broken by ice flows, rock walls and deep gullies.

Winter ascents on Creag Meagaidh have a remoteness and scale that make them a serious proposition. The base of the cliffs can be reached in two hours' walk from the nearest farm at Aberarder, above the Newtonmore-Spean Bridge road but, as quite a few climbers have discovered, in bad weather route finding on or off the mountain is difficult, and to get back to the valley can be a fight for life in a blizzard.

Weekend after weekend Bugs and I left Edinburgh, our plan shrouded in secrecy, to make our base in the bothy behind the Loch Laggan Inn, from which we investigated and mapped out the girdle. Jubilantly we told ourselves that this would be the longest expedition of its kind in Britain, longer than the Eigerwand! But conditions were always atrocious and one thing we agreed upon was the need for good conditions. We were not the only ones interested in the project and Tom Patey, the speed merchant of Ullapool, had a proprietary interest, having already climbed what would be the middle section of the traverse on his aptly named Post Horn Gallop. In typical Scots mountaineering, and even more Patey, fashion, he of course denied any interest in such a worthless outing. Being well versed in such matters we knew that this meant the opposite, but the rules of the game decreed that we must appear to believe him.

After many weekends at Laggan all we had accomplished were several examinations of the face, a frightening encounter with a blizzard, a new route on a lowly valley crag and a craving for Glenmorangie malt whisky. One Friday night we arrived late at the Laggan Inn to find Aberdeen climbers there in force, led by the legendary McArtney. I had not then met Jim McArtney but I had heard of his ability with axe and crampons, and after a few drinks with him I began to appreciate his ability with the spirit. Bugs kept giving me black looks. 'They're here fae the girdle, mon,' he whispered. 'Dinna drink tae much!' Eventually, convinced by Bugs' dark mutterings, I crept out with him into a snowstorm and drove up to bivouac in the barn at Aberarder Farm, where we were joined a short while later by the Aberdonians. They were downstairs in the barn and we were upstairs; at Bugs' insistence we rose before dawn, cooked as silently as we could, and tiptoed out before first light on a miserable morning like a pair of James Bonds, in inky blackness stole through the farmyard, waking what seemed like a dozen barking dogs, and by the light of head torches walked up the frozen hillside leading to Coire Ardair. As day broke the weather showed signs of improving and by the time we arrived at the frozen lochan under the cliffs the mists had parted and we could see the magnificent forms of the Ardair buttresses. Unfortunately I had a terrible hangover from all the whisky I had drunk, and as we climbed up to reach the start of the traverse line I was sick. Bugs attributed this to English weakness, uncoiled the rope and set forth.

The first problem, moving from left to right across the cliffs, was the Bellevue Buttress, but running across it was a gangway or band, steeped in snow, which finished on the edge of Raeburn's Gully. The first ten feet were awkward but thereafter it was simply a case of dagger, axe and crampons, and a crab-like movement sideways along a perfect ribbon of hard snow. Two rope-lengths of this were like a bad dream to me, but after a bar of chocolate I began to feel better and to enjoy the climbing. Although not difficult, perhaps grade II, this was superb, with tremendous, almost Dolomitic exposure; it must be one of the finest passages of its kind in Scotland. Each pitch offered something new; at one point there was a pinnacle to climb, at another the band of snow narrowed to a mere sliver, but by midday we stood in Raeburn's Gully with an easy but magnificent traverse behind us, which Bugs decided we should call 'The Scene'.

Eagerly we crossed Raeburn's towards what we considered would be the crux of the girdle, the Pinnacle Buttress, largest on the Ardair cliffs. From our explorations we knew there were two possible crossing places, a low and a high line. We decided to look first at the lower one, but just as Bugs was about to launch himself at an improbable icefall that barred our way it began to snow. After a few moments' hesitation Bugs got to work with his axe and placed an ice piton as he moved out on to an almost-vertical wall of ice. His progress became painfully slow and the falling snow steadily increased in density. 'It's brewing up!' I observed.

'I'm coming back. Watch the rope!' Bugs' ice piton popped out, immediately he moved sideways to it and he slithered back to my stance.

'Let's take a look higher up,' I suggested, and moving together with rope coils we cramponed up to the second possible crossing place. It looked difficult and entailed traversing Smith's Gully, one of the hardest of Scottish ice climbs, but it appeared more likely than the lower line, as far as we could see through the falling snow.

Indecision gripped us and we hung around waiting and waiting until it was obviously too late to make an attempt on the Pinnacle that day. Finally we climbed the top sections of Raeburn's Gully and exited on to the summit plateau of the mountain whence, aided by our knowledge of its topography, we hurried back to the Spartan comfort of the barn.

Later that evening we went down to the Laggan bar with the Aberdonians. 'What climbs did you make today?' I ventured to ask McArtney.

'Och, just a couple of the Post routes. And what did ye climb, mon?'

Bugs' eyes narrowed and his brow furrowed more than usual and before I had time to reply he named some climb I had never heard of, let alone ascended. 'Och, ye can nae trust the Aberdonians,' Bugs confided over a 'Morangie when we reached the bar. 'It might be they're nae interested in the girdle, but Patey is and he's Aberdonian, dinna forget!'

I found all this very amusing and it certainly gave a spice to our doings. There was never anything unfriendly in this jockeying; I climbed with Tom Patey a short while later in Applecross, and when I mentioned our attempts on the Ardair girdle he gave his honest opinion on what he considered the best route for tackling it, but of course he declared his own disinterest.

Next morning the weather was fine and, rising early again, we retraced our steps and cramponed down Raeburn's Gully to our point of retreat; the sun was shining as we climbed over the summit cornice and the sky was blue. At the highest of the two possible crossing points Bugs led the first rope length to a belay on the edge of Smith's Gully, then I took over the lead. The steep black ice in the couloir looked difficult and I moved gingerly down after cutting steps with my longest axe. That day I had brought two axes, one a medium-sized Charlet, the other a short axe with a fourteen-inch shaft, shaped from an ex-War Department model, which had once been Robin Smith's. I cut out into the bed of the gully with the Charlet and, balanced on the ice, looked up the fissure above my head. Whoever called it a gully was an optimist; it was more of a hanging chimney chock-full of ice. Jimmy Marshall had led the only ascent so far and gazing up at it I could understand his reputation for ice climbing.

I stopped staring upwards and continued cutting. The gully here was like a bowl, below which the bed steepened, and quite a long way across. The ice was peculiar, with a black shiny surface of great hardness which when broken revealed myriads of small crystals like diamonds. 'Damn!' The head of the Charlet flew off and disappeared with a clatter down the ice; the shaft had broken. Just then from Raeburn's on our left came a hail and Jim McArtney, climbing solo, appeared, moving at an incredible speed. Quickly he was gone again with a farewell wave, leaving me marvelling at such a beautiful display of front-point crampon technique. A few minutes later two more Aberdonians followed in his wake; the difference between their movement and McArtney's was the difference of chalk and cheese. It was a terrible blow for all who love the Scottish winter scene when this powerful figure perished so tragically in an avalanche on Ben Nevis in January 1970.

Luckily I still had my second axe in reserve and I cut my way up to a ledge on which I fashioned a stance in the banked snow and brought Bugs across. 'Did ye see McArtney watching us?' he asked.

'Oh, you Scots are awful suspicious men!' I remonstrated as he led off on the next rope length.

This proved reminiscent of our traverse of The Scene, not too difficult but its position and great exposure giving it a feeling of openness as one balanced along a narrow ribbon of hard snow. I joined Bugs, well tied to a rock pinnacle; looking across the face to our right, it was obvious that the next lead would be the crux. The fault we had been following finished dramatically with steep rock and shale but below and to the right I could see a horizontal fissure trending away from us; the problem would be to join the two up by climbing the bare sections of thirty feet or more in between.

From the end of our gangway I stepped on to steep rock with my Grivels rasping, balanced across some shale, moved a few feet further right and found myself stuck on nearly vertical earth. 'What to do?' I kept muttering to myself. Half an hour passed as I hopped first on one leg then the other. 'Why not cut steps in the shale?' I poked rather feebly with the axe spike and then the adze. 'No good!'; the ground was firmer than it appeared. Above my head was a large ice boss so I climbed up to this and carefully fashioned a channel round which I fastened a sling. Protected by my running belay I climbed cautiously down the shale for about fifteen feet, then made a difficult rock move to the right, with crampons sparking, to swing into the horizontal crack.

I managed a kind of mantelshelf and, placing my right leg and thigh inside the crack and using the upper lip as an undercut, shuffled slowly along the face. The position was wildly exposed with nothing underneath for hundreds of feet, but after a few moves I found another ice formation that I succeeded in converting into a second running belay. These shuffling antics were most painful and I began to get cramp in my leg, but luckily the crack finished with huge handholds and swinging down on these I was able to get to a ledge. Thereafter followed some step cutting over hard snow, then easy cramponing to reach, at the very limit of 150 feet of rope, a perfect vertical crack in the rock face into which I banged a twelve-inch channel ice piton to the hilt. 'Clip in! Relax!'

I decided it had been quite a pitch and this was confirmed by the difficulty Bugs had in following. He arrived with a grin as wide as a banana but all the same dropped his Edinburgh reserve to exclaim 'Mon, that was a hairy lead! Jeez! I've never seen such unusual winter climbing.'

The rest of the Pinnacle Buttress proved an anti-climax; after one more rope length we could amble along solo over perfect snow banked on to large terraces till we reached Easy Gully.

We rested there and looked at the way ahead. Behind us lay over 3,000 feet of climbing, before us was another 5,500 feet. It was now late on Sunday afternoon and we both had to return to Edinburgh; either we had to miss work and bivouac or call it a day and climb up Easy Gully to the summit. We wavered for quite some time but in the end, saying 'We'll come back next weekend', we raced up to the top of Meagaidh and thence home.

We never got back together on the girdle. Although Bugs completed all its sections in separate forays, the complete unbroken traverse, which we had meant to do once we knew the whole route, had to wait for several years. Shortly after the crossing of the Pinnacle Buttress I went back to Yorkshire and Bugs left Scotland for the sterner joys of Antarctica.

In the end the climb was accomplished in a single day, solo, 8,500 feet of serious climbing with many difficult sections, by the man most versed in Scottish winter tactics, on or off the Bens – Tom Patey. Maintaining his disinterest to the last, one day in the winter of 1969 he raced across the whole of the Coire Ardair precipices – one of the greatest achievements in British climbing history.

9   Alpamayo – The World's Most Beautiful Mountain

'Remember that the most beautiful things in the world are the most useless.'

(John Ruskin)

The sun was nearing its zenith, adding to the burdens already imposed by altitude, rucksack and weary legs. Ahead of me Ned Kelly stood like a sentinel astride the path, camera perched on tripod ready to film the next sequence of our march. His task was proving tiresome, it entailed running ahead of our column, shooting film, being left far behind, then a lung-bursting dash to overtake for the next shots. I had marvelled at Ned's dedication during the past four days' journey, especially the way he had managed almost singlehanded to carry immediate filming requirements.

'OK, Ned?' I asked, drawing level.

'Bloody hot!' came the reply.

'Never mind. We should reach our base site tonight, if the *arrieros* don't lose any more *burros*.' It had taken four hours that morning to find one mule, which galloped off when a puma had been sniffing round.

'They are a prize bunch,' agreed Ned. 'Trying to film this march is a play without actors – just scenery.'

'I'll push on and make sure Terry has a brew waiting at the lake.' Talking was an effort, the altitude made demands and a cough which had developed at the unhygienic *hacienda*, Colcas, at the start of our march had left me hoarse.

'When is this Alpamayo dame going to put in an appearance?' grumbled Ned. 'I bet she's all melted away in the heat.' It was hard to imagine that somewhere in the valley ahead, despite the tropical sun, was the most renowned pyramid of ice in the world.

I plodded away on the track up the *quebrada*. Rounding a hillock I stumbled into a herd of fearsome black bulls, frisking despite the heat. A glance was enough. Maybe they were not vicious and were used to humans wandering amongst them, but I didn't feel up to playing toreador and legged it up the hillside. 'Leaders of expeditions shouldn't take risks,' I assured myself guiltily.

Across the valley an Indian woman tended a herd of goats, an idyllic scene that belied the hard realities of Andean living. In the copper mountains – the Andes – avalanches, floods, malnutrition, cold and heat all take their toll, and men die young.

I rounded another hillock at a slower pace. A white fang of ice rose into the sky at the valley's head, gleaming in the sun and shaped like a crooked finger. Alpamayo? The world's most beautiful mountain? It looked small, unbalanced, neither the perfect pyramid nor trapezoid, the two aspects that have made the mountain famous. 'If that's Alpamayo, it must have toppled over' was my reaction; it didn't compare with the impressive photographs we had seen, and I felt disappointed. Menlungste, our frightening neighbour in 1964, put it to shame in comparison; it seemed Helvellyn to the Matterhorn.

I went on along the track cut by Peruvian engineers to the Alpamayo lake. Several times in past years its waters have caused flooding and tragedy in the lower valleys. Once the retaining walls of the glacial lake collapsed and six million tons of water rushed down into the Santa valley, destroying everything in their path. Flooding had been such a regular occurrence that the Indians called the white mountain above the lake Alpamayo, which in their language, Quechua, means 'flooding the land'. Nowadays, government engineers come up the track to measure the water level and, if need be, this is lowered artificially before danger point is reached. It seemed strange that the valley should be so sparsely inhabited with such an easy approach. Further down there had been evidence of terracing and a canal system from Inca times, including one canal six miles long, and people had thrived in the valley. Now, apart from one Indian family, it was deserted. Despite the efforts of the engineers, memories of the disasters keep newcomers away.

My eyes were riveted on the head of the valley as I trudged its level pampas. Above the depression that must contain the lake rose a steep wall of rock, overhung by ice from the Alpamayo glacier. Toppling séracs, waterfalls and avalanches thundered down its flanks in stark contrast to the lush valley below. It was not apparent how we could reach the base of the mountain; there was no way up the rock wall, at least not for heavily laden mules, and the valley appeared to end at the lake. I began to grasp for the first time the immensity of the scale – not the equal of the Himalaya but nonetheless massive. Alpamayo's summit was perhaps 7,000 feet above our heads, yet looked but a short climb.

It took two hours more to reach the rendezvous with Terry at a small hut of grass and earth used by the engineers for shelter on their visits, and sited under the retaining walls of the lake, hundreds of feet high and composed of loose boulders and glacier debris. The thought of this mass moving along on a vast wave of water made the throat catch.

Terry Burnell was crouched inside the hut, stirring a pot of tea, when I arrived and flopped beside him. A moment later we were joined by Dave Bathgate, back from a trip with Roy Smith to the proposed site for base camp. Dave, one of Scotland's best ice climbers, had been so keen to get a closer look at the snows that he had pushed on ahead of our mule train. Roy and

Terry had already made a reconnaissance. It was obviously not possible to get to Alpamayo directly from the valley, so they had climbed the steep hillside to the west, into a subsidiary valley under the Santa Cruz mountain. This Hobson's choice for base had at least two things in its favour: wood to burn and running water.

'What's holding those mule guys?' Dave demanded from under his huge black Stetson hat. He had come down again to help drive the animals up the last steep section to base, leaving Roy to work at the site above.

'They should be here soon. Meantime I need a brew.'

'Plenty in the pot,' grinned Terry as he passed over a pint of tea. Terry is one of the Rock and Ice Club's best tea makers, which means something in a club where hard climbing and brewing are synonymous.

Dave and I went outside to study the mountain and await the mule train. I crept into the shade of the hut wall and began to think about future plans … the establishment of base camp, the way on to the glacier, the icefall, the ridge, the traverse along the exposed crest to the summit and, most important of all, the film. But no, all that was too far ahead; too much planning at this stage was useless. Variables such as weather and human performance would dictate the strategy; flexibility should be our plan.

So I thought of the history of Alpamayo, famous in mountaineering circles for decades, its aspect familiarised by Kinzl and Schneider's fantastic book of photographs, *Cordillera Blanca*. Of its many outstanding pictures none compares with those of Alpamayo. Erwin Schneider, who has climbed and surveyed so many mountains, was responsible for climbing Alpamayo's near neighbour, the Quitaraju, which we came to know well above our first camp. It seemed fitting that today we were guided by his and Kinzl's map of the Cordillera Blanca.

The first attempt on Alpamayo was by way of the north ridge. In 1948 a Swiss expedition safely negotiated the difficult icefall and reached the ridge, only for its cornices to collapse, carrying Lauterberg, Schmid and Sigrist down 650 feet of the north-west face. They escaped with only minor injuries, one of the luckiest falls in climbing history, cushioned as it was by the cornices that had carried them away. The Swiss left Alpamayo alone after this, but before they quitted the range they had climbed the Nevado Santa Cruz (20,655 feet), and dubbed Alpamayo 'the world's most beautiful mountain'. Many others have agreed with this opinion since then, and in 1966 (the year of our own climb) a poll held by *Alpinismus,* the German mountaineering magazine, confirmed the mountain's appeal by an overwhelming vote of its readers.

Next on the scene was the French expedition of 1951, who thought they had reached the summit of the peak along the north ridge route chosen by the Swiss. The difficulties they overcame were many, and only a few climbers at that time in mountaineering history could have equalled the attempt of the

French aces, Leininger, Lenoir, Jongen and Kogan. They reached the top of the ridge in the dark and did not realise that the true summit was still a long and difficult traverse away and 200 feet higher. A storm broke and they had to bivouac on the descent in an ice cave, providentially found by Georges Kogan at the grimmest moment of their predicament. With great determination and good teamwork they managed an orderly retreat in appalling conditions, upheld by the supposed success of their enterprise. Their subsequent book was translated into English as *The Ascent of Alpamayo*.

Various authorities who knew Alpamayo realised that they could not have reached the true summit of the mountain, and there resulted one of those controversies which make mountaineering all the more interesting. The claim was finally examined by the Swiss Foundation for Alpine Research who, studying the evidence on an objective basis, concluded that the French had reached only the summit of the north ridge. The mountain was still unclimbed.

New attempts were launched, but none could emulate the French performance, let alone reach the summit, until 1957 when a strong party of four Germans arrived in the cordilleras of Peru. Led by the redoubtable Gunter Hauser, they strode from peak to peak, knocking off last problem after last problem, and soon they had notched ten first ascents in nearly as many ranges. At the top of their list remained Alpamayo; they looked on their other climbs as training for an attempt on the Queen of the Blanca. Unlike other suitors, Hauser's party turned their attention to the south ridge. In the southern hemisphere this is the equivalent of northern slopes in Europe and means less sun, icier conditions, but Hauser saw one big advantage in his proposed route: it went straight up to the top and obviated the long traverse from the north side.

After a hair-raising climb in bad conditions, a minor fall and a cold bivouac with resultant frostbite, the German party successfully carried their attempt to the true summit of Alpamayo at 20,100 feet.[1] Hauser, Huhn, Knauss and Wiedmann could be more than satisfied with their efforts.

This did not end the story; the mountain still fascinated climbers by its shape and beauty, its cornices, flutings and formations. The north ridge appealed to many; it is an elegant route, and the traverse of the summit crest posed a high-standard challenge. The Japanese repeated Hauser's route in 1961, followed by a New Zealand party and two American expeditions, during one of which the American climber, Ed Bailley, died of pulmonary oedema on the edge of the Alpamayo glacier. A light party from California went to the mountain in 1965 and reached the north ridge after the usual difficulties in the icefall,

---

1. Map height at the date of the expedition in 1966; two subsequent parties, American and New Zealand, made plane table and theodolite readings of 19,610 feet and 19,510 feet respectively.

but they had then withdrawn, judging the climb too serious for a small party.

So now it was 1966, and our turn to add to the saga; the north side of the mountain had still to be climbed. I remembered Hauser had said that from the summit the way up from the north 'looked knife-edged and horribly dangerous'. To make our task more arduous, we hoped to make a full-colour, synchronised-sound 16mm cine film. I wondered how we should fare. On paper we were an experienced party, a blend of youth with older hands, but I now knew something of the psychological problems of human interaction during an expedition. Time and again expeditions have shown the foibles of human incompatibility, climbers who can enjoy each other's company on British or Alpine mountains quickly losing sympathy with one another in relationships constricted by expedition involvement. If things didn't go well I had only myself to blame, for the party had been gathered by Chris Bonington and me, with myself as leader only after much inner searching on my part.

It was becoming obvious that Chris was not going to join as planned. He had gone off to Ecuador a few weeks ahead of our party, on a photographic assignment for a magazine, but he should have been in contact long ago. As the days slipped by, it became worrying; something serious must have happened to detain a man like Chris, and throughout the expedition our fears grew as we received no news. It was with deep regret that we heard on our return to Colcas that his son had been drowned in Scotland. Chris had returned home immediately he received the news, to be with his wife.

My musings were interrupted by a swooping condor, largest bird of the Andes, then by Ned coming into view with John Amatt, the youngest and tallest member of our party, carrying the filming equipment. The ebullient Kelly, a television producer of wide experience but with no great climbing pretensions, was already making his presence felt. Somehow Ned gave the impression of being just a cheerful, tubby fellow out for laughs. In fact, his good humour and wit hide a deeply thoughtful person, a diplomat used to handling people and getting the best out of them, a talented performer in many fields, and physically fit. Everything augured well for a potentially first-class film; we had the manpower with a six-member party, the possibility of good filming conditions, the mountain's fame, the historical and geographical detail of the tropical region not far from the Amazon, and the wildlife of the country. We meant to capture it all, the toil and the thrills, the life of an expedition. We had one disadvantage: Ned was on his own as far as shooting the film and recording were concerned. I had shot 16mm film in the Himalaya but none of the rest of the party understood the techniques involved in film-making. It all depended on one man, and it was a big responsibility for we had much at stake. A thousand and one things could go wrong.

Ned and John dropped their equipment, grabbed mugs of tea and sought the shade alongside Dave and me. For once Ned was in a serious mood.

'Well, my leader, what do you think of her in the flesh?'

'The icefall looks difficult but the mountain is just not as I expected. It must have fallen over! I've seen lots of peaks more impressive than this one. Anyhow, we'll soon get a closer look, if the bloody donkeys ever arrive.'

At last round the corner staggered the first animal, looking truly pathetic, its knees buckling under a huge load, and soon we were surrounded by the beasts and their grinning drivers. 'Alpamayo, señor?' asked one of them.

'Si, si,' I grunted, picking up my pack and heading up the hill, hoping by setting a good example to keep the train moving instead of stopping there and then for the night. But we didn't get far before we had to stop because of thrown loads. This had been happening all along the march. Dave and I struggled to replace a load, slipping on the steep ground. Dave, a typical Scots climber, generous and good-natured under a dour, hard surface, really let fly with invective. For once it seemed to impress the drivers who actually hurried at their work, frightened by the bad humour of the stern-looking gringo.

The climb into the subsidiary valley proved the hardest of the day and it was a pleasure to see Roy Smith waiting ahead of us beside a small river. The site for base camp at last, and what an impressive place it was, with Santa Cruz towering above the upper valley, the Pilanco group in the opposite direction, and in the distance Champara, incredible peaks all.

The *burros* refused to cross the rushing stream and no amount of whipping or beating by the *arrieros* would move them. The RSPCA would be kept busy in the Peruvian mountains where mules are normally driven with ten-foot bull whips. In the end we offloaded the equipment and started to manhandle it across ourselves. The *burros* milled about, kicking up clouds of dust, while the drivers shouted and bawled at the top of their voices. I struggled to make myself heard above the din and insisted on paying off at once. The days are short in the Blanca; by six o'clock it is dark, and as soon as the sun sets the temperature shoots down and it begins to freeze. Paying off the *arrieros* in the last hour of daylight and trying to convince them they should set off immediately, back to the warmth of the hut by the lakeside, proved difficult. The drivers spoke only Quechua and we had none of their language, of which no dictionary exists because it has no written form. Ned tape-recorded and filmed the event as I paid off in a mixture of Spanish and Anglo-Saxon expletives. Later the tape had to be censored for use in the film; it gave the sound editors a good laugh, but at the time only the oaths seemed to be understood.

While this was going on the loads were moved and base camp established. I couldn't persuade the drivers to go, so left them on completion of payment and crossed the river to give Roy a hand with an immense load. By far the strongest member of our party, he had hoisted a bag on his back that lesser men couldn't move. He grinned as I ran to aid him. 'Just carry my half-frame camera, I can manage then by myself.' Handing over his most precious possession, he strode off with the 140-pound load as if it were nothing. I followed him, noting with relief the *arrieros* drifting slowly down the valley with their mules, obviously still not certain that this was what we meant them to do. I only hoped they had understood my request for them to come back in three weeks' time.

At last we were alone with our mountain. Behind us lay the months of effort: planning, fundraising, customs formalities, night after night working at a typewriter or collecting and packing food and equipment. That first night at base was incredibly beautiful; above our heads was the Southern Cross and about us the peaks of our dreams. These halcyon early days soon pass and then it is hard to recapture the first romanticism. As we sat round a blazing fire, I firmly etched the scene into my memory, knowing from experience that these were unrepeatable hours. Soon it was too cold even by the fire, and the warmth of a sleeping bag became preferable to a starlight tryst with my own feelings.

Next morning we rose late and the sun was high as Roy and I set out to prospect the route to the glacier. Immediately behind our camp a steep scree slope rose to the east, with rock buttresses at its head. From other expedition reports we knew that this must be the easiest way to cross the subsidiary ridge between us and our goal. I estimated our base height as 14,500 feet and the top of scree as 16,500 feet – 2,000 feet of hard slogging.

As Roy and I were leaving, there was a loud explosion. 'Good God! What is it?' My heart was pounding like a steam hammer.

Ned subsided in hysterics, 'It's the pneumatic blow-up tent, it's blown up!'

I had thought the night before, when John had been pumping away at the tent, that perhaps we ought to allow for the heat expanding the air more at this altitude than at sea level. The tent lay shattered, but luckily John had patches and rubber solution and vowed it would soon be as good as new.

John had made a brilliant job of his post as expedition equipment officer. Twenty-one years old, he had shown real flair as publicist as well as organiser; few suppliers had refused his approach on the lines that it was an honour to be invited to contribute their products to our famous expedition, a novel enough method. We must have been one of the best-equipped parties ever to visit the Andes; if good equipment was the arbiter, our success was assured.

The scree proved of the most tiresome kind as we slowly climbed its fine stones. I was on the look out for signs of previous parties and was relieved when after a thousand feet we found a rusty tin. My cough was proving troublesome and Roy had to keep waiting. 'You shouldn't have come,' he remonstrated.

'I know, I know,' I replied irritably. 'But I must get a look at the route for myself.' I coughed and coughed and envied Roy his strong physique, copybook of the layman's ideal adventurer. He bounded off up the scree, stripped to the waist, muscles gleaming and rippling in the sun. I must be mad, I thought, to be leader of a party with fitness like that in its ranks. However, my ego recovered as I recalled a favourite maxim, 'It's brain, not muscle, you need on big mountains', and I set off in the wake of 'The Corporal'. The scree reminded me of the Great Stone Chute in Skye, recalling earlier and less-organised mountain days. This chute narrowed at its head between enclosing rock walls and we could see that it ended at a series of rock buttresses.

The last part of the slope, with the smallest stones I have yet climbed, was torture, one pace up, one down. We traversed to the left and gained some hard snow lying in the shade and quite wintery, then kicked steps to the rock, which we scrambled up in a fever of excitement. Roy traversed left along ledges, while I tried to climb directly upwards. I made rapid progress over shattered rock, then stuck in a shallow groove on more solid ground. 'Just my luck,' I grumbled to myself. 'Roy will be up by now, and here am I stuck like a fool, balanced on tiny holds and can't get up or down.' But no, just to the left was a hidden finger jug; a quick pull and I was on easier rock, gasping and coughing, but driven upwards by that competitive urge known to all climbers but seldom acknowledged. Excitement gripped me; from the top of the buttress we would see Alpamayo clearly, one of the famous views; would it be as good as other parties had made out? I had to get there first, and was jubilant to see Roy's head emerge out of an icy groove below me. I shouted to him over my shoulder, scrabbling upwards with only 200 feet to climb. I was no match for the super-fit Smith however, who stormed past and ran the last section up a loose gully to the top.

'It's fabulous,' Roy gasped as I joined him. At first I was too dazzled by the brightness to make out the scene before me, then I too caught my breath at the sheer majesty of the Queen of the Blanca. There it was, Alpamayo, the perfect symmetrical pyramid, gleaming like a white cathedral in the bluest of skies. The kind of mountain a child might draw who had never seen one, Alpamayo of all the photographs and all the superlatives towered above our heads.

I looked down to its glacier sprawled at our feet. We were standing on what the Swiss had named the 'Col des Drus', at a height of 16,700 feet. To reach the glacier would mean descending easy slopes for hundreds of feet, a tiresome loss of height after the slog up the scree but at least a descent without difficulty. The icefall straight in front of us was impressive even from this distance. The leader of the Swiss expedition of 1948 had said that 'the crevasses were so big you could bury the Trocadero in them', and from our viewpoint it was easy to believe this. The glacier creaked and groaned like a beast in torment; the glaciers in this part of Peru are among the fastest moving in the world, and clearly the passage through the icefall would be our first major difficulty. Roy and I went down into what was the Alpamayo valley proper. It seemed obvious to us that the safest way through the icefall would be up at the valley's head where the ice flowed off, and below Quitaraju, a fine snow mountain of just over 20,000 feet. Surprisingly this mountain has been climbed several times since the first ascent by the ubiquitous Schneider; it is from its slopes that Alpamayo assumes its most beautiful form, a perfect trapezoid, even more beautiful than the pyramid shape above our heads.

Satisfied with our reconnaissance, we headed back to base and found some hard work had taken place in our absence. We were now established for a long and comfortable stay. From under the folds of the cooking tarpaulin came the aroma of a stew. The weather, so perfect earlier in the day, had changed; cloud was building up fast and soon it began to snow. The cloud always built up from the Amazon basin, from the east, but we were rarely to be troubled by its presence.

The whole party was keen to start operations in earnest. It is good for morale to keep things moving and, although the weather was threatening, activity was a must at the beginning of an expedition when everybody was bursting with enthusiasm. The problem was who to put in the lead. Clearly Roy should be in the vanguard but, thinking it over, I decided to ask Terry and Dave to start out next day, backed up by the others, to establish our first camp and from there to prospect a way through the icefall. They were much akin to each other, quiet and hard working. Dave I guessed would climb well on the ice and Terry had that essential big-mountain experience from the Himalaya in 1964. We should need plenty of help and manpower behind these two for film work would ensure that everybody had a worthwhile task and not just supporting roles. I didn't want to sound authoritative, and in any case few climbers like being told what to do. I left it to Dave and Terry to find the route, but suggested that they try as high up the valley as possible.

Next morning, in bad conditions, everybody but myself carried loads to establish our two icefall pioneers in a camp on the moraine of the glacier. Later the weather improved and I was able to sunbathe as I worked at the logistics of supplies, then I began to prepare a meal for Roy, Ned and John. Hardly was the fire lit when Roy came galloping in long before I expected. 'It really made Ned gasp when he saw the hill! He's decided to leave climbing films to men like Terray and Rébuffat in future and go in for the glamour stuff.'

'It's certainly impressive, that first view,' I conceded. 'But you should see Menlungste, it's twice the scale of these Andean peaks.' I was consciously playing the one-up game.

'Mount Kenya puts it in the shade too,' retorted Roy.

'Mount Kenya? You're kidding!'

'Not at all, you should see it from the plains.'

'I don't believe it,' I asserted in annoyed tones, thinking that the corporal knew little of the gentleman's code in one-up battles. John and Ned interrupted our by now heated argument, pushing in under the tarpaulin as snow began to fall once more.

'They've put camp low down the valley,' John reported. 'Terry insisted it should be by running water.'

'Sounds a good idea to me; it will save carrying fuel in the long run. How is it with you, Ned?'

'Well, to be truthful, I'll need the biggest stepladder in the world to get up that peak. It's steeper than the hills I'm used to. Auntie would not be pleased at me going up there!'

Next morning the four of us carried loads over to the moraine camp. Our acclimatisation was improving and we reached the camp quickly and dumped our burdens. We could see nothing of Dave or Terry on the icefall; mist lay over the whole glacier like a blanket. We soon tired of staring into the fleecy whiteness and retreated, racing at breakneck speed down the scree to our base.

The following day the weather was fine once more. Roy and John set out with more loads for Camp I, while Ned and I filmed the climb to the Col des Drus, working on establishment shots and panoramas. To get even better views of Alpamayo, if possible more beautiful sparkling in fresh snow, we traversed the ridge to a point several hundred feet north of the col, whence the mountain attained a perfection of symmetry. By the time we retraced our steps, Roy and John had gone back to base. Leaving the film equipment safely cached, we hurried down after them.

Roy and John were waiting with unhappy faces. Before we had time to ask why, Roy blurted out 'They're making a pig's ear of it between them! You know that couloir in the middle of the icefall, well, they're in there. What a route to try! They must be crazy. So far they've used ice stakes and fixed rope galore and aren't halfway.'

This was a jolt, not made easier by John's attempting to enlarge on Roy's report. Later I began to feel guilty, realising that it might not be our route-finders' fault; after all the weather had been bad all the time Dave and Terry had been at Camp I until this morning. From the col it was easier to spot a line through the icefall than from the camp. From there, the route they had chosen might appear easier. It was not the time that it would take to force this passage that mattered; we knew that the Japanese had been held up for nineteen days in the icefall in 1961, paradoxically because of dry conditions. No, our worry was safety. A party at the right time of day could perhaps pass quickly through, but to attempt to film in the middle of an avalanche couloir, day in, day out, sooner or later spelled disaster. We must find a safer alternative.

Roy asked to go over and join the other two on the moraine and look for a safer way. I had no alternative but to agree, and early next morning Roy, John and I crossed to Camp I in time to meet our pathfinders coming in, looking burnt and tired. I thought it might be difficult to dissuade them now that they had climbed so high, but their route was proving so slow and dangerous that they readily agreed we should try another way. Dave, as ever a willing horse, offered to accompany Roy next morning and have a look from higher up the glacier, enabling Terry to have a rest day. Looking up the couloir from which they had just returned, I felt relieved at this compromise; it looked evil and dangerous, obviously scoured by avalanche at regular intervals.

John and I returned to base once more, my cough becoming a monotonous accompaniment to every other minute. Ned was typically concerned for my welfare, pleading with me to treat the ailment more seriously, and asking, 'If you died who would look after my chilblains?' I didn't intend to miss the fun now and took massive doses of cough suppressant with obvious relish, acting out my role as expedition doctor.

Good news came next day. Roy and Dave, working on our suggested high route, had found a way through the icefall. They reported it was not without the threat of danger in several places from hanging séracs, and crevasses had to be crossed by flimsy bridges, but it would have been hard to find any route without some danger in that chaos of ice. We all agreed that Roy had done a first-class job, so much so that Dave and Terry returned happily next morning to retrieve all the gear from the couloir of avalanches.

The successful route through the icefall began at the head of the Alpamayo valley where stood a grim reminder of a previous tragic attempt on the mountain, Ed Bailley's cairn, on the place by the glacier where the American climber had succumbed to pulmonary oedema, a high-altitude condition caused by acclimatisation problems. Pulmonary oedema is prevalent in the Andes because it is so easy to go to high altitudes there; even bus routes ascend higher than Mont Blanc. All intending mountaineers in the range should know the condition's syndrome, and the precautions to be taken against this dreaded possibility.

The push forward was now a reality, but this spotlighted what was to become my acute worry – the liaison of filming and climbing parties. It seemed certain that, weather permitting, with our size and strength of party we should succeed in our climbing ambitions, but the film was another matter. A lung-bursting summit dash was no good here; if our film was to have its logical conclusion, the cameraman and all his accoutrements must be there too. This meant we could not allow our climbing party any lead; if necessary they must mark time, an idea that in good weather conditions appeals to few mountaineers. It was apparent that the film would in places double or treble the work involved, as it is necessary on occasion to shoot over the same ground several times: for every foot used in the final production several are wasted or cut. And there is of course the equipment to be carried. Cameraman on a high mountain is one of the hardest tasks anyone can undertake, and the operator soon begins to feel responsible for all the extra difficulties and trouble being caused. In short, the cameraman needs encouragement from all concerned. I am afraid that at times our party gave Ned a rough passage, but happily he always rose above our pettiness.

Communication is probably the secret of good leadership; by the end of our expedition I had lost this essential requirement for many reasons, perhaps the main one being that, apart from Ned and myself, the others had never really understood what would be involved in attempting to make a high-standard film. The front men soon began to find filming a chore, a feeling that built up over the weeks. Perhaps they had a right to feel this, for they were the people who suffered most from the slowness of our advance.

Henceforth our route from base descended from the Col des Drus to Bailley's cairn, cutting out any more supply carries to Camp I which was well stocked. For a few days everybody hauled supplies to the new position ready for onward transport through the icefall, then the whole party moved into Camp I on the moraine which already housed Roy, Dave and Terry. We had now split firmly into two parties of three: spearhead the three original inhabitants of the moraine camp, filming party Ned, John and myself. Three is not a particularly good number for climbing but somehow we seemed happiest working this way.

In their prospecting Roy and Dave had stopped above the icefall on slopes below the North Col, and it now needed a further reconnaissance to climb to the proposed site for our next camp at the col and to estimate what lay ahead. The morning after we had all moved into Camp I, Dave and Terry set out to make this inspection, leaving their tent at an unusually early hour in order to climb the slopes to the col before the sun made this an agonising toil. The camera party, strengthened by Roy, set out at the more reasonable hour of five o'clock to begin the work of filming in the icefall and roping up difficult or dangerous sections. Five o'clock is still an uncomfortably early hour to move out; it means rising around four to cook in a freezing tent where the only warmth is to be found inside a sleeping bag, wearing a down jacket and every stitch of clothing one owns. Lighting the stove is a trial, and once it is lit, although life becomes slightly better, the ice which has formed overnight melts off the tent walls and showers one with water. But the hardest thing of all is trying to force any form of food down the gullet. Some, but very few, climbers can eat hearty breakfasts at this hour; the majority seem to be able to stomach a hot drink and little else. If I take more than a drink, I am invariably sick once I start to climb, a malady which soon affects the whole party – if a single member is vomiting it usually ends with one and all doing the same.

Dawn in the Andes is indescribable, but one rarely bothers to notice; as we tramped along the moraine slopes towards Bailley's cairn, it was the last thing my eyes paid heed to. Five o'clock is no hour for romanticising, but rather the time for counting the cost and harbouring evil thoughts against one's companions. We reached the cairn in silence, but now the sun had struck the pyramid of Alpamayo and clearly etched the gigantic cornices of the north ridge, along our proposed route. The cornices are always largest on the west (our) side of the Andean mountains, for the prevailing winds and the intense radiation of the sun work together to produce continuous formations, large and precarious. The cornices of the north ridge looked like huge Swiss rolls, and even from the glacier's edge one could appreciate the unusual feathery consistency of their snow caused by the moist prevailing winds from the Amazon basin in the east.

After a rest and some film work, we set foot on the glacier, which creaked and groaned as if waiting for its breakfast – us if we fell into one of its open crevasses. The first part was straightforward as an easy gully led from the flat, dry bed of the glacier and through the first séracs. Our crampons crunched and bit the ice, and now the first rays of the sun reached us. This was the time to start being human again, to talk and laugh and even to sing, though the altitude of 16,000 feet soon put paid to that. We halted at the gully's head, ready to begin a traverse into the more chaotic sections of the icefall; here was an outstanding camera position and Ned insisted on stopping to erect camera on tripod. Bubbling with enthusiasm, we could all appreciate the uniqueness of the setting; framed between the séracs was Tayapampa, a shapely ice mountain and northerly neighbour of Alpamayo. We had made sure that our clothing was colourful, and we must have been a vivid sight for any eye at six in the morning with orange rucksacks, red sweaters, powder-blue anoraks and the like. All this helped our film contrasts but was apt to be too much for comfort in the midday heat. At least we could all understand the need for tripod filming; to try to keep a camera steady above 16,000 feet and hold one's breath while shooting by hand is nearly impossible.

After the traverse we entered a mad wilderness of ice – caverns, bridges, towers, gigantic ice-buildings – a moving, twisted world full of hidden menace and obvious dangers. There was no way through other than by walking under tottering séracs; either one accepted the risk or abandoned the ascent. A short descent and we were confronted by a monstrous leaning tower of ice with a narrow snow bridge at its base, poised over one of the biggest crevasses I had seen anywhere, and subsequently called 'the Cat Walk'. On first view I had to confirm with Roy that this was where the route actually went. It must have been 200 feet from our side to safe ground on the other, and the whole passage was menaced by hanging curtains of icicles, which had outstanding beauty for film purposes but lethal danger for the climber. If one of the larger stalactites should break off and hit someone, it would be the end, for they were thirty feet long and thicker than a man's body. I have heard many mountain passages described by the cliché, 'a sword of Damocles', but if any deserved the description it was surely this one.

'We must put rope across,' I said to Roy. 'If anything falls while one of us is crossing, it will be the chop!'

Roy was soon at work smashing an ice stake into the ice at our feet; next moment we nearly fell into a crevasse which opened under the shock of Roy's massive blows. 'Sorry!' he grinned as we leapt back. Roy drove the stake home into firm ice, then set out on the dangerous crossing, uncoiling fixed line as he went. I winced when he stopped in the middle and hammered another three-foot stake into the base of the ice tower itself, but he was soon over and 250 feet of rope was stretched across the traverse. To the purist climber this may sound like taking safety too far, but the passage had to be filmed from the middle to get the best result and both hands would be needed for the camera. Our cameraman was visibly disturbed by the prospect of filming in the middle of such a dangerous passage. 'Come on, it's easy,' John and I urged, and technically it was, but one dared not look too closely at the bridges over green depths. We descended an ice groove, crossed into a chimney formation and reached a cave in the ice tower itself. Here was the place to film from and we belayed Ned to a piton to begin work while we continued crossing with our loads. The camera whirred, and once again I marvelled at the operator's dedication; while climbing he was often visibly 'gripped', but once filming started the dangers or difficulties of a situation were forgotten – it was the work that mattered.

The last fifty feet of the traverse were along a wide snow bridge that was taken at the gallop. All this section was menaced by icicles; though beautiful I hated them and their dagger points as I hurried under that curtain of spite. Gasping and choking we landed at the end of the bridges, to join Roy on safe ground. John was immediately behind me, and then we brought Ned across.

The altitude was affecting all of us but Roy who had already been higher than this; he puffed a pipe and took our loads off our backs. The sun's power magnified many times by the snow and ice was burning us badly, covered in glacier cream though we were; I had the distinct feeling my skin was frying, our throats were parched and lips began to crack. No one who has not been in full sun in an icefall can properly appreciate this frying sensation and its horrible discomfort. We hurried across to the shade of a monster sérac and huddled under its icy base, only to begin shivering almost immediately.

We were over halfway through the icefall, and waiting round the corner lay the last major difficulty. Dave Bathgate called it 'the Sugar Bowl'; it reminded him of that humble utensil and the ice in its depths had an unusual sugary consistency. We moved to the edge of the bowl and gazed down; it was indeed an impressive obstacle. The route lay in a semicircle but first one had to descend a hundred feet into its bowels, then a traverse led round its inner rim by way of slender ice bridges, followed by three crevasses in a row and finally a steep snow slope up for 150 feet to a cornice which was taken direct, out over the upper rim of the bowl. It was not as dangerous as the Cat Walk but still had plenty of menace, in that it meant trusting the flimsiest of bridges.

'More fixed rope?' I suggested wistfully.

'It's not as bad as it looks from here,' Roy informed us.

'I think you had better rope the bridges,' Ned interjected. 'It looks a difficult place for carrying and filming.'

John wanted to see if we could arrange some kind of Tyrolean bridge from one side of the rim to the other, 'It would make a great film sequence hanging out on a rope a hundred feet above that lot.'

'It's the altitude that's got him,' Ned laughed. In fact we did spend some energy on this idea later, but somehow when we finally managed to stretch a rope from rim to rim, anchored round ice bollards, no one would volunteer to swing out into space and make the crossing.

During the discussion Roy had pragmatically hammered in a stake and dropped a rope into the bowl, and down we went. It was eerie inside what was plainly a large crevasse, and the ice scenery was as if from a moon-shot sequence. There were no second thoughts about the need for rope over the rickety bridges. Roy and I traversed round them and arrived on a hog's back of ice in the middle of the bowl. Here we placed an anchorage in the form of a stake, then, fixing rope as we climbed, leapt the crevasses and ascended the steep snow leading out of the basin. John came past and climbed the slope above our heads, out over the projecting cornice via the groove cut and enlarged on previous ascents. When Roy and I joined John we were above the icefall on a flat snow plateau – the monster lay conquered at our feet.

We had been hearing voices – Dave and Terry returning from their reconnaissance. Dave's Stetson appeared, a good investment for it gave first-class protection from the sun. Then we saw Terry loping down. We were right under the west face of the mountain, and immediately above us rose the only piece of rock visible on the whole mountainside from our moraine camp, the diamond buttress. This was a truly pleasant situation after the claustrophobic icefall; a cool breeze blew and the view was extensive. I felt sorry for Ned down in the bowl, crouched over his camera.

Dave and Terry looked happy and Terry, normally quiet and taciturn, was quite loquacious as they met us. 'It's a piece of duff!' he reported.

'The ridge looks easy.' Dave did not seem quite as certain; perhaps after the business in the icefall he didn't want to commit himself.

'We'll be on the top in a couple of days, once we put a camp on the col,' Terry insisted. 'What a view from there – mountains everywhere, and down in the next valley on the east side is a fabulous green lake.'

'What about the cornices?' I asked.

'Well, the whole ridge is just one big cornice this side, but over on the east face a band of rock runs parallel to the ridge for several hundred feet. If we make for that, we should be safe,' Dave replied.

This was good news, and we happily watched Dave and Terry go down into the Sugar Bowl, just at the right moment for Ned to film them. The light is a real problem for filming in the Andes; once the sun is high in the sky, filming is not really practicable, especially around noon when there is little shadow and blinding light. This lack of contrast is a worry, particularly on cut-in shots to match earlier sequences.

From our plateau we had a clear line of sight to Quitaraju and could just see over the Col des Drus to Santa Cruz. Looking down the Alpamayo valley we could follow our whole march from the descent off the high passes. I could well imagine how good the view must be up at the North Col and couldn't wait to get there; however, it was time to start down. The thought of the Sugar Bowl and the Cat Walk was not to be relished. Later we became blasé and crossed much later in the morning, in retrospect a dangerous practice, but fortunately we were allowed to go unscathed, although a large avalanche fell over our route during our descent at the end of the expedition. Dangers faced every day dull one's appraisal of them; indeed a few days later we happily stood filming hour after hour where originally the mere creaking of ice had made us catch our breath.

We collected Ned, cached the film equipment and loads and hurried down to our tents on the moraine.

It was time for big decisions. The plan evolved was for Roy, Dave and Terry to move immediately to the col while John, Ned and I acted as porters to lift loads to Camp II and as camera crew. The front men would get to work on the ridge and prepare a way to the north summit with fixed lines, so that this section could be filmed and, even more important, to ensure that it was feasible to put cameraman, camera and tripod high enough to film the final traverse along the mountain's crest to the summit – the highlight of our climb. Once we had climbers at the col, which was in direct line with Camp I, we could bring into play one of the important new aids to expedition mountaineering, namely, two-way transistor radios.

The mountain seemed to wear a friendly countenance next morning. I had been surprised at Terry's assessment of the ridge, but we kept assuring each other of an easy climb and believed our own stories. Part of our plan was that the spare man at the col should come down each day, solo, and collect one of the loads dumped above the icefall. Only two climbers could work on the ridge at a time, and the slopes down to the icefall, though steep, were straightforward. The film-and-porter team, after that day, would carry from Camp I right through to the col. This was a long way; it could take seven hours or more, most of the time in scorching sun.

The front men would have no luxury life, eating only dehydrated food, but at least they had the interest of finding and preparing the route and climbing on steep rock and ice, always moving into unknown territory. Those behind have far less responsibility and better food and rest, but the monotony of carrying loads every day over the same ground, if we hadn't had the film to think about, would have been sheer drudgery.

Roy, Terry and Dave, once established at Camp II, worked away at the ridge while we filmed, humped loads, and sunbathed down on the moraine. Progress from our point of view seemed agonisingly slow, but until the ridge was fully roped and ready to climb and film, it was pointless to put six men at the col to eat twice as much as our present party of three.

It was at this stage that contact began to be lost between us, that essential contact of understanding in small matters, mutual trust and good will, which makes the difference between happy relationships and a bickering group of individuals. The party at the front resented our hints of slow progress, doubtless feeling we were having an easy time and in no position to judge. When I did arrive at the col with my first carry, I could appreciate the difficulties; from the col the ridge didn't appear too difficult, but when one moved northwards towards Tayapampa it was possible to see the whole ridge in perspective – 2,000 feet of steep climbing with the last 700 feet up an ice gully and steep snow slopes. It could have been climbed quickly in a day, but to climb it fixing rope every inch of the way was a different matter, particularly on the upper section where ropes could only be fixed to three-foot channels driven fully into the ice.

All the same, the carry to the col was a tiring struggle for us, especially as we were attempting to film as well as carry. One particularly heavy load took the combined efforts of John and myself to move it up to Camp II. John carried this sixty-pound load over most of the last section, and I felt annoyed later when he was not given any credit by the others for his efforts.

One can make much of these things on high mountains. Men even at 18,000 feet are the same animals as at sea level, with the same weakness, the same strength, but the environment is different, the social veneer is dropped completely, and the qualities of self-sacrifice and of selfishness appear undisguised. Our party were in no way untypical and I was no exception to being selfish.

We had our lighter moments. One day Ned was filming directly above a bergschrund on the steepest part of the slopes leading to the col. Concentrating on the picture in his viewfinder, Ned ran out on to the exposed slope for a better position, minus axe and unroped. Finishing his reel of film, he suddenly realised his situation, balanced above the void on crampon points. 'Jesus! How did I get here?' he screamed, clinging to his precious camera and leaning almost flat against the slope. 'Help, for God's sake, help!' He wasn't joking and I had to act quickly; running across to give him an axe and a rope had me gasping, but Ned soon recovered once he had a belay. 'Auntie rescued again by the old consumptive,' was his comment.

Our evenings down on the moraine were good entertainment. Part of the film equipment was a tape recorder and we had several pre-recorded tapes: symphonies, *The Goon Show*, the Beatles. We also played back our own recordings of the expedition; these caused great merriment for the language was invariably bad in tense situations. We made up songs, tried impersonations, and Ned gave us the benefit of his years in television with stories and impressions. Laurence Olivier as Richard III became our favourite: 'now is the winter of our discontent' will for ever conjure up for me the inside of a mountain tent, tucked in sleeping bag and wearing every stitch of clothing, talking through the long Andean nights.

Then came a panic. 'Running out of rock pegs' – Dave's voice on the two-way radio.

'You can't be,' I retorted. 'It's a bleeding ice mountain!'

'You forget we're following the rock band out on the east face.'

'Sorry, I get you, of course. How many do you need?'

'Well, the band is about ten rope lengths, so we could do with another dozen or so.'

'It means going back to base. Can't you make do with ice pitons?' I suggested hopefully.

'No, the rock is bad and the cracks poor. We need some American hardware for this job.'

'OK. I'll go down now and come up again tonight. John can bring them up first thing in the morning and meet Roy at the top of the icefall. That way we won't lose much working time.' Off I raced, up to the Col des Drus, then down the rock buttress and the scree to base. It only took an hour: our load carrying had not been in vain.

We had hired a young Quechua Indian boy to guard our camp while we were away, armed with an ancient muzzle-loading rifle. We had laughed at his weapon until we saw him in action; a marksman with lightning reflexes, he had killed a *vizcacha* (Andean hare) with a single shot before our eyes. After this we treated him with respect whenever he held his rifle, feeling our camp safe from raids by 'El Bandidito' with young Daniel standing guard. 'Tea, Señor?' he smiled, handing me a pint of it. This was a surprise for it was the first work he had done since we hired him. He seemed incapable of using a tin opener and washing up. I heaped praise on him, hoping that whenever we returned to base in future he would repeat the service.

I picked up the bag of rock pitons lying at base and set off on the return journey. All went well until I reached the rock buttress where the first bad weather for many days arrived in the form of a heavy thunderstorm. I froze in a hail shower as I climbed the rocks, fought my way through a snow blizzard to the Col des Drus, then sploshed in torrential rain to arrive at moraine camp in the dark. The weather, as so often after a thunderstorm, was set fair again next morning, and John delivered the sorely needed pitons into Roy's waiting hands above the icefall.

Progress accelerated at last, and two days later the route had been prepared to within a hundred feet or so of the north summit. It was time to move the whole party to the North Col and, regretfully now, we said goodbye to moraine camp, leaving a single tent erected on a platform for emergency, a splash of colour in an otherwise drab world of glacier debris. The col party were having a rest day while we quickly moved up to join them. The final stages of our carefully planned and executed climb could begin.

Once at the col, the air of tension that had built up between the two parties dissipated and Ned soon had everybody laughing. We were well placed to achieve our objectives – summit and film, the weather was the best I had seen anywhere in the mountains, and our present camp was a haven of security, pitched in the most impressive of mountain settings – a resting place fit for the gods.

Towards sunset I climbed above the tents on to the col itself, alone in an ice kingdom. Northwards lay Tayapampa, the Pilanco group and Champara, eastwards the multi-summit Pucahirca and behind that peak the Amazon basin, dark and mysterious; westwards the view was dominated by Santa Cruz, and lastly, due south and immediately above our tents, was the north ridge of Alpamayo, steeped in climbing history. Its fangs were drawn now, with fixed lines in place, but we still had to climb and film it, and reach the true summit 700 feet beyond its crest.

After the three weeks of slow build up, everyone wanted to climb the mountain there and then, without further delay. Roy and Dave were at fever pitch to make the attempt, and Ned needed an ascent for long shots as well as getting the cameras up with a summit party. It didn't need any planning – tomorrow must be the day.

Roy and Dave were away before dawn, followed by Terry and myself as soon as it was light enough for Ned to film our departure. Ned then set out with John along the ridge towards Tayapampa to shoot our ascent in long focus. We tied on to the rope and I took a firm belay as Terry stepped out over the first hanging cornice and traversed on to the east face towards the rock band. Out on the cornice the exposure was considerable and to climb off it required a slightly downward movement across clear ice; here the fixed ropes started and I thankfully clasped them and moved up to join Terry. Large steps were cut in the ice and it was child's play except for the fact that we were on or under the biggest cornices any of us had seen. The altitude began to affect me as I tried to move too quickly. Terry had been at over 18,000 feet for a week but I was fresh to this height; it brought on my cough with a vengeance. One more rope length and we reached the security of rock.

'It made a lot of difference, this rock band,' Terry remarked. 'Pitons into rock are more my idea of safety than ice stakes into bad ice.' Looking upwards I could appreciate his comment; the rock band zigzagged its way up through ice, in some places thirty feet across, in others only a foot wide or completely overlaid by snow. How fortunate we were that so much of it was bared – over a thousand feet. Another year we might not have been so lucky.

The band was shattered red granite, loose and friable, but the angle was such that most of the way one could put feet against rock and swarm up the fixed ropes, using a prusik clamp for aid. A different story when Dave, Terry and Roy had first climbed the band which they judged 'Severe' in standard. After another hundred feet the rock was overlaid with ice and the route traversed to the west and out on to cornices over the west face. I prusiked up and landed in an ice cave into the wall of which were two ice stakes buried to their hilts, for belaying and hanging a descent rope for quick returns down the face and back to the tents. Terry pointed out the finer points of this descent. 'Look out over the face,' he ordered. I hung out on the rope over a huge cornice and drop. 'Can you see the bergschrund?' I could make it out about 300 feet below. 'Well, it's a twenty-foot leap downward to clear it and pretty gripping!' I peered up to my right and could just discern a faint break in the cornice line – was that where the Swiss had fallen? What an escape! The fall line from that point landed in the basin where our own tents nestled; if they had missed this they would have gone down into the icefall and certain death.

Another ice passage and we were back on rock. The sun was fully on us now and I moved like a man in a dream, drained of all the energy I had possessed earlier in the day. Actually we were climbing fast although we never caught sight of Roy or Dave, and I had to keep asking Terry for a rest. We were over 19,000 feet and well on our way to the north summit. Just before the rock petered out we came upon a second cave. We crawled inside for a breather and Terry showed me where he had found a hammer-axe embedded in the ice; it could only have belonged to the French, perhaps to Kogan who had discovered this very haven when things looked their worst in the blizzard. Four men in this icy grotto for a night … my heart warmed to the initiative of that team of French aces.

Above the cave the rock band ended and we embarked on a traverse leftwards to an ice couloir. I suppose it would have been too easy if the rock band had been bared to the summit, but I left the rock feeling as a shipwrecked sailor might on abandoning land he had just swum for. The traverse was easy and Terry climbed past into the gully, set at fifty degrees and pure ice. After one rope length it became steeper still, and I suppose the next 400 feet had an average angle of sixty degrees. Terry led cheerfully, using the ropes dangling down in absolute trust. One section had a vertical lip and even with a rope fixed it was a strenuous pull out and over this projection. I appreciated more and more the French team's performance and why our own front men had taken so long to prepare the route.

The ropes made it straightforward, but near the top of the ridge my heart sank when one of the ice stakes popped out of the ice as I pulled on to a belay platform to join Terry. 'Don't go to pieces,' he laughed. 'The ropes are all joined together in one continuous length, and the corporal has driven a three-foot stake into solid ice at the top. He broke three hammer-axes belting it home, but it would hold you, me and everybody else at once if it had to!'

We decided to have a rest, and I looked back whence we had come; far below I could see the tents and along the ridge northwards Ned crouched over a camera, filming our progress. I saw with alarm that the filming position was actually a giant cornice; both Ned and John were out over a dangerous drop. We shouted ourselves hoarse but it was no good, they couldn't hear us and they happily continued their work.

'Must press on,' I suggested to Terry, and off he led up the last sections of ice, which were the steepest of all. Suddenly the slope eased back and we arrived at the top of the north ridge and the end of the fixed rope. An easy traverse, sinking deep into snow, and we had reached the north summit of Alpamayo. We were on the very crest of the mountain at nearly 20,000 feet and along its edge, over 600 feet away and possibly 200 feet higher, was the true summit. We could at last see our goal but between us and its arrow-tip of ice lay some of the most horrifying ground I have seen on a mountain – mushrooms of ice, knife-edged and corniced ridges, weird formations the like of which we had never before encountered.

At our feet was a coffin-type trench cut in the snow and inside were Dave and Roy's rucksacks. Terry and I were to enlarge this into a shelter of some dimensions and leave in it our loads containing food, stove and bivouac equipment, to serve as a supply dump for future filming operations, and for Roy and Dave if they took so long to reach the true summit that they had to bivouac.

We looked expectantly along the switchback of a ridge but couldn't see anyone; what had happened to our teammates? Terry and I moved along a little way to enlarge our vision; from there the crest plunged into a crevasse set on the ridge itself. This was followed by an ascending knife edge which swung to the east into a minor peak of its own, then there was a sizeable drop into a fissure directly under a mushroom of ice. This last looked impossible to get round, with overhung sides and composed of unstable feathery *névé*. Voices came from the rift under the mushroom, voices which floated across as if we were out on a fine summer's day in our own lowly homeland hills and not perched on an ice crest at nearly 20,000 feet in the Andes.

Dave emerged from the fissure and attacked the mushroom. This was the tensest part of the whole expedition and Terry and I froze in our steps, willing Dave round this fearsome obstacle. Balancing on crampon points he gingerly cut away, fashioning a groove in the mushroom itself. Underneath him the ice plunged thousands of feet down the south-west face. Working swiftly with his short axe, he prepared a channel big enough to take his body, then swung boldly on to the side of the bulbous formation. We could only hold our breath, privileged to watch an ice technician of the first order dealing with an exceptional problem. From the rift we heard Roy's voice urging caution; at least Dave knew that if anything did go wrong he was tied to one of the strongest of men who would do his utmost to save him. Dave balanced off the mushroom's side on to a knife-edge of snow; he was round and safely off the weirdie but the next section looked the crux of the climb. Above his head was the summit edifice, standing proud like a giant arrow; to reach the tip he had to stride a steep ice groove to a col, then he would be out of sight, but the final thirty feet of the summit tip was obviously the steepest climbing of the whole ascent.

Roy began to sing a tuneless dirge, interspersed with occasional shouts of encouragement; we could hear as plainly as if we sat beside him. Dave disappeared and we waited for his reappearance with dry mouths, as tense as if we had been leading ourselves. A few moments, then over the top of the mushroom appeared Dave's Stetson and his flashing axe cutting into the summit tip itself. Eighty-degree snow is not pleasant to climb anywhere in the world, but here there was no other way. As Dave said later, he climbed up 'by preparing footholds and handholds that would just have to do'. Roy had tied a second rope length on and the lead was into a double century of feet. Twenty feet to go. 'Oops!' Dave slid down three feet as the snow gave way, but fortunately he had his axe buried into soft whiteness. It was no place for a fall, balanced out on the Amazon face of the mountain above 5,000 feet of space.

Dave confessed later that he nearly gave up at this point. We, aware of the great lead we were witnessing and its gravity, urged him on with all our willpower. Next moment it was over, he was balanced like a dwarf on the topmost ice of Alpamayo, a dream had come true, our expedition had reached what so many parties had failed to attain.

The summit was so small that Dave had to climb a short way down the opposite side before Roy could try to join him. Dave ran a fixed rope back down the steep summit wall, tied round the tip itself. 'Well, either it will come down for certain or it's safer than it looks,' I thought as Roy tested it to the utmost, pulling up the final wall, but rope and summit stayed in position for Roy to stand, a red blotch, on the tip beside the black dot that was Dave.

We clicked away with cameras and Terry was obviously sorry not to be in the summit party. 'Let's go?' he pleaded.

'No, someone has to climb it for the film and none of the others may feel like repeating or making that climb. We'll come up again in a couple of days.'

Terry hid his disappointment and showed as ever his willingness to be accommodating and try his utmost for the expedition's aims. I was worried over the prospect of filming this last section; the cameras must come just beyond the north summit for a chance of successful coverage. It would need every ounce of determination if we were to succeed.

We waited until Dave and Roy were off the summit and safely back inside the rift; they were climbing strongly and didn't need any help from us. Shouting our congratulations, we set off down.

I am afraid I was a passenger on that descent; the altitude affected me to such an extent that I could hardly move. 'I'm knackered,' I kept telling Terry in between coughing and vomiting.

'Take your time. It's still early and we'll be down in a couple of hours,' he replied. I had climbed with Terry since he was a youth; although small, he is wiry and strong, and as careful on a mountain as any climber I have been with. I was in good hands, and he shepherded me down the north ridge slowly, a rope length at a time.

It was with relief I reached the abseil down the west face, so dreaded when seen earlier in the day. It proved an easy slide down to finish with. Even the leap to clear the bergschrund was negotiated swiftly, with the indifference known to tired men. Dave and Roy were on the abseil before Terry and I had reached the camp. We stopped and shouted our news to Ned and John, long returned from their filming, and cooking in the tents. Ned came out with a mug of tea and thankfully I grasped this victory offering – of all gifts the best!

Soon we were all safely resting at the camp. We had made it – and by rights we should have been pleased with ourselves. Somehow I felt hollow inside; at that moment it did not seem much of a victory. We had been on the mountain from 17 June till that day, 9 July – over three weeks, a long time to take for such a climb. We had placed 1,700 feet of rope in position on the ridge, and used stakes and pitons galore. Lying in my sleeping bag that night and thinking the climb over, I realised that this preparation was what had taken time, but it was entirely necessary for filming requirements. Here was the dilemma: one cannot have an elegant ascent and an award-winning film, the two are incompatible.

The next day was spent filming on the ridge, posing for close-ups, balancing on ice, cutting steps, climbing the rock band. After several hours' filming, we reached the cave with the abseil rope fixed in position, and decided to call it a day. At the end of the descent Ned nearly came to grief. Jumping off the lip of the bergschrund he disappeared, rope and all, straight into its icy depths. What a plummet! Luckily he landed astride a narrow bridge of snow, still attached to the abseil rope. Roy, who had stood by for such an emergency, fished him out bodily, none the worse for his fall but badly shaken.

Food now became our worry. We were using up supplies fast, and argument raged when I insisted on rationing our remaining stocks. Food more than any other topic – sex, climbing, home or comfort – dominates conversation in high mountain life. Existence is so basic in that situation, and human fuel is the most important consideration.

The second day after our initial success, still in perfect weather, found us setting off again for the summit. Terry and I were in the glamorous task of film stars; the others had the unenviable job of film crew to Ned's cameraman. Cameras, tripod, film were all cheerfully shouldered and slung on backs, behind Terry and me. The timing was important and we had to work closely as a team. Without the fixed ropes, filming would have been impossible; as it was, on some of the handheld work Ned was near to collapse through holding his breath while shooting. Everyone gave of his best, and just at the right time of day, into the afternoon with shadows lengthening, we reached the north summit.

Cloud began to build up from the Amazon; there was not a moment to lose. Camera and tripod were carried quickly along the crest, with Ned belayed by Roy in the most exposed positions. Filming began immediately Terry and I started out on the last lap to the summit.

It was every bit as difficult as it had looked, but we were following Dave's well-prepared route, with a fixed line to make for. I could only marvel at Dave's skill as I crawled round the ice mushroom and struggled up the steep snow wall on to the summit tip, protected from above by Terry who had led our rope on this part. It was an out-of-this-world situation, balanced on that incredible top. A light mist blew across, concealing our view and camera team, then just as swiftly it cleared. We could see so much that it would take hours to describe: Huascarán, the highest mountain in Peru, Huandoy, Taulliraju and a hundred others. It was all stored in the mind never to be forgotten, as clear today as it was then.

Dave decided to repeat his ascent and agreed to lead John. This was a bonus for Ned who could film their ascent as well, in case the shots of Terry and me had faults. As our two ropes crossed each other, it was a boisterous occasion, with much shouting and laughter.

Back on the north summit, Ned informed us that his film stock had run out, not one foot to spare: good budgeting and, as they say, it was either 'in the can' or useless. Freed of all yokes, the descent began in high humour and turned into a madcap race to see who could get down first. Ned, who had put so much into his filming, could not stand the pace; he must have thought it a crazy stunt to be engaged in. Roy patiently stayed behind with him and, just as Terry had looked after me when I was suffering from altitude sickness, Roy carefully watched Ned down the ropes behind the fleeing horde. We arrived breathless at the tents after swallow-diving the bergschrund. Soon everyone was off the mountain for good; it was nearly all over.

One or two of the party were clearly sick of filming, the food rationing and the over-close contact of their companions. It was with obvious relief that the film was carefully parcelled up and plans laid for a quick evacuation down to base and its prized delights of solid food.

Next morning everyone was awake and working before dawn. Tents were downed, bulging loads prepared and packs hoisted up for the final descent off the mountain. Roy, Dave, John and Terry were first away, leaving Ned and me to follow at a more leisurely pace. Ned was in high spirits and in retrospect he had reason to be; his film, so carefully planned and executed, was to be a success, and throughout the expedition he had done more than his share of work, especially load carrying.

We lounged, talked and gazed at the view, reluctant to be leaving this basin that had been the scene of some of the best mountain days of our lives. A little later than was probably wise, we started down, bowed as the others had been under heavy loads. On the slopes above the icefall I suffered the worst attack of coughing of my life and a blood vessel burst in my nose. Blood poured out of my mouth and nose, upsetting Ned more than myself. When we could move again, we had an accident in the icefall. Rounding the Sugar Bowl, one of the bridges collapsed and Ned, plus precious film, plunged into a crevasse. After his fall into the bergschrund, he must have thought he was fated.

I managed to hold him, but he had damaged a ligament in his leg and sprained an ankle. He had difficulty extricating himself and getting back to solid ground, and the rest of the Bowl was taken with great caution. Luckily John had waited for us, a thoughtful act for which in our predicament we were grateful. We must have looked a sight – Ned limping badly and my face covered with blood; from our appearance we could have fallen down the slopes above the icefall. When we reached the Cat Walk, part of the overhanging ice tower had just avalanched. Our initial fear of its danger was proved correct; the fixed lines were buried and it was a more hazardous crossing than ever, balancing over ice blocks resting on the bridges. John confirmed that Dave, Roy and Terry were safely through; he had watched them cross before the avalanche. Only the knowledge that we had to cross spurred me on; gritting my teeth I jumped and bridged from block to block. I hardly dared breathe as first John and then Ned came over to join me, aided only by the moral support of a rope. Then began for Ned a painful descent of the lower part of the icefall. His ankle was swelling up like a balloon, but he determinedly kept going. We moved slower and slower, suffering in the intense heat, for it was midday already. Finally, in the late afternoon, we struggled off the glacier bed and up on to the moraine.

It doesn't do to relax before the valley is reached! A moment's carelessness is often harshly repaid. We were lucky, but not so lucky that Ned and I had not to stay at moraine camp for several days before he could walk again. The rest of the party had gone straight through to base camp and, while Ned was recovering, they moved all the spare equipment down from the moraine to base, ready for the day when we could start the trek back to civilisation.

The expedition had in fact achieved finality. It was all over and, due to transport and petty argument, disintegrated. In retrospect I blame nobody but myself. It is the leader's responsibility to make sure this doesn't happen; personal example is the key factor in avoiding this kind of ill feeling. The leadership of the Alpamayo party had meant much to me, and I think in fairness to myself the planning and organisation which I directed had been good. I must still take the blame for allowing the expedition to reach a low level of comradeship and ill will.

I have said before that one can make too much of these things: all the members of the party are still friends, and I know that each one would gladly relive the adventure tomorrow, given the chance.

In the end our efforts proved worthwhile. One evening in October 1967, the telephone rang from Geneva airport and Ned's voice boomed cheerfully out of the earpiece. He was on his way home from the 1967 Trento Festival of Mountain Films. 'Well, old son, we have won,' he calmly reported. 'We were awarded the Mario Bello trophy for mountain films.' Yes, our film, *The Magnificent Mountain*, the film we had all toiled so much to make, was the success we had dared to hope. I could only choke a 'Well done, Ned!' at the time, but whenever I see the film now I am transported away from my daily round, back to that magic land of Peru, and to our mountain – Alpamayo.

To be truthful, it never gleamed brighter than the day Ned and I turned our backs painfully on our moraine camp, Ned limping, I bent under a heavy load. Above our heads shone Alpamayo, a beautiful thing in a beautiful world.

10 Granite Walls and Iron Curtains – Yosemite and the High Tatra

'Man is a tool-using animal ... without tools he is nothing, with tools he is all.'

(Thomas Carlyle)

I walked slowly down the valley towards Camp 4, stopping to rest every little while to look at the scenery and wipe the sweat from my eyes. My rucksack was bulging with equipment, souvenirs and presents I had collected on my way from Peru. I had flown to Mexico City, then hitch-hiked many hundreds of miles to Yosemite Valley in California. The journey by myself had been a good antidote to the strains of over-close contact with human beings that an expedition imposes.

The last three miles down the road seemed an eternity but, trudging along, my mind was occupied with questions and contradictions, and wonderment at the people and places I had seen: Machu Picchu and Cuzco with Ned Kelly, especially an eerie night bivouacking in the ruins of the fabled 'Lost City' of the Incas; the slums of Mexico City; the ruins of the Maya civilisation and the Latin America of today, obviously in political ferment; the Mexicans, gayest and noisiest of people, though openly hateful of Americans, *los gringos*. More than once in Mexico I met with hostility until I realised I was being mistaken for an American and made it clear that I was not from the States, when this attitude changed dramatically and the famous Mexican hospitality was warmly extended.

I stopped beside the Merced River to watch some blonde-haired girls diving into the glinting water and giggling right prettily. I could see that Yosemite was something more than a centre for rock climbing, but despite such distractions and the myriad signs of man's presence and work in this national park, one was never far from impressive views of rock faces. I limped past a campsite quizzing myself – how on earth do Americans manage to move the masses of equipment and caravans they haul to such places as Yosemite?

The heat was getting me down; in mid-August it is too hot for comfort with midday temperatures of ninety and above, but I still kept trudging along, my mind switching to impressions of the last few days of wandering in Arizona, Utah and California. What contrasts these states presented! Such beauty in their deserts and wild country, yet man's effect on nature as manifested in cities like Los Angeles had staggered my senses. I had always agreed with the view that among the faults of the English insensitivity was the worst, but the average American now made me see us as positively aware as a nation. American generosity on the other hand outstripped any I had experienced. The white American who gave me a lift from Fresno to the Yosemite park boundary was typical – ninety miles out of his way to get me to my destination, but some of his attitudes to life had appalled me. We discussed the recent Watts riots and he startled me by declaring, as a confessed liberal, how hurt he had been by this outburst. 'We have always treated our n*****s well and I have nothing against them as long as they know their place, but if this is how they are going to treat our kindness, I say let's shoot them down without mercy!' This was still simmering in my thoughts as I drew level with Yosemite Lodge and saw Sentinel Rock on my left and then El Capitan directly ahead. El Cap made me gasp at its scale and line and swept away my grasshopper thoughts of the last few hours.

I turned into Camp 4, the Yosemite climbers' campsite, very different from my imaginings and full of cats, dogs and the other animals that Americans keep as pets, including a full-grown baboon on a chain. Camp 4 used to be the only site in the valley to which one could bring pets and had something of the appearance of a zoo. Shortly after my visit it became a summer gathering place for beatniks and the park authorities closed it – a pity, for the mixture of climber and hippie might not have proved too incompatible. As I approached a clump of trees I saw what must be climbers, surrounded by battered cars, piles of equipment, dirty pots, all very noticeable as in Yosemite they rarely own or use tents.

Trying to appear nonchalant, I walked across and broke in on their conversation to introduce myself. 'Gee, are we pleased to meet you?' came a chorus. 'Royal let us know you British guys would be coming. We've been waiting for you all summer!' I felt inadequate, although I had known of the Californians' keen expectancy of visits from British climbers. Royal Robbins, one of the most famed of American climbers, had visited Britain shortly before I left for South America and had stayed with me for a few days in Yorkshire, convincing me I must visit Yosemite and impressing me by his great ability on rock.

A pot of coffee and many friendly questions broke down my reserve, and every few minutes I was introduced to other people coming back from climbing, swimming or motoring in the valley. Around the camp were endless boulders and I joined a group to try one or two problems and get the feel of Yosemite rock. After managing one or two of these I was invited to go out next day by a young climber from Los Angeles. 'You will really like *Peter Pan*,' he told me. 'It's a fine piece of crack-climbing at around 5.8.' The valley specialists seemed automatically to assume all British climbers to be good rock climbers and, although I roughly understood the Yosemite grading system and that

5.8 was a high standard, I didn't want to spoil this fine image by backing out, so I agreed to climb with him – let the morrow look after itself! Tiring of the heat and the ordeal of well-meant but incessant questions, I excused myself and wandered over to the bar of the Yosemite Lodge.

Here I met Chuck Pratt, one of the acknowledged top American climbers, especially noted by his contemporaries for his free rock climbing. I found Pratt vastly different in manner from my mainly youthful questioners; he seemed completely relaxed and had a ready chuckle. I soon heard this when I told him of my proposed climb for next day. 'That climb is hard, boy!' he exclaimed. 'You've stumbled on the outpatients' department, they're so close in they are just wanting to burn you off!' I had heard how competitive they could be in the valley and the treatment a stranger might receive in the wrong hands, but I shrugged it off and didn't show any more interest – a big mistake! The beer we drank made me still more unconcerned, and later even a Mercedes 200SL running over my foot on the way back to Camp 4 was treated with indifference.

Next day I felt far less happy and began to regret my temerity as we approached the base of El Capitan and our proposed route. Besides the famous major climbs of the buttress there are many short ones that finish where the crack-lines peter out or on top of a pinnacle whence one rappels down, and *Peter Pan* was one of these. Looking up the wall was overpowering. I have never seen anything more impressive in the way of rock architecture, so smooth and so high, the vertical height of more than 3,000 feet dwarfing most granite faces I had known.

Our climb, though relatively short, was something of an undertaking. We had made the big mistake of not carrying any water and the first pitch soon had me dry-mouthed and swollen-tongued. On the second awkward-looking pitch I discovered the limitations on Yosemite rock of rock-climbing footgear of the PA type, so popular in Britain. My young friend led this pitch first by an undercling flake (undercut layback), then by overcoming a small roof to reach a jam-crack, which he followed to a fine-cut ledge. This section was graded 5.8 and I followed with difficulty, confidence undermined by my footgear. I found I just couldn't 'edge' like my leader who was wearing kletterschuhe. Edging means the use of small side footholds, often so fine that my PA-type boots wouldn't hold. Most Yosemite experts climb in kletterschuhe of one kind or another, with a special heavy model designed by Royal Robbins or the Kronhofer type being favourite. After a great struggle I reached the stance at last. My thirst had become acute and the sun's heat made one feel as if one was in the middle of the Sahara.

The next section was the crux of the route and turned out to be one of the most sustained pieces of crack climbing I have come across. The first thirty feet were too wide to jam by hand and foot and had to be climbed by wedging feet across the crack and pulling in opposition on the edges of the fissure. My leader placed a piton at the beginning of the crack and at thirty-five feet there was a bolt in position to protect an awkward mantelshelf on the upper part of the fault, which was wide enough to chimney up. It was reminiscent of the strenuous Derbyshire gritstone cracks but on a bigger scale, the whole lead being a hundred feet or more, with few resting places and only the piton and bolt for protection. My leader quickly and smoothly overcame these obstacles, and my respect for Yosemite rock-climbing standards grew with every foot he climbed. When it was my turn, a combination of thirst and strenuous climbing made the possibility of collapse real. My struggles with the crack grew weaker and weaker and only the rope's assurance kept me moving upwards. I arrived at the belay on some enormous chockstones where the chimney disappeared into a roof and slumped into the shade of the crevice.

The last pitch consisted of sensational bridging out over the closure of the chimney, mercifully of an easier grade and relatively short. Immediately we were both on the finishing ledge, we began our descent, rappelling from stance to stance. Every minute I came nearer to collapsing from heat exhaustion, and the Californian was suffering too. The slight up-draught breeze was hot, heat came out of the cracks in the rock, pitons and karabiners were hot to touch. Climbing in such conditions without water is undoubtedly dangerous; several times on the way down I felt dizzy and when we reached the base of El Cap at last, the short walk back was a trial of tremendous proportions. Back at Camp 4 we guzzled and guzzled pint after pint of water. We were told that the temperature had reached ninety-four in the valley so a hundred degrees on the face was a safe estimate.

That evening I met Chuck Pratt again in the Lodge bar and he was soon chuck-ling at my story of the fight for *Peter Pan*. 'That was tough for a first time,' he conceded. 'Visitors should be warned that it takes time to adjust to the climbing here. How about an easier and more classic ascent tomorrow? The *Lower Cathedral Spire*?' I readily agreed and studied the description of it in a borrowed guide; it was graded 2 and 5.6 with a 5.8 variation.

For the uninitiated, Yosemite climbers use a numerical grading system divided into three categories. The first in the valley guidebook is the overall grade of the climb, numbered 1 to 6, taking into account the length, serious-ness, protection available, etc.; second is the grade of free climbing, running from 1 to 5, the highest grade being further subdivided by adding decimal places – 5.1, 5.2, 5.3 and so on. The top free grading used to be 5.9 but now there are harder pitches in the valley and the system allows for higher grades to be added to the scale from 5.10 upwards. Finally, the third category covers artifi-cial climbing, if any, the grades running, as in Britain, from A1 up but with A5 as the hardest grade.

The Cathedral Spires are quite a walk from the valley floor, so we left early to get this over before the sun was too high. We toiled up scree slopes, luckily shaded by trees; as we gained height El Capitan on the other side of the valley came into view through the branches.

When we stopped to rest Chuck told me some of the El Cap story with which he is closely concerned, having climbed most of the major routes and led on several of the hardest first ascents, such as the renowned *North America Wall*. The development of Yosemite climbing is, I feel, the direction we should follow in mountain exploration. The first major El Capitan route – the *South Buttress*, known in the valley as the *Nose* – involved siege tactics and fixed ropes and took forty-five days before it was completed in November 1958. This was a real breakthrough in the climbing of steep granite walls, and for the first time some of the aids and equipment were used which have since made Yosemite world famous for the development by its climbers of new methods. Bongs, for example, were first used on this ascent, in the form of the legs off a stove, later to be developed into the cowbell-type piton in vogue today.

Since 1958 a series of climbs has been pioneered on the faces of El Capitan which were and remain among the biggest undertakings on rock anywhere. Slowly the Yosemite climbers developed an expertise on massive granite walls unequalled in rock-climbing history. To improve on the ascent of the Nose the valley experts realised they must do away with siege tactics, but know-how and equipment were not yet equal to a major El Cap ascent in a continuous unbroken push. The next successes were the *Salathé Wall* and *Dihedral Wall* in 1961 and 1962 respectively. Shortly afterwards siege tactics were dropped, fixed ropes became obsolete and since then only continuous unbroken ascents have been considered correct. The evolution of further specialised and better-quality equipment has made possible a steady process of cutting down on its quantity, on numbers in a party, and on the time spent on routes. The next big climb on El Capitan, the *North America Wall*, was accomplished in the mid-sixties in a single push by a party of four, and then the *Muir Wall*, again an unbroken ascent, was climbed by a party of two. The times for some of these climbs by today's valley experts are impressive – two and a half days for the *Nose* – and the cutting-down process has reached the stage where some of the El Capitan routes are actually ascended solo.

This paring down has much to commend it to the rest of the climbing world. The initial problems of El Capitan were so gigantic that, with the then knowledge and equipment, they had to be tackled on expedition lines, but with the development of know-how and specialised equipment Yosemite climbers have shown that anything possible for a large party is also possible for a small one. If we learnt from their example we should perhaps see an end to the ludicrous spate of large parties, massively equipped, setting out for objectives in distant ranges with unjustified expense.

However, any of the big climbs on El Capitan remain major undertakings on the grandest of scales, requiring careful planning, preferably cool autumn or spring weather, American hardware and first-class teamwork, for the climb might still take a week or more, making the carrying and hauling of supplies an intricate problem.

Chuck pointed out to me the line of *Salathé Wall*, first climbed in 1961 by Royal Robbins, Tom Frost and himself; this he rated the finest in quality of the climbs although not the most difficult. After hearing him talk about it I felt sorry not to have the chance of a go at it myself.

Our spire came into view, looking like a Dolomite tower, and soon we were roping up by the notch separating it from its near neighbour, the Higher Cathedral Spire, under the eastern face of this huge needle of rock. The climb was easy to start with and Chuck and I led through on long run-outs, using little or no protection. We came to a large ledge where I belayed and Chuck, clad only in breeches, kletterschuhe and a sunhat, set out on the crux pitch. He moved rapidly and then it was my turn to follow; I noted that he had not placed a single piton or running belay, contrary to the beliefs of some climbers at home who thought American climbers simply moved from piton to piton. On stepping off the ledge I had difficulty in making the first balance moves rightwards across an almost-vertical wall, and it took me some little while to work out the best sequence of holds. My mouth was dry when I eventually joined Chuck, but this time we had water to refresh us and soon climbed the easier upper stretches of the spire to its summit. From this tip the view was breathtaking: above us rose the Higher Cathedral Spire, across the valley were El Capitan, the Brothers, Washington Column and Arches, well-known features of Yosemite climbing, and far below in the valley bottom were the dark green of pine and light green of meadow, through which meandered gently the Merced River.

We heard the ring of steel on steel, and looking down the other side of the spire to ours we could see two small dots on the rock wall across an interven-ing valley. 'Must be T.M. and Gorty Webster,' Chuck decided. 'That's a new route they are trying, T.M.'s had a go at that face before. If they get down tonight you must meet T.M., he's the funniest guy I've ever met and keeps everyone in a constant laugh.' We sat and watched for half an hour or so till the rock warming under the sun told us it was time to descend. A series of lengthy rappels took us down the side of the spire, and a swift, perspiring run down the scree slopes led us back to the auto and the bar at Yosemite Lodge.

The next day I spent bouldering with some of the young climbers at Camp 4. I have always enjoyed this sport immensely and have never been able to understand those who declare themselves 'mountaineers' and above such lowly problems. However, to enjoy bouldering one usually needs to be fit, for if its problems are worthwhile they are almost always extreme and near one's limits. Dozens of boulders are dotted around Camp 4 and over the years the Americans have discovered many teasers. After a lengthy expedition and a month at sea before that, I was unfit. I no sooner failed on one problem than I was marched to the next, to fail yet again and finally, at what was said to be the ultimate in finger strength, *Kor's Wall*, I couldn't even start and gave up my feeble attempts in disgust.

But I was impressed by my companions' performance; mainly young climbers, they were dedicated to their sport and had given up jobs or study to spend the summer in Yosemite, in some cases thousands of miles from their homes. They were very serious in their approach and openly competitive, which I suppose is not out of keeping if you are thinking of soloing such a climb as the north-west face of Half Dome, second in the valley hierarchy to El Cap itself and a multi-day expedition, which one of them had done shortly before my arrival. Of late this same seriousness of approach, moving towards utter dedication and an inability to relax, can be more frequently encountered amongst the leaders of the latest generation of British climbers. Perhaps this will become the universal attitude to climbing in the years ahead; the more mountaineering and rock climbing are popularised, exploited and commercialised the more inflexible and competitive will be the attitude of the top practitioners. They set the style for the mass of climbers and as the sport becomes professional, with a personality cult built up by the popular communication media and even a spectator attraction, some of the elite climbers will worry increasingly about their image and the need to justify their reputation. All who love climbing as it has developed over the last hundred years should ponder these things.

More disturbing than the boulders about Camp 4 used to be the bears. Food left lying about attracted them and the climbers often made a bundle of their foodstuffs and hung it from a branch on the end of a climbing rope. If the bears smelt food they would rip a tent open and even attack the occupants if they got in the way. That evening a full-grown grizzly appeared in the camp, causing panic among tourists and climbers alike. Lying asleep in the open, I woke up to see this enormous bear up on its hind legs pawing the tree next to where I lay – it had smelt the food hung from one of the branches by Chuck. It took a while to persuade the bear to turn its attention to a nearby tourists' frame tent where there were plenty of 'goodies' stacked in their larder, and to leave our meagre supplies alone.

I enjoyed some fine slab climbing with Chuck and another local climber during the next two days. The slab climbing like the crack climbing at Yosemite is outstanding; the only comparable slabs in Britain are those in Glen Etive in Scotland, and even they are neither as fine nor extensive. The weather was superb, even if too hot at midday, and Chuck in his post of unofficial clerk of the weather confessed he had lost count of the number of days since the last rain – in April or May he thought.

Then, just before I had to leave, I met T.M.; he had abandoned his new route and was at Camp 4 to see Chuck. Without waiting to be introduced he told me he was T.M. Herbert and that I would climb with him and Gorty Webster or never see Yorkshire no more! He has never had any Christian names; he was named T.M. at birth and T.M. it has been ever since. He too is very much part of the story of modern Yosemite developments and, with Tom Frost, Royal Robbins, Yvon Chouinard and Chuck, he has taken part in some of the valley's biggest first ascents; with Yvon Chouinard he was responsible for the *Muir Wall* of El Capitan.

You don't argue with a man like T.M., so next morning found me leading the first pitch of Gorty Webster's own route on Glacier Point Apron, which finishes on an eminence known as the Patio Pinnacle part way up the face. The Apron has the finest sweep of slabs in the park, smooth to the touch, huge in bulk and lying at the deceptively easy angle of fifty degrees; but on this occasion they were not deceiving anyone as I had climbed on them two days before with Chuck, making a 5.8 ascent, and knew exactly what to expect. In front of T.M. and myself were Gorty and another Yosemite expert, and following closely behind them I reached a thin move about eighty feet from the ground, to find a piton into which I gladly clipped. This piton had been placed by Gorty merely for protection but, I am ashamed to admit, try as I might I couldn't climb the next slab without using it to stand on. Even so it was still a thin move to finish off the lead and gain the stance occupied by the first pair who, like good hosts, pretended not to notice my offence. But T.M.'s comments, though he was still on the ground a hundred feet or so below, could have been heard in Camp 4 a mile away.

From this stance we had to climb a shallow corner for about 250 feet and the next pitch of a hundred feet or so was ascended comfortably by all. T.M., who allowed me to lead again, demonstrated on the way up how easy it was to climb the first pitch without using the piton, which he removed from below before making the difficult moves. By the time I reached the next stance Gorty had led the pitch above. T.M. joined me and we crouched on the belay ledge, alarmed by the grunts and groans of the second man as he tried to climb the groove. I could see only three pitons ahead of him although he still had to climb about 120 feet.

T.M. started on this section immediately in the wake of the complaining second and at once placed a piton, then after making what appeared to me some trying movements he placed another, but still he hadn't reached Webster's first pin, left in position for us by his unhappy second. T.M., famed for his colourful language, kept up a stream of comment and yelled up to

Webster his opinion of him and his climb. Still having trouble he placed further pitons as he continued his upward progress. It is an interesting point about American climbing that an ascent is considered free as long as the climber doesn't actually use pitons to aid his progress; he can lead a pitch with one or five pitons for protection and it doesn't matter ethically as long as they are not used for direct assistance.

T.M. finally reached the stance 150 feet above me amid great hilarity. 'It's 5.9 all the way, boy, 5.9 all the way!' he shouted down, and with these and other cheering words in my ears I set out to follow. I made a poor show of bridging, jamming and laybacking the groove. It was striking how the American pitons of hard steel had bitten into the 'flared' crack of the groove, often only gripping for a couple of inches, but certainly providing greater security than any other type of ironmongery. I was almost strangled by T.M.'s desire to further Anglo-American friendship by pulls on the rope but, to be truthful, as last man removing the pitons I needed them.

When I arrived I pointed out that the British system of nuts on slings could have been used instead of pitons. 'Same thing!' was their opinion. I believe that nuts are now becoming accepted in Yosemite and they will make a big difference to climbing there, especially on the massive combined artificial-and-free routes that require so much 'nailing'. Yet the more I think of it, the more I believe that the Yosemite climbers in 1966 were right in considering the principle of the nut and piton to be almost the same, given that the nut is often speedier to place. We saw in Britain during the last years of the sixties that, expertly handled, nuts are almost as sound as pitons, one can use them for protection almost anywhere on rock climbs and they have been responsible for a dramatic increase in general standards. But one is left wondering if they are a good innovation. The first person I ever saw using one was a climber in Llanberis Pass in 1952, leading *Brant Direct* on Clogwyn y Grochan. He was using ordinary screw-thread nuts on slings and we immediately nicknamed him 'Whitworth'. I remember his being told off resoundingly by the pass clientele of that era. 'If you can't do the climbs as they're meant to be done, go somewhere else!' It may be that in time climbers will adopt a similar attitude to nuts as has slowly evolved to the use of pitons for protection on free routes in Britain where they are now kept strictly to a minimum.

The next pitch was a short overhanging jam-crack and then we moved on to the middle of the open slabs of the Apron. At first the climbing was not too thin, with good frictioning and fair side-holds, but this led to a minute stance with a single expansion bolt to tie into. Three of us clung to this while Webster led 140 feet up the Apron with only a single bolt in position to protect him, and seeing the efforts of his second T.M. and I decided we didn't like the look of the way ahead and said so. Our call for a top rope was quickly answered and once we had tied on to this, I for one felt better. We lowered the tone of seriousness by moving together up the slab with a short length of rope between us. Nevertheless, it was indeed a thin pitch, a hundred feet to the first running belay, a bolt in position, then another forty feet to join the first party on their stance. It was wonderful slab climbing on warm, dry granite, but I was glad to be on a rope from above. T.M. followed a few feet behind me, shouting with his full power of invective exactly what he would do to the man stupid enough to pioneer such a route!

At the stance the only belay was again a single expansion bolt; on Glacier Point Apron these are absolutely essential on many of the climbs and it would be asking for trouble not to use them. Unlike piton usage, the ethics of bolt placing are strict in Yosemite, and the valley aces will often chop a bolt out of a climb if they feel it in any way superfluous to requirements.

The next pitch was another hard lead and again I found my PA footgear very limiting. I am not exactly sure why kletterschuhe should be so much better on Yosemite rock; partly it is because of the smoothness of the rock and the lack of friction value but perhaps also because of the valley's prevailing weather. I have noticed in Britain that, during our occasional fine summers, after a long drought the rock tends to lose much of its 'frictionability'.

A long exposed traverse to the right led at last to the top of Patio Pinnacle, actually only a knob of rock sticking out of the face. Above us the Apron steepened, hundreds more feet of smooth, clean granite, formidable in appearance, but for us the way was down again. T.M. kept us in such a state of laughter that I hardly noticed the slick teamwork as rappel followed rappel. From the foot of the Apron we quickly removed ourselves to Yosemite village to drink beer and talk climbing.

Regretfully I said goodbye to Yosemite and its climbers. I had intended going to New York from California as I had promise of work on a community project in the Harlem ghetto, but news from home was bad. My mother had contracted an incurable illness before I left for South America and ahead of predictions her end was near, so I wanted to get home immediately before it was too late. As we sped through the night in Gorty's car to San Francisco's airport, I had a chance to think over my short visit to Yosemite, which had proved one of the most interesting weeks of my life.

Although I know such generalisations are meaningless, I found myself agreeing with its devotees that the valley has the best rock climbing in the world. Only in Norway can Europe boast anything like the Yosemite faces, and even then only a northern enthusiast would compare, say, the famous Trolltind Wall with El Capitan. It is not a question of size but of rock architecture. The Yosemite walls require special techniques and equipment, pitons that can be used over and over again, and something better than wooden wedges for the long continuous-width cracks which are a feature of so many routes.

To me the most striking thing about the valley's climbers was their dynamism; they have not become static as have many European schools of mountaineering in the last decade. Some of these reached a peak in the early years after the last war, stayed on that peak for a time, but are now vastly out of date, so rapid has been the progress of modern techniques. Perhaps every climber has now heard of such Yosemite inventions as the Leeper, Bong and RURP.[1] I was shown the URP, about as big as a thumbnail, then recently developed for use as a balance aid by hammering it into a hairline crack and pulling on the attached nylon tape. Several brilliant designers have been at work in the valley, refining and restyling, adopting and adapting, and the present-day climbing world owes much to the equipment and thinking of Yosemite climbers. They have given much attention to ethics; each piece of new equipment has its place and its carefully evaluated usage.

Performances have steadily improved. One has only to contrast Royal Robbins' fantastic solo ascent of the *Muir Wall* of El Capitan in nine days in 1968 with the sieges of the Trolltind Wall by the French, also in 1968, and of an Eiger Direct by the Japanese in 1969. This kind of ascent, though requiring great ability, is not progressive; Yosemite has long left such tactics behind. The French and the Japanese achieved nothing new; using all-out methods they made first ascents which future generations would have been able to climb with classical elegance, in a manner more in keeping with the essential challenge of mountaineering.

Certainly one must give Yosemite weather its due; it is reliable and does not produce the extremes that may be encountered on the Eigerwand, but still the ideal must be Yosemite-style ascents as practised today which have proved siege tactics to be neither desirable nor necessary.

When I got back from the States I heard that a group of Polish climbers had been in Britain, climbing in Snowdonia, the Lake District, Glencoe, and had left an invitation for a party to visit the Tatra mountains. In February 1967, I was instructing on the survival course in the Cairngorms, along with a fellow Yorkshireman, Tom Morrell, Jim McArtney from Aberdeen and Jim McDowell from Glasgow among others. The four of us sat round the supper table one evening talking about places we would like to visit and someone mentioned the High Tatra of Poland and Czechoslovakia. We all agreed we should like to climb there. Why not write to the Polish climbers and ask for information and advice? I agreed to do this, and through the good offices of John Hunt, who had himself visited the High Tatra, I was put in touch with Andrzej Kus of the Polish Mountaineering Federation, Klub Wysokogorski. Soon we had received an official invitation to the Polish High Tatra for July and August.

---

1. R.U.R.P. – Realised Ultimate Reality Piton; U.R.P. – Ultimate Reality Piton (smaller than the R.U.R.P.).

A few weeks after the survival course I was at a Rock and Ice meet on the sea cliffs near Swanage, my first visit to Dorset's climbing ground. Tom Morrell and another young Yorkshireman, Rob Wood, were with me, and after doing routes on some of the other cliffs we set out to repeat one of the hardest existing climbs on Boulder Ruckle. Nowhere I have climbed is more serious or more fraught with objective dangers than this sea cliff; the tide must be watched carefully, the rock is loose and the upper part of this limestone bulwark is often steep and crumbly ground with no secure belays.

Our route began from a shelf a little above the sea, and the first pitch followed a crack and groove that swung diagonally from left to right. At ninety feet there was a small ledge with a piton belay and above this perhaps fifty feet of steep wall climbing, finishing with the usual Boulder Ruckle earth slope.

All was well until Rob and I reached the ledge, though both of us had been frightened by the loose rock, particularly a passage over an immense detached flake about fifty feet from the start. As there was no room to bring Tom up to our stance, Rob carefully climbed the wall above my head and gingerly scaled the last broken sections to the clifftop and a belay. Unfortunately, as events turned out, although Rob and I were attached to double ropes, there was only a single overweight nylon rope between Tom and myself and to make matters worse this rope was new, first time out.

Usually I take in a rope round my waist but for some reason on this occasion I took it in on a shoulder belay and stupidly – although almost everyone does it – I was not wearing gloves. Tom dealt with the first forty feet in fine style, climbing almost too quickly for me to take in his rope and, grinning, he shouted up that he couldn't understand the climb's reputation. He reached the flake of rock, huge and detached, and began working his way over it, bridging to avoid pulling too much on this obviously loose feature.

Suddenly his right handhold gave way and in an effort to save himself he caught hold of the edge of the flake. This enormous object simply broke off the wall and Tom, holding a large piece of rock, swung into space. He fell in a giant parabola, swinging from left to right and – an interesting note for those with a penchant for Boulder Ruckle climbing – at every running belay between Tom and myself the rock crumbled as his weight came on the slings. At the end of his swing the tug on me was as if a leader had fallen, not a second, and turned me round sideways; the piton belay held but to my horror the rope jumped off my shoulder. Immediately Tom began to fall vertically down the cliff. 'God, he'll be killed!' I thought, and automatically grabbed at the swiftly running rope with both hands.

The pain of burning on my hands was incredible and I let go! I let go, then grabbed hold again, the pull on the rope jerking me forward so that I could see Tom falling. I gripped the rope more tightly, feeling it cut through my fingers to the bone, and stopped his fall about ten feet above the ledge. But my hands were done for, I couldn't hold on and had to let him fall on to the platform. I took my hands off the rope and looked at them; they were a terrible sight, blood, blisters and dangling flesh, but surprisingly the pain was not unbearable – that was to come!

Tom was unhurt and I shouted down to him that my hands were burned and I would need rescuing. Luckily several of the Rock and Ice were to hand and the ropes that came shooting down could have evacuated Nellie the Elephant! I tied on to a rope from Nat Allen and, still attached to the double ropes from Rob, I somehow managed to climb to the top of the cliff. Tom had come round an easier way and was most concerned about having come off, but I knew my injuries were my own fault and the result of incompetence of a kind I had never been guilty of in twenty years of climbing. I had been careless; I didn't expect Tom to fall simply because I had never known him to fall before, and because of my confidence in him I wasn't watching the rope as I should have been.

For the next month my hands were covered in burn dressings; the pain was unbearable at times and even a week after the accident brought tears to my eyes. After a month, when the dressings were removed, the long slow process of getting my hands back to normal usage began. I spent night after night soaking them in salt and water to heal the wounds. The tendon in my right forefinger was cut and three months later I still couldn't bend or use this finger. The doctor advised it should be amputated but luckily a surgeon climber I know examined my hands and recommended wax baths. These worked miracles and six weeks later I could use all my fingers, including the right forefinger, although I have permanent scars and neither the finger strength I once possessed nor the full use in manipulation. I would now recommend anyone holding a rope to wear gloves; rope burns are painful and serious, as I know to my cost, and are best avoided!

Despite this setback, our plans to visit the High Tatra proceeded and towards the end of July the four of us, Jim McArtney and myself in my van and Jimmy McDowell and Tom Morrell in Tom's car, set out to drive in convoy over the continental roads. A typically disorganised group of climbers, we lost each other somewhere on the German autobahns and didn't meet again until we arrived at Zakopane, the main centre for the Polish Tatra.

Jim McArtney and I were almost arrested in East Germany; we only had transit visas but as we did not understand German or Russian, we didn't grasp this fact. Jim, an ardent communist, wished to see as much of life behind the Iron Curtain as he could. East Germany opened our eyes and Jim insisted we drive here and there to talk with and stay amongst the East Germans. For five days we toured round the country, surprised to discover that this was no socialist state but a policed country with Russia as overlord. We were turned away at Checkpoint Charlie in Berlin, and when we finally tried to leave East Germany at the Polish frontier we were in trouble. The Russian officer to whom we were 'referred' was luckily a man of some humour and when McArtney grabbed a water hose used for dousing down the road outside the police station and pretended to give the officer a dousing, the Russian suddenly whirled on Jim, grabbed the hose and proceeded to soak him instead. This was seen by everyone as a great joke, and after a glass of vodka we were allowed to go on our way.

The Polish people we met soon dispelled our fears that their country would also be dominated by the Russians. We were taken to their homes, treated with courtesy and friendship, and usually plied with vodka or beer till we could take no more. We had many adventures, for travelling with Jim, the most spontaneous person I ever met, one never knew what would happen next, and it seems surprising now that we ever reached our journey's end.

Zakopane, a ski resort in winter and venue of the world championships before the last war as well as the main Tatra climbing centre, was thronged with tourists as we roamed among its fine Alpine-style buildings against a backcloth of towering summits and high granite walls. Finding Tom and Jim McDowell was an easy task, everyone had seen the 'English' climbers – much to Jim's disgust. We were to meet our Polish hosts of the Klub Wysokogorski at Kuznice, a ski-lift station outside Zakopane, and there we found our interpreter and our friend, Tadeusz Jankowski. He soon had our camping organised at a nearby village and then took us to a tavern where he explained to us how mountaineering is organised in Poland, its traditions and latest developments.

The Klub Wysokogorski has funds from the state and branches throughout the country; it runs the only two campsites allowed in the Polish Tatra, publishes a quarterly magazine, *Taternik*, covering members' activities and news of climbing abroad, and is responsible for cut-price training courses for young people and novices. But we understood that climbing in Poland is still seen as an activity for individuals rather than organised masses as in some communist societies.

Next day we walked up through pouring rain to a mountain hut perched on an alp-like pasture at Hala Gasienicowa (meadow of the caterpillars!) in the Sucha Woda valley, directly under the peaks at the western end of the range. There was also an Alpine-style mountain refuge and in the evening, after cooking ourselves a meal, we walked across to it and were introduced to an instruction course of young climbers and guides. These subsidised courses are surprisingly cheap and seem an example of the benefits available under Polish socialism.

We spent several hours with the instructors, until it was too dark to see, attempting problems on the walls of the refuge, some of such difficulty that they frustrated our efforts. Despite inferior footgear, mostly slippers or basketball boots, the Poles showed themselves adept at this pastime. Tadeusz explained that, apart from the Tatra, some limestone gorges near Krakow and one or two isolated sandstone pinnacles in the west, there are no climbing grounds in Poland, and buildings are the only source of practice for many climbers!

We were amazed at the number of people amongst the hills, far more than one would find around Mont Blanc at the height of the season. Few, however, are climbers. The Tatra form a national park extending through southern Poland and northern Czechoslovakia, an immense attraction to tourist, hill-walker and skier alike. Throughout the park runs the best system of mountain tracks and paths that any of us had seen, and the staff of the park maintain them in good order and they are well marked. All visitors other than climbers are asked to stay on these tracks, for the fauna and flora of the area is in some cases unique and by such methods it is hoped to preserve them. It was surprising to me how the average person respected this request, only the bona fide climbers moving off the paths to reach the foot of the climbs. This started our party discussing the problems in our own overcrowded mountain areas and the possibility of operating such a system in, for instance, Snowdonia. We concluded it wouldn't work, but at least in the Tatra something has been done to conserve and preserve the area without strict legislation, for the system is voluntary.

Next day, in fine weather, we crossed a pass on Zamarla Turnia, one of the peaks at the head of the Sucha Woda, then tramped through the valley of the Five Polish Lakes and crossed a second pass to the Morskie Oko valley, the main area of Polish climbing. To start our day we made a detour to look at the classic rock climbs on the face of a peak called Koscielec, literally laced with routes in a manner reminiscent of British crags. In the valley below us as we crossed the first pass I counted nineteen lakes, some small, a few large; it was this contrast of granite mountain and valley lake which made the Tatra beautiful in my eyes, despite the absence of glacier and permanent snow.

After spending the night in a hayloft we returned to Zakopane and were taken to the headquarters of the mountain rescue organisation for a conducted tour of their services. Our overall opinion was good of the planning and way this is operated. The rescue teams are full-time professionals paid by the state, and their equipment is first class, including twenty-four-hour radio contact with the refuges throughout the range. At each hut a rescue leader reports and deals with minor accidents, but a major rescue is the work of the Zakopane team who operate winter and summer with a party always on standby. The rescue service is free to climbers!

Later we went to a bonfire at a Gural celebration in the hills above Zakopane. The Gurals are the real highlanders of Poland, whose toughness and drinking prowess are legendary throughout the country; their dress, singing, music making and dancing are reminiscent of parts of the Austrian Tyrol. A deal of strong drink and strange singing brought our day to a convivial end, with our two Scots admitting that the fiery pepper vodka was almost as potent as Scotch.

Early next morning we started back to the Morskie Oko valley, this time to set up our tents in the Klub Wysokogorski campsite for the rest of our stay. The club is the only organisation allowed by the park authorities to maintain a permanent campsite in the valley. Although it was full, Tadeusz explained that most of Poland's leading climbers were absent since, for the first time, it had been possible for a large number of them to visit the European Alps; the club had chartered an aircraft and about eighty Polish mountaineers were in Chamonix. Others were in the Hindu Kush, a popular area for Polish expeditions, the Caucasus, the Pamirs and Turkey.

Over the next few days we made several good friends and I was surprised how frankly our questions about life and politics in Poland were answered. Each evening, after the last tourist had departed, we gathered in the refuge to sing till the late hours and to discuss every kind of topic, from the war in Vietnam to the merits of Tatra climbing. During one particularly noisy session, kept alive by liberal quantities of beer and vodka, Jim McArtney made a speech in which he declared that the Tatra mountains were almost as good as the Cuillin of Skye which, as I made plain to Tadeusz, from an Aberdonian was about the highest possible commendation.

One thing that struck us was that nearly all the climbers were at or had been to university. Apparently only in the last few years had the workers earned enough money or enjoyed enough leisure to indulge in such activities as mountaineering, and as in the early days of British mountaineering there was no tradition of working-class climbing. In Poland of course this situation is accentuated by the lack of facilities near the modern industrial cities, but slowly it was changing; some of the young people attending instruction courses were the sons and daughters of factory workers and, as elsewhere, once the mountain bug is implanted it never ceases to flourish.

Another impression was that Polish climbers are physically fit and hardy creatures, sleeping in the open in any conditions with a minimum of equipment and protection. There is a big difference between, say, Yosemite where sleeping out is more comfortable than camping in summer because of the heat and the Tatra where the summers can produce cold and wet weather or worse.

The Morskie Oko valley is indeed a wonderful place, with two large lakes trapped beneath granite walls and towering over the Morskie Oko lake itself the 3,000-foot face of the Mieguszowiecki, one of the highest summits of the range at 7,518 feet. Mirrored in the lake are the pine forests and often Mnich, the Matterhorn of the Tatra.

From the campsite the cliffs were easily accessible and the two Jims set about the big face-climbs while Tom and I concentrated on traversing the ridges. My hands troubled me whenever I attempted demanding routes, and the folly of being too ambitious was brought home to me early in our visit when, on a climb with Jim McArtney, I was leading a pitch of V-superior (the Poles use the

Welzenbach grading system as in the Alps). I had led out perhaps sixty feet of rope, obtained a good thread runner and could see a large ledge about fifteen feet up. Between this ledge and myself was a corner groove split by a thin finger-width crack and I started to jam up it. This hurt my hands but I had almost reached the ledge when my fingers suddenly started to cramp, I couldn't feel the rock and was in danger of falling out of the groove backwards. I was wearing heavy boots and luckily on the corner of the left wall was a small, sharp-cut hold, ideal for a boot; I stuck my foot on this and balanced across swiftly without handholds, the kind of thing one might do on a boulder as a 'no-hands' problem! Shaking with fright I grabbed the edge of the ledge with the palms of my hands and threw myself into a mantelshelf to land, panting but safe on the balcony. This taught me a lesson and from then on I was content to traverse the ridges, which was no hardship, for the Scots' comparison with the jagged Cuillin was an apt one; often the firm granite ridges were knife-edged, though technically easy.

Meanwhile, the Scots were repeating some of the hardest climbs of the area and delighted our Polish friends with a quick free ascent of the direct climb of Mieguszowiecki. The climber who led the first ascent of this grade-VI route a few years earlier went with them to the foot of the face and he and other watching Poles shouted their encouragement every inch of the way. There was some confusion when, after completing the hardest section, the two Jims decided to make a direct line for the summit instead of following the more devious original line; the Poles thought they had lost the way or were in trouble, but ended full of admiration for this new direct finish, and their enthusiasm over the success overwhelmed us.

We were surprised at the amount and variety of climbing available in what is actually only a small area of the Tatra, ranging in length from 300 to 3,000 feet and some of the hardest courses requiring bivouacs. The guidebooks to the region run to fourteen volumes, with new routes and developments published in *Taternik*. When it rained it was almost impossible to climb; the rock, such wonderful granite when dry, was like soap when it became water soaked and most of the Poles did not bother to go out in such conditions. On one occasion our party were making a climb when a thunderstorm broke about our heads; try as we might we couldn't climb the finishing pitches and had to traverse off. Our Italian Vibram soles were most ineffective and slipped off any but the largest holds and the softer soles of the Czech-made boots worn by the Poles and Czechs were far more efficient when the rock was slippery.

Towards the end of our stay, in a large and sociable party we did a most enjoyable crack-and-groove climb on Mnich. This relatively small summit is by far the most striking peak of the Tatra, more reminiscent of the Aiguille du Fou of the Mont Blanc range than the Matterhorn to which it is popularly compared. Some of the Polish climbers following us were surprised at our not inserting pitons, but we managed to find good protection everywhere using nuts and slings. We gave the Poles a demonstration of their use but they remained unconvinced, arguing along similar lines to the American climbers in Yosemite. In fact Polish rock-climbing ethics are similar to those in vogue in the USA, France, and Italy – if you want to place a piton for protection you place it and only 'extreme' rock climbers attempt to keep such use to a minimum. We formed the opinion that the Polish climbers had a more traditional approach to mountaineering than ourselves; they were not on the whole orientated towards crag or cliff climbing but were more interested in greater mountaineering. Much winter climbing is done in the Tatra and at that season the mountains must provide superb sport, with the major climbs and traverses demanding great fitness and stamina. We were told that the traverse of the whole Tatra range was one of the best of winter climbs and from our own days on its ridges I can believe this. When it was first accomplished it took thirteen bivouacs; this in a region of heavy snowfalls and severe blizzards gives some idea of the scope and standards of the winter expeditions available.

The evening before I left Morskie Oko, I gave a talk on our Alpamayo expedition and my Yosemite visit, illustrated with colour slides, to a packed audience in the refuge. This created tremendous interest, as the Peruvian Andes and modern American rock climbing were outside the Poles' experience. With question and counter-question the show lasted nearly four hours, exhausting poor Tadeusz as interpreter but happily his flagging efforts were revived by free beer provided by the hut guardian.

The enthusiasm of the Poles and Czechs for mountains and climbing and their essentially romantic approach was refreshing to me when set against the increasingly materialistic attitude among British climbers, and the more surprising because found in a supposedly communistic society. When I left next day – my fortunate companions staying on for a short while – I had no doubt as to the worth of climbing friendships and was happy to feel that the love of mountains can transcend frontiers and political barriers.

11   Mukar Beh, 1968

'Before the unconditioned, the conditioned dances.'
(Poems of Kabir: Rabindranath Tagore)

'Day XIII. Thursday, 25 October. Foul weather. Only two inches of each end of Pemba's tent showing above the fresh snow which must be two to three feet deep. Climbing now out of the question. The problem is to get out as soon as possible, but not safe today. Food and fuel are abundant, so will sit here until conditions are more favourable and hope that we don't get ten feet of fresh snow!' (End of diary.)

Unfortunately for the diarist, the Australian Geoff Hill, it probably did snow as much as ten feet that October day of 1967. Geoff, Suresh Kumar from Bombay and Sherpa Pemba were literally buried alive the same night by a cornice forming over their tent on a ridge of the complex Mukar Beh.

Ever since 1961 I had secretly cherished the ambition to return to Kulu and try to climb Mukar Beh. As with many such plans it took several years' gestation, but in the autumn of 1967 I was at last thinking in the constructive way that turns mere ideas and ambitions into action. I was closely following news about Mukar Beh, including details of the topography of the mountain via Bob Pettigrew, leader of our 1961 expedition and for several years after, a teacher at Rajkumar College in Gujarat, India. From Bob I learnt of the various attempts on the mountain: of his own reconnaissance, of the false claim by a party of Indian mountaineers to have reached the summit, easily disproved by Bob, of the attempts in the autumn of 1967, first by a party of Americans led by Bill Staniger and, immediately afterwards, by the ill-fated party led by Geoff Hill.

This amounted to feverish activity by Himalayan standards, and when I heard from Bob of Geoff Hill's interest in the mountain I thought my own effort would be forestalled. Geoff had already pulled off a spectacular first ascent in the Kulu area in the spring of 1967 as a member of Bob Pettigrew's party to Papsura (21,167 feet). He had stormed the summit in alpine fashion, after bad weather and an accident had made the possibility of success most unlikely.

The news of the disaster which overtook Geoff Hill's party on Mukar Beh reached me in November and caused me to rethink my whole strategy for the mountain. I had intended travelling alone to India, to meet Sonam Wangyal, the Ladakhi, in Manali and to attempt Mukar Beh in alpine fashion as a party of two. From the information available as to route possibilities, it was obvious that the only approach to the mountain, because of political considerations, was by the Solang valley north of Manali. This meant that to reach the actual summit ridge one had first to climb Ladakhi Peak, 17,525 feet, then Manali Peak, 18,600 feet, and finally Mukar Beh, 19,910 feet, all joined together in sequence along a continuous ridge.

On paper or off, this appeared a colossal task for a two-man party. The distances involved seemed too great, especially as base would be as low as 11,000 feet and even then, as it turned out, well above the snow line. Eating my words as to my intention of always making expeditions in future with ultra-lightweight parties, I cast around for others who might be interested in the project. At Glenmore Lodge, during successive survival courses, I had made good friends with the deputy principal, Liam Carver. Liam, bulky and solid, with many years' experience in the mountains behind him and an authority on winter survival work, expressed his interest despite, as he said, 'being beyond the madcap adventures of youth'. That made two of us. Bob Pettigrew had emphasised in his letters the worth of the part played by one John Ashburner as a member of the Papsura expedition and how, as a friend of Geoff Hill, he would be interested in any plans for Mukar Beh. John was working at Allahabad in north India; as an agricultural engineer he was part of a team trying to design and develop a tractor wholly made in India. I had not met him but friends of his who had told of some of his exploits while he was honorary secretary of the Cambridge University Mountaineering Club made him sound a likely lad. An exchange of letters, including one from him in the forbid-den-to-Europeans Garhwal Himalaya, showed him to be the type of person to suit a small lightweight party on the mountain. A letter to John Banon, local secretary of the Himalayan Club at Manali, located Sonam Wangyal who, besides being with us in 1961 and climbing the Manikaran Spires, had also been with John on the Papsura expedition; he could be relied on to the hilt and beyond. He had remembered my promise to come back and try Mukar Beh.

We hadn't much money between us but luckily two of the party were already in India: getting there is the most expensive item in any Himalayan budget. A grant from the Mount Everest Foundation gave Liam and myself the start we needed to raise the necessary funds and I was fortunate enough to be awarded a Churchill Travelling Fellowship to India. On returning from the Alpamayo expedition and America in 1966, I had become interested in social problems – demography, criminology and so on – and decided to enrol for a three-year course in Social Psychology at Leeds University. India remained a country of unparalleled interest for me and I wanted to study its history and culture and its problems of present-day life in depth. The Churchill Fellowship awarded to me in January, 1968, by the Winston Churchill Memorial Trust was to lead an expedition to attempt Mukar Beh and afterwards to travel and study throughout the Indian subcontinent social problems of India today. All my expenses were thus paid by the trust but Liam Carver and John Ashburner were not so lucky; they had to meet part of their share of expenses out of their own pockets. Their finances, like my own in normal circumstances, being strictly limited, expenditure had to be kept to a minimum.

We assembled in New Delhi towards the end of May 1968, and elected to travel from there to the mountains on ordinary service buses. Our total baggage was about four hundredweight, made up into fourteen packages of varying sizes – rucksacks, kit bags, sacks. The journey to Manali getting on and off buses was tedious, dusty, hot and tiring, but we did achieve our objective to keep it cheap. No one batted an eyelid at so much baggage. Indians often travel with all their worldly possessions, household effects, chickens, goats, which makes for insanitary conditions and terrible overcrowding, but at the end of our road at Manali, the three of us with our fourteen pieces had made the three-day bus journey for under £5.

'I'm afraid I've had enough. I need a rest,' John Ashburner said as he and Wangyal stumped into Camp III, perched on the ridge between Ladakhi and Manali peaks. 'The way off Manali looks really terrible, loose rock and difficult climbing, and after that Mukar Beh is still difficult and a hell of a way. And the ridge connecting the two is heavily corniced!'

I could only sympathise with John; for a fortnight he and Wangyal had been out in the lead, preparing the way and carrying heavy loads. Four of us had been shown by events to be not as man too many. Loads had been carried from base at about 10,500 feet to a first camp at 13,000 feet and from there to another camp at 15,000 feet on the broad shoulder of a ridge leading on to Ladakhi Peak; from that point one could either traverse over its summit or across its eastern face to reach a third campsite at 17,300 feet on the ridge rising 1,300 feet to Manali Peak.

The sheer logistics and scale of the undertaking were brought home to us. We had used up all our tents in placing three camps, one at each site, with a bivouac construction left at our base at Beas Kund in case of retreat or emergency. We had been on snow from 9,000 feet upwards; the previous winter had been the worst in living memory and snow was lying at an unusually low altitude. Initially Liam and I had acclimatising difficulties but fortunately John was still used to altitude from his trek in the Garhwal earlier that year and Wangyal never seems to notice such problems.

Our plan had worked successfully so far, the idea being to follow the classic snail's pace of Himalayan build-up – Camp I, Camp II, Camp III. It had been Liam's task to haul supplies from Camp I to Camp II, mine from Camp II to

Camp III and John's and Wangyal's to prepare the way from that point onwards, during the preceding few days. The culmination of the plan was that when the route was successfully prepared over Manali Peak two of us would make an alpine-style dash for the summit of Mukar Beh, climbing from Camp III. This, as we well realised, would still be quite a feat if only because it involved the 1,300-foot climb up Manali Peak, followed by an 800-foot descent to the col between it and Mukar Beh, then a quarter-mile of switchback traversing along a heavily corniced ridge, leading to a final ascent of perhaps 2,000 feet to the summit of our goal. This added up to a final push of approximately 11,000 feet of ascent and descent, by any standards a marathon effort, especially as most of the ground was at 18,000 feet or higher.

The key to success was in building up Camp III into a well-stocked site, and in preparing the route over Manali Peak before making the final attempt. From Camp III to the Manali summit was easy going, along snow ridges and an open but steep snowfield to a corniced rock ridge before the tip of the final cone, but the descent on the other side was of some difficulty the whole way.

John and Wangyal had cut bucket steps up Manali Peak but had stuck on the descent to the col. On this section we had decided we would permit ourselves to place fixed rope, for it was here that several of the previous attempts had fizzled out, defeated by the magnitude of the task ahead. The American Bill Staniger with a Sherpa companion had almost completed the descent off Manali Peak, leaving a rope in position to facilitate their retreat. He had been most generous in sharing his knowledge with us and strongly advised us to rope the whole descent for, as his photographs made plain, retreat from the summit slopes of Mukar Beh would be no easy matter, even with the aid of a fixed rope on the re-ascent of Manali Peak.

'I'm sorry, Dennis, it's too much,' John reiterated. 'Wangyal's climbing like a steam engine but I'm a bit gone and getting jiggered.'

'No wonder, seeing you've carried a load every day for a fortnight,' I consoled him. 'I feel like that myself and I've not shifted half the weight you have.'

It was true that I had been finding the going hard, especially carrying a load and climbing alone as I had done that day from Camp II to Camp III. This trip brought home in capital letters the seriousness of small expeditions. Whichever route was taken, either over Ladakhi Peak or traversing its eastern flank, was serious; on the first alternative, in many places a single slip would mean a certain death fall, and on the other route avalanche danger was acute. In fact, large areas of the face had avalanched, and to make a safe crossing, or at least not take too many risks, meant leaving Camp II at first light.

To be alone in the midst of Himalayan peaks is a salutary experience, with sharpness of impressions heightened to an unbelievable degree – the colour of the rock, the heat of the sun, the sweat running down over glacier cream, the rasp of your own breathing. You are so alive you feel and notice everything at once, and the twin moods of happiness and fear are almost overwhelming to strained nerves taut as piano wires. I felt the need of company badly after being alone crossing and recrossing the avalanche channels.

'OK, Wangyal?' I asked.

'OK, Sahib.' The same old toothy grin, the glinting eyes, unprotected despite the blinding light, the obvious enthusiasm.

'I'll stop here with Wangyal and take over in front, and you go down and rest,' I suggested. John hesitated, but it was clear he needed some respite; he was the youngest member of the party, his face was burnt and lined with effort from non-stop work in the welcome but searing sun of the last two weeks. 'Down you go, before the avalanches start a-rolling. I'll watch you down to Camp II.'

A flurry of packing, 'All the best, chaps!' and he was gone.

I watched as he ploughed down the track sunk deep into the snow by successive journeys. It made me hold my breath to see him moving over those slopes, avalanche-furrowed and debris-strewn, reeking of danger. But soon he had crossed the menacing passages on to safe ground, and I scrambled back along the ridge to join Wangyal at our tiny Whymper tent.

The Himalaya is not all work, danger or boredom. If the weather is good, lying out on a foam mattress in the afternoon, feeling the sun's heat on the body, reading and drinking pints of tea, is a pleasant experience. Wangyal speaks little English so conversation was minimal, but his untiring work at brewing and cooking made him the best companion anyone could wish for in such a situation.

At three o'clock next morning we were awake and at five we were climbing the deep-cut icy steps; our crampons bit firmly into the iron surface, obviating the need for a rope though on the heavily corniced summit crest I should have enjoyed its security. It requires real mental discipline to stop and rope up under these circumstances, on easy but dangerous ground and at six o'clock when the flesh may be willing but the spirit is often weak. At six-thirty we stood on the summit pinnacle of Manali Peak, a fine mountain in its own right. The clarity of sight from its rock spire was magnificent; to the east were the well-remembered mountains of Deo Tibba and Indrasan, with Ali Ratni Tibba sticking up immediately behind them like a giant tooth, but dominating the whole panorama was the aptly named Solang Weisshorn to the north-west. And in front of us was Mukar Beh.

The weather was superb and had aided our progress for many days, but I began to get a creepy feeling that it wouldn't last. This seemed silly with no cloud on the horizon, but each day now there was bound to be a slow build-up before the complete break when the monsoon arrived.

The way off Manali Peak did look off-putting, to say the least; the rock is atrocious, shattered and broken in some places into almost vertical shale. For half an hour we stared at this prospect. 'Let's start down, Wangyal,' I proposed.

'OK, Sahib,' came back the expected reply, perhaps the only English Wangyal really knows!

We fixed a length of rope round the whole summit edifice, then running out courlene rope, previously carried up by Wangyal and John, we started our descent, Wangyal climbing down first. The rocks were so loose that it was frightening, and although Wangyal moved carefully, huge blocks shifted if he touched them, or simply splintered off the face. After the first rope-length the situation improved somewhat, when below the summit pinnacle we got on to rock plastered in snow and ice and cemented by the firm grip of frost. From under the snow we dug out a piece of white bleached rope, obviously the one left by Bill Staniger. Here and there it stuck out of the ice but after so many months in position we weren't sure how safe it would be and daren't risk using it. Wangyal was in his element on this ground, kicking off stones, jabbing his crampons into the ice, singing with delight at being in action again.

After about 300 feet the face overhung, then in a single sweep shot towards the Chandra river on the Lahoul side of the range. The exposure was extreme, perhaps 5,000 feet of space under our feet – no way down on that line. An easier alternative presented itself in the form of a slabby arête which jutted out from the face, finishing in a shelf directly above a ridge broken by a series of steps down to the col.

Climbing out along the slabs on crampons, belayed by Wangyal, I began to feel quite scared; the rock crumbled under the touch and at the first piece of firm granite I came to I hammered an American knife-blade piton into a hair-line crack. The piton only bit for an inch but, tied off with tape, my experience with American hardware had shown me it would hold. I also attached a fixed line to it, which Wangyal at first refused to handle when he joined me, but after my demonstrating its firmness he happily clung to it on the way back.

I belayed to a chockstone in a crack just below this and Wangyal came across to me, then continued through, down the face below. Carefully we unearthed belay points for the fixed line or used snow or ice bollards until we stood just above the col and the start of the switchback ridge leading to Mukar Beh. With a final burst of energy Wangyal slid down a chimney to the col and moved on to the ridge, to run out the last of the fixed rope. Over 600 feet was in position and we could feel satisfied; the way was open to Mukar Beh. I called to Wangyal to come back but was alarmed to see him take off the rope between us and start solo along the heavily corniced ridge. He tripped happily along, oblivious to danger, but eventually he guessed from my shouts that the attempt on Mukar could wait! He was keen to see the way ahead, but nothing was to be gained by taking such risks. From where I stood I could follow the whole route;

after the ridge a short slope led to an immense transverse crevasse to bypass which would probably provide the first real difficulty, then a huge snowfield set at a reasonable angle could be traversed diagonally rightwards to land one under the summit ridge which looked steep and proved to be the crux of the climb. Wangyal turned about, tied on to the rope again and we reascended Manali Peak, unroped on the summit and soloed down the steps to Camp III. It was late afternoon by the time we got back and we worked out we had been climbing for eleven hours. I concluded that to climb Mukar Beh from Camp III would probably necessitate a bivouac, even with the aid of our fixed ropes.

Unwisely I decided to have a rest day before Wangyal and I made our attempt. The rest day was blessed with marvellous weather, and we lay in the sun and ate and drank our fill, expecting to be climbing throughout the following day and possibly to bivouac as night fell. Next morning we awoke at three, prepared a drink and got ready inside the tent but were amazed on crawling outside to find ourselves wreathed in cloud and mist. 'Hell, a break in the weather!' How I cursed my decision to have a day off. But there was nothing to be done; it was snowing lightly so, unbuckling our crampons, we crawled back into our warm sleeping bags to wake again at dinnertime with the tent still swathed in thick cloud.

Later the cloud cover began to disperse and by sunset we had no weather worries, it would obviously be fine on the morrow. But we soon ran into another trouble – our single Primus stove, in spite of its high-altitude burner, would not ignite properly. Wangyal pricked and pumped from three in the afternoon till dark, to no avail. We ate our dehydrated rations cold but without a hot drink life was sorrowful. At three next morning the story was repeated; the tent filled with fumes, flames and unvaporised paraffin and by five o'clock we still hadn't prepared so much as a drink. The noxious fumes made me retch but Wangyal remained unaffected. Kicking the offending stove out into the snow, we donned our equipment and set out.

No food and drink was just too big a handicap; Wangyal was moving slowly for him and I felt like a sponge, drained of all liquid and sustenance. Halfway up Manali Peak we about-turned, descended to Camp III, picked up the stove and hurried across the face of Ladakhi Peak and down to Camp II in search of a stove that worked.

John greeted us with amazement when we reached the tent; he was just about to move up to Camp III to await our return from the summit! He looked much fitter; the rest had clearly done him good. After cooking us a large breakfast he volunteered to go up at once to Camp III and try for the summit next day, in company with the indefatigable Wangyal. They would take the good stove from Camp II and I would follow them to Camp III next morning so as to be on hand in support.

This seemed a sound plan. The paraffin fumes had really unsettled me and John was now fit and raring to go. It all hinged on Sonam Wangyal who typically didn't utter a word till he had picked up the good stove and put it in his rucksack, then he said 'OK, Sahib, Jaldī, Jaldī'. I watched them leave with envious eyes.

I got up before it was light next morning, managed to make some tea on the troublesome stove and set out with the dawn for Camp III. Anxiously I searched the faces of Manali Peak and Mukar Beh for some sign of John and Wangyal but caught not a glimpse of anything which might have been men moving over the slopes. Carrying additional food supplies in my rucksack, plus sleeping bag and personal equipment, I moved slowly along the track across the flanks of Ladakhi Peak. No movement or sign of man's presence showed itself. I guessed that Liam would probably be leaving Camp I with more supplies about then, but until his solid figure breasted the ridge to Camp II, I was once more solitary in the middle of the great alone.

A small snowslide immediately ahead halted me in mid stride. I sunk in my axe and balanced on crampons, trying to decide if the slope was safe, my mouth dry and my heart pounding, then scurried across a runnel till the altitude slowed my pace. Suddenly my mind somersaulted to fatalism. 'If it avalanches, it avalanches!' The sun caught the face ahead of me and soon I was in its welcome warmth, to begin cursing it half an hour later as I plodded through the bright early morning. But I was still elated by the sharpness of everything. At my feet the slope dropped into a small basin, then shelved into a chaotic icefall that finished its journey in the valleys of Lahoul, perhaps 10,000 feet below. On the eastern horizon cloud was massing, the weather could not be far from truly breaking as the monsoon continued its inexorable build-up from the plains. It was probably raining already on the Punjab plain; how the Indians look forward to its coming, bringing cooler weather, their water supplies and relief to sun-scorched earth and man alike.

Camp III was empty, so John and Wangyal had set out. Seven o'clock; I sat down to make some breakfast on the good stove lying inside the tent. Looking up to Mukar Beh I detected a slight movement; two little black dots emerged from the immense barrier crevasse which John said later was 100 feet wide with a 120-foot upper lip of vertical ice. They had been able to turn this on the right and then easily gain the huge snowfield. Slowly eating my breakfast I watched them race across, it looked all over with Mukar Beh but, as they were to find out, it was almost the beginning of their difficulties.

They reached the summit rocks at nine o'clock but the 800 feet to the top occupied them until almost midday; the rock was incredibly loose and shaly, held together only by its covering of snow and ice in much the same fashion as the descent from Manali had been. Holds and whole ledges crashed down at the merest touch and John said it was the loosest ground he had ever been on. Luckily, of all Wangyal's abilities his best is climbing on such ground. He forged away in the lead, kicking, scrambling, cascading down streams of rocks and boulders, often marking time as the slope collapsed almost as fast as he ascended, but slowly they gained height.

Watching was as agonising as taking part, for it all seemed to be happening so slowly and the cloud was building up with each passing hour. The final rope length to the top was the worst of all and John, tied only to a loose rock for a belay, was kept on edge to the last by Wangyal, who though actually on the summit of the mountain shouted down that there was worse to come! By midday they were both on top, Liam waved from Camp II and I shouted and yodelled myself hoarse at Camp III, then set out to meet them.

It was going to take them almost as long to get back as it took to climb to the summit, cloud continued to increase and soon the first wispy snowflakes were falling. The weather was living up to its promise of a complete break. John and Wangyal slowly and carefully abseiled down the shivering rocks to the snow-field, abandoning a rope. Wangyal, ferreting about for a belay at the foot of the rocks, was surprised to find an old rusty tin. How did it get there? At least one party had got further than the pundits had allowed. But no one had trodden the summit before Wangyal and John for it had taken them several hours to the top from where they found the tin, and no visible trace did they find on the peak itself, on which they built a cairn.

The storm hit them as they started up the fixed ropes to Manali Peak. The ironmongery they carried buzzed with static electricity, and as they hauled themselves up the rope visibility was almost zero. I had long since returned to Camp III, expecting they would have to bivouac but I kept a billy of tea on the stove, hoping against hope they would get down before nightfall. When it was almost dark, through the gloom, mist and snow, the reverberating peals of thunder and the mad flapping of the tent fabric, I heard a shout and looking out was delighted to see two figures tottering, it seemed, through the night along the last easy ridges from Manali Peak. A great performance; they had started climbing at 3.20 that morning and arrived back just sixteen hours later, at 7.20 p.m. on 23 June 1968.

The three of us crowded into the small Whymper tent while the wind whistled around us and snow built up continuously, making the tent poles groan like a beast in torment. John and Wangyal slept the sleep of the climber while I lay awake with Wangyal's head cradled on my arm. How one warmed to this funny little black man, this chota wallah (small man) with a heart like a bucket and the blackest skin outside Africa. No Tibetan, Ladakhi, Nepali or Indian I have seen has skin quite the shade of Wangyal's; at times he resembles a lump of coal, blackness heightened by his flashing white smile. I have had many friends and climbing companions over the years but none for whom I felt more affection than Sonam Wangyal.

The night passed as such nights do and next day, taking advantage of a slight and temporary improvement in the weather, we evacuated ourselves plus all our equipment and surplus food back to base in a single day! The probability of the true monsoon arriving, instead of the minor harbingers we were experiencing, urged us downwards.

Near our Camp I, sited on the slope above a ridge, we found a tent pole sticking out of the snow on the ridge itself, about a hundred feet lower than our tent – Geoff Hill's camp. We dug and dug and soon unearthed rucksacks, clothes, ice axes, crampons; they had been well equipped but had made the mistake of placing their camp on a narrow ridge, a site, I hasten to add, used by previous Mukar Beh parties. They had the great misfortune to be caught in that exposed position by one of those rare but major Himalayan storms which defy all previous experience, especially in the amount of snow that falls, the like of which is seen in few other mountain ranges of the world.

The others had long since gone home. Liam back to his work in the Cairngorms, John, his task in India finished, to lecture at the National College of Agricultural Engineering at Bedford, Wangyal to Manali and his job of road-building foreman with the Mountain Roads Commission of the Indian Government. I was travelling alone in the state of Rajasthan where I visited universities, schools, Mogul monuments, Amber City and Jaipur.

From Jaipur I went with a young Hindu friend, a trainee doctor practising Indian, not Western, medicine, to visit first a shanty town inhabited by outcastes or untouchables, then a famous Swami or teacher.

I have seen people living in squalor in Bombay, Calcutta, Karachi, even in the *barriadas* of South America, but nothing like the conditions in which people lived in that shanty town outside Jaipur. Human excreta, flies, filth and starving children were everywhere. The monsoon rain poured down, turning the dwellings made of old paraffin cans, straw and bits of timber into shower baths, and the ground inside and out into a quagmire. 'Let's go!' I pleaded. The young Indian looked at me for a moment with amused contempt, then remembering the good manners of his caste, the Sindhi, he took me to meet the Swami in his spotlessly clean but Spartan abode not far away.

The Swami, an old man, was the young man's great uncle; he greeted us with typical Eastern courtesy and over tea we talked of many things. My young friend's brow furrowed when I asked the sage his opinion of the outcastes and their seemingly inhuman plight. The old man gazed into my eyes for a long moment then replied 'Few Westerners understand our country. Your people ruled this India for 200 years but only a handful of them ever probed its secrets. You will not come to terms either with India or yourself on this visit. Come back again with your wife and children, live here in the same manner as we do, then you might one day understand something of our life, our customs and history, God willing! You will soon be married, soon have children, and perhaps you will find the call of Mother India irresistible and then you will return to us.'

I thanked him and went off to complete my study tour.

The Swami was right in suggesting I should be getting married. Soon after my return from India I married Leni, a keen climber and skier from Nottingham, and we now have a son, Stephen Dillon. I hope the Swami proves as far-seeing when he said that some day we should return to India and live there for a while.

12 Questions and Conclusions

'The glass is falling hour by hour, the glass will fall for ever, but if you
break the bloody glass you won't hold up the weather.'
(Louis MacNeice)

Tracing my climbing career in this book has been a fascinating experience.
It has brought home to me the good fortune I have had, ever since I was a
small boy, in my friendships and climbing companions and in getting to know
well many outstanding human beings and some men who must be reckoned
brilliant climbers by any standards. In the last few years, since I began to study
again – an occupation neglected since my early school days – and to become
aware of the make-up of character, I have pondered two of the questions that
everyone asks: why people climb, and why some develop what amounts to
near genius at the sport while others of apparently equal initial ability attain
only average proficiency. Why, for instance, should Joe Brown be such an
outstanding rock climber? Or Tom Patey a whirlwind of speed on mixed
ground (rock, snow and ice intermingled)? Unlike some activities, climbing is
not easily analysed, partly because both its motivation and its rewards are
so variable.

No one has ever produced a blanket answer to the question, why do people
climb (I hope no one ever will!), because the sport is so egocentric – a personal
activity with a personal motivation. I cannot put my own reasons clearly,
let alone attempt to speak for others, but I can say that climbing has given me
a chance to be truly myself. Sometimes it has made my objectives in life sufficiently clear for me to know exactly where I was going, by giving me something on which to concentrate a hundred per cent, something to go all out
to achieve without constraints of any kind, and in doing this I have not felt
divided within myself. Yet this is only part of my answer; if climbing didn't
involve an element of aesthetic appeal I for one would have tired of it long ago.
And above all, in climbing I have sought friendship, without which the rest
would be meaningless.

During a study into personality and climbing at the University of Leeds
Institute of Education, the researcher, Jeff Jackson, found that top climbers

– men who consistently climbed at the very highest standards – had a special personality bias and, what is perhaps more interesting, that most of the top climbers who took part were shown to have similar personalities.

Another study at the Leeds institute showed that the most important physical attribute of the climber was balance, more important than strength or a low anxiety rating. This is confirmed by a second investigation carried out by the Catholic University of Louvain in Belgium, which in trying to ascertain 'the physical qualities necessary for the sport of high-standard alpinism' found that balance was again the most important factor.

From my own experience, and quite apart from these studies, I also would say that the key to very high climbing proficiency is balance, physical and mental, and the interaction of each with the other. I came to this conclusion one day when I was watching Joe Brown on *Vector* on the Tremadoc cliffs during a televised ascent. Standing on minute footholds, Joe puffed at a cigarette and carried on a conversation with the commentator below through a tiny radio microphone hung round his neck, while TV technicians made adjustments and everyone else stood by awaiting the next transmission. Completely relaxed, he rested in a position where I and perhaps most other climbers would barely have been able to stay on the rock. Why? Because, I decided, his physical sense of balance combined with an acute balance of mental faculties enabled him to do so. Strength has little to do with such a performance and anyone else with the same gifts of balance and mental control should be capable of similar feats. My only unanswered query as I recount this episode is, if Joe is so relaxed, why should he smoke a cigarette? Force of habit? Perhaps, but I think not. This gets us into the deep waters of theorising. Despite his modesty and legendary ability, Joe is only human. He knows his worth and place in British climbing history and, rather like being the fastest gun alive, he too can and occasionally needs to play to the gallery. Smoking a cigarette in a position where others can barely stay in contact is part of the role, and a foible that I for one can take huge delight in.

The early days of my climbing career were the period richest in meetings with memorable personalities, some of whom have appeared in previous chapters. This is not, I think, nostalgia but is due to the fact that in those days climbing still had something of a mystique about it and gatherings of its practitioners had an aura of the eccentric, the unusual. Everyone seemed more clearly defined when numbers were sparse compared to the tens of thousands of today's participants, and the close-knit groups who climbed together regularly in the forties and early fifties allowed us to know and recognise the exceptional men among us. Something of this spirit is still alive today, although I feel it is fast disappearing; but at least mountaineering is still practised by all levels of society, from lords to labourers, and attracts every type of personality and this, together with its aesthetic appeal, is a reason for suggesting that it has a possible element of educative and social value.

I have always been sceptical, however, of attempts to cut across cultural and national barriers in the belief that climbing on an official exchange basis can be used for ulterior purposes such as helping to bring about world peace, improving international relations and so on. The very nature of mountains and the individuality of the men who climb them would, in my opinion, preclude such aims being achieved. The debacle of the 1962 expedition to the Pamirs by a joint British and Russian party was a case in point. I am not naive enough to believe the fault lay solely with the Russians; the trouble may have been that the parties set out with the wrong motive, attempting to improve international goodwill instead of concentrating on enjoying themselves on the mountains.

By contrast, how good climbing can be as a basis for friendships was proved to me when I was lucky enough to take part in the international meet of young alpinists organised by the Belgian Alpine Club in the Ardennes in May 1969. This simply brought together for a week individual climbers from many parts of the world and, in an informal atmosphere with little in the way of directives, let the participants get on with it. Perhaps the fact that Belgian breweries had donated unlimited beer contributed to the meet's success, or the Belgians may have a flair for these things, but the week was unforgettable and I personally made many good friends from all over Europe.

To be convinced that climbing friendships do not always thrive in an atmosphere of international representation, one has only to witness the competitiveness which develops between representatives who attend the international meets held in Chamonix under the auspices of the French École Nationale de Ski et d'Alpinisme and the French government. On occasions the competition is rather like a battle to see who comes out top, with the various national representatives striving to outdo each other in the severity of their ascents.

The international meet in Belgium emphasised for me the vast changes in the mountaineering world since my own youth. I could sit and talk with German, Dutch, Spanish, Czech, Polish, Austrian climbers about mountain philosophy and mountaineering in all parts of the world. It is not only in Britain that the structure of society has changed during the years covered by this book. Affluence and leisure have enabled climbers everywhere to spend more time in the mountains than ever before.

This has resulted in vast strides in proficiency and one is tempted to say that the standards attained by the greatest of today's climbers – men like Bonatti, Brown, Robbins, Messner, to name a few – are nearing the limit of human capabilities. But if one considers this further, it is of course nonsense. With one exception that I have heard of, no one has applied to climbing the type of training routine and the dedication of an Olympic athlete. The exception, and he only in a specialised manner for a special kind of climbing, is the American, Gill, who has systematically applied himself through gymnastics and rock-climbing training of his own devising to the art of bouldering. He is capable of feats, strictly within the problem-climbing limits he has set for himself, which other American climbers cannot emulate.

Through the amazing gymnastic ability and strength he has developed, Gill has shown what future rock climbing standards might become. Many people would not be prepared to go to such lengths and most would feel, on the present basis of mountain ethics, that actually to train for climbing, other than by being fit, is the antithesis of what the sport is all about – and this is my own point of view. But attitudes are changing, and increasing popularisation and professionalism may lead some climbers to accept the life of the ascetic, dedicated athlete for the sake of the material rewards open to leading performers.

At the beginning of the 1970s the biggest single difference since the days when I began to climb in 1947 is the ever-increasing crowds who swarm in such popular areas as Snowdonia, the Lake District, the Cairngorms. The trickle of newcomers to climbing in 1947 became a river by 1960 and will soon reach flood proportions. Because of these numbers the traditional basis and values of British climbing are breaking down with the disappearance of a once wholly amateur sport. The serried ranks of professionals stretch through climbing instruction, journalism, lecturers, equipment designers, manufacturers and retailers, and as in any boom there has been no shortage of exploiters. Mountaineers do not live in a vacuum between days on rock or hill, much as some may desire to do so. They are affected by the pressures of the society in which they live like anyone else, by the materialism and commercialisation which are the dark side of the age in which mankind has made the greatest technological discoveries and achievements in our history.

Until the early fifties the public en masse was indifferent in the sport of mountaineering. The ascents of Annapurna in 1950 and of Everest in 1953, however unwilling the participants were that it should be so, were hot news to the publics of their two countries, whose anxiety and interest were matched by all the forces of modern mass media. For the future, with further advances in knowledge and techniques, one can envisage such exciting possibilities as a complete traverse of the whole Annapurna range or of the Dhaulagiris by a light party supported by airdrops, or four men attempting a face climb such as the southern flank of Lhotse Shar, but one can hardly imagine the climbers, however much they wished it, escaping an enveloping cloud of publicity.

Television, that medium of such possibility, but so misused, has probably done more to change the public image of climbers and climbing than any other; slowly its moguls grasped that the sport is good television and, with appeals to the leading climbers that the public has a right to be informed, spectacular has galloped after spectacular. Climbers taking part have become household names, producers have been highly satisfied and the TV addicts cry for more! Starting out with the best intentions in the world we, the actors, have slowly prostituted the sport we love so dearly. If one does accept that the public has a right to be informed – and I am not so sure of that – then one should also insist that the instruction should be correct and matter of fact. I have been as guilty as the next for I have helped in a small way the production of climbing television, and it is amazing how one enters into the spirit of the thing.

The producer makes a suggestion, 'Could we have someone swinging out into space on a rope?'

'Yes, easily,' comes back the reply from willing climbers. 'It would make awfully good television.'

So the public at large sees a climber dangling in space, or two men paddling through the waves in a rubber dinghy to reach the foot of a sea cliff (as if this is standard equipment carted about by climbers!), we see our heroes bivouacking for the night on ledges when actually, as soon as the day's filming is finished, they slide down their abseil ropes to join the ground crews in the nearest public bar.

On the surface, what harm is there in such mild deceptions? Unfortunately one thing has led to another; fame is now openly sought by some and there have been claims to first ascents by climbers who have apparently never been on the routes claimed and, even worse, the exploitation of such scandals by climbing journalists. Whose fault is this state of affairs? It is mine and every other climber's who, like me, although he has acted innocently, has not sufficiently considered the future well-being of our sport. Its founding fathers were men of vision; they laid a firm basis for the direction it could follow to its best advantage. Technical progress was not to be eschewed but it was always to be allied to aesthetic appreciation and ethical considerations, factors that we have ignored to mountaineering's detriment in recent years.

British climbing is at present being reshaped by pressure groups completely outside the traditional basis of individuals and clubs. Many of the old established clubs don't seem to realise this; their members do not appear to grasp the size of the numbers now taking part or wishing to participate. They have lost contact with the latest newcomers to the sport who are taking their lead more and more from the climbing photographers and journalists, training and quasi-educational organisations, suppliers of equipment and the mass media in general. The coming flood of new climbers will accentuate this trend and if today's climbers, who are still in touch with the traditions of the past, direct descendants of Ruskin, Stephen, Mummery, Young, Kirkus, Linnell, Dolphin, Brown and their peers, do not act, climbing will soon become just another commercialised spectator sport with the same sort of ethic as football or horse racing, and with ratings like boxing, far away from the idealistic concept of mountaineering as a physical and aesthetic recreation for individuals.

The problem of the future resolves itself into control of the training and instruction offered to would-be climbers. Clubs and individuals can no longer cope, or certainly will not be able to do so in the years ahead, and the process is already well advanced of taking away from that basis the introduction of beginners to the mountains. No one, I am sure, wishes to deny these beginners the right to safe and expert tuition, but only a blind optimist would say that the present set-up of instruction is making a good job of it. A vast training programme is mushrooming, encompassing many different organisations with, to my mind, some very woolly thinking and clouded motives. We have educators talking about 'character building', militarists talking about 'courage', strategists who declare that 'expedition participation' is awfully good training for Britain's changing role in the world! No one I know of has yet attempted to assess the effects or worthiness of the latest rash of certificates, awards and general programmes of bodies outside the mainstream of British climbing or even of those under the umbrella of the British Mountaineering Council. To me some of these programmes are anathema, but I would rather, I must admit, have a wall littered with worthless pieces of paper than one dead body!

My biggest criticism of our present instruction programmes is the lack of any attempt to implant an aesthetic appreciation of climbing and mountains or knowledge of the tradition and history of mountaineering. The stress is on technical proficiency at schoolroom level; hence we have thousands of newcomers who are able at map reading, the use of belays and so on, but with little or no feeling for the hills other than seeing them as a vertical gymnasium. This, of course, is a vast generalisation; some of our mountain centres, instructors, guides are doing a good job within the present framework and some of the training and educational bodies employ instructors who themselves have a reverence for the mountains and an understanding of the days when Leslie Stephen could write of them as a playground. But in the main one has only to meet some of the products of the vast sausage machine that is in operation to realise that there is some truth in my assertions. Again one may ask whose fault it all is, and once more the answer lies with ourselves. It has been a slow, insidious process, illustrated in its final stages by the decision of a friend, prominent in climbing instruction, to quit the task. 'I am getting out,' he declared. 'The job of climbing instruction is falling more and more to the schoolroom scientist – teachers, educators. There is no substitute for experience, but only a few of us seem aware of this.' It is also illustrated by a man like Eric Beard, a good instructor and an asset to any mountain centre, who was unable to get a permanent job because he hadn't the necessary pieces of paper.

It is unfortunate that the educators have seized upon climbing as a way of making the man out of the boy, of character building, of implanting or testing courage. I cannot see how such claims can be justified. Undoubtedly mountaineering is still rich in characters, but not of the type talked about by official bodies. Some climbers in my experience have been antisocial, some criminal; the outdoor community as a whole has been no more inclined to be virtuous and self-sacrificing than the non-climber, yet from such a premise as the character-building one, meaning I suppose producing people of high moral values, has come much of the impetus which has made these bodies favour mountaineering for training purposes. Speaking as a climber, I would agree it is no bad thing that young people are given the chance to taste the sport, but it is regrettable that they are put on to mountains for the wrong reasons and even more regrettable that this will result in an eventual change in the sport's whole character. This use of mountaineering is partly responsible for the growing emphasis on achievement as an end with too little attention to the means by which the goal is attained. We must recognise in our own climbing and teach to those who are coming after us that a glorious failure is better than a meaningless victory.

Only concentrated action by those climbers who dislike the system which has developed above their heads will reverse its trends. Given the numbers who now wish to climb, I will concede the need for training centres and instruction courses since, as I have said, the old way of introducing beginners to mountaineering is no longer viable, and centres and courses imply the necessity for professional instructors. The very word 'certificate' is abhorrent to me in this connection but if, as it appears, such things are inevitable, let there be a national school of rock climbing, mountaineering and mountain activities, set up by the old established climbing organisations with government funds but complete autonomy. Only persons who have been through this school should be in charge of the instruction of potential future climbers.

There might well be different grades of instructors but the chief instructor cadre should have been through something like a guides' course in the Alpine countries. The full course for guide or chief instructor should take him at least two years and should include, besides practical mountaineering activities, and such associated disciplines as ski-mountaineering, avalanche control, survival and rescue, the history of mountaineering and the literature and art which it has inspired. At the end of the course the student should have the equivalent of a university qualification.

In this way beginners would know there was no doubt as to the worth of their instructors, since those responsible for climbing tuition would be well informed and in touch with both mountaineering history and the latest developments, dedicated to a profession and not mere armchair experts.

In my experience it is the armchair expert, the dabbler at the sport who has seized upon it as a lucrative way of making a living, who is mainly responsible for the commercialisation of present-day climbing – although I must admit again that persons such as myself have contributed innocently to the process.

The present decline in the aesthetic regard for mountains is best reflected in the barren state of climbing literature in the last decade. It is no accident that members of the university climbing clubs are mainly from the practical disciplines. The sport nowadays hardly attracts an artist; how different from the early days of mountaineering! But it is no wonder, for most articles in the popular climbing press make one think of a treatise on mechanical engineering or a blow-by-blow account of a heavyweight tussle, with a style to match. There are bold exceptions to this, particularly in the old established club journals, which prove that there are climbers about who can produce worthwhile, even outstanding work, but art requires certain conditions in which to flourish and climbing in Britain in 1970 is not very stimulating for the creative mind. The general climate of opinion calls for the technical, nut-and-bolt type of description, cheap journalism and the mere reporting of facts; a mountain writer of the calibre of Geoffrey Young might find real difficulty in being creative in the midst of such mediocrity.

A surprising phenomenon of the last few years has been the demand among British climbers for a national club. This again seems part of the malaise that wants certificates and awards and approves of the mass popularisation of climbing. I have put forward the need for a national school for instructors, but a national club is another matter, although it is difficult to argue against the new breed of climbing politicians who seem hell-bent on getting everyone steamrollered into a single organisation. They point out correctly that with a single national club we could have insurance schemes, lecture programmes, magazines, yearbooks, training programmes, reduced rail fares, etc., etc., and that an all-embracing organisation is called for to speak for all British climbers and to organise truly national expeditions.

Such claims ignore completely the fact that the traditional set-up of small intimate clubs has everything to recommend it; it has given to British climbing an almost unique flavour with its parochialism, individualism and lack of organisation on any but the smallest scale. Our climbing has thrived in such conditions – in my experience the only anarchy that really works! The tradition of spontaneity and individualism is precious and infinitely worth preserving. It is still deeply engrained in local clubs and in climbers themselves, and if we allow it to be swept away climbing will be the poorer. A national club could only work if the existing clubs surrendered their sovereignty, and I hope they never will. Let us turn our backs on the institutionalisers and retain our fuddy-duddy, un-with-it clubs; if they give support to the British Mountaineering Council, it should be enough!

Perhaps in this last chapter I have put too much emphasis on the affairs of men and not enough on the mountains. Yet men and their interaction one with another is one of the most important aspects of any climbing venture, even a book. I have spoken out because, though I may be judged a pessimist, I feel there is danger ahead for our beloved sport of mountaineering. Why bother? Why not let the new generation reform, revolutionise and change as they wish? My answer is bound up with my own story of a change in attitude as I have grown older.

When I was thirteen I disliked all climbing organisations, especially such clubs as, say, the Alpine Club. I laughed at the old traditions and, along with many others, looked on the clubs and their members as 'the establishment' and was ready to strike a blow for freedom for all young climbers from their influence and constraints, even by some such deed as blowing the top off Napes Needle or maybe blowing up the Alpine Club itself! Some of the Bradford Lads, including myself, actually did plan to take the former action. Luckily for the Fell and Rock Climbing Club, whose motif is the Needle, our efforts were frustrated by our gelignite expert getting drunk in Wasdale Head and so failing to meet the other dynamiters who, intent upon their explosive deed, were travelling over to Great Gable from Borrowdale on foot.

Since those days I have slowly come to realise that the founding fathers and their descendants were no fools and that the traditions they established were sound. Climbing needs a little organisation and a lot of anarchy; freedom is its greatest attraction. Today's newcomers and the well-meaning but wrong-thinking organisation men, if they do not appreciate these facts, may change irreversibly the basic structure of climbing, may even have begun the process by which climbing as a sport for individuals would disappear for ever.

But it is not necessary to finish on a sour note. There are already the first signs that the wholly technical, mechanical nature of some modern climbing is beginning to pale in its attractions. Solo climbing is much in vogue in this country for the first time. Perhaps this is only because the possibilities of pioneering new routes are denied by the overcrowding of British hills, but I think not. Talking with some of the cult's leading exponents leads me to believe that it is rather a reaction against the barriers which have arisen between man and mountain, and a desire to establish a closer relationship between the rock and themselves. Once climbers become fully aware of what is at stake they will react.

It may not be possible for newcomers to experience the kind of days we spent in the Lake District in the 1940s, but this may not be a bad thing. Man has reached the moon, and the youth of today is bound solely by their own imagination and sense of adventure in climbing as in other spheres.

For me climbing is still an all-consuming passion. I have my bad days and good days but through it all the desire to climb is always present. With a wife and family I cannot move around the world as freely as I once did, nor do I wish to be away from them too much, but this has made me value my mountaineering expeditions all the more. It is possible for me to enjoy climbing as much as I have ever done and I hope to do so till I die.

I feel truly happy to have lived the days described in this book. Mountains have been an inspiration throughout my life; their forms have always affected me, either to love or hate. They stand above the daily round, still mystic, magical and secretive, and I hope for me they will ever be so. It was so for most of those who climbed before me and I hope it will be for those yet to come. Paraphrasing the ancients, I believe it is something to have lived as we have lived, and even more to have climbed as we have climbed.

Acknowledgements

Several persons have helped me in the production of this book, some with personal reminiscences, others by clarifying dates and events. In this connection I would particularly like to thank Harold Drasdo, Jack Bloor, Jack Bradley, Pete Greenall, Nat Allen and Bob Pettigrew.

For help with photographic material I wish to thank John Cleare, Erwin Schneider and Wolfgang Linzer and, in the preparation of such matter for the press, Roger Pearson.

My biggest debt of all is to Eveleigh Leith; any merit the final production may possess is due in no small way to her abilities at editing, retyping and preparation of the final manuscript for publication.

I would thus take this opportunity of thanking them one and all and I do hope the finished result justifies their interest.

D.G.
Brantwood, Coniston
15 April 1970

About the Author

Dennis Gray first climbed as a schoolboy, with the 'Bradford Lads', a group that emerged in the 1940s and remained united for many years. In 1954, when called up for National Service, he was posted to Manchester where he would go on to climb with the finest talent in the country: members of the Rock and Ice club – Joe Brown, Don Whillans, Merrick 'Slim' Sorrell, Ron Moseley, Nat Allen, and many others.

A brief posting to Innsbruck in 1955 gave him his first taste of Alpine rock, and countless more Alpine visits then followed throughout the sixties, as well as a visit to the Himalaya, which led to the first ascent of the Manikaran Spires. In 1966 he led an expedition to film the first complete ascent of the north ridge of Alpamayo in the Cordillera Blanca range in the Peruvian Andes, and two years later led another which made the first ascent of Mukar Beh in the Kulu valley in India.

Gray became the first general secretary of the British Mountaineering Council (BMC), a position he held for eighteen years until 1989, before later guiding in Morocco, the Atlas Mountains, and the Himalaya. He then returned to academia and has written three papers about various aspects of development in China, after some time spent lecturing in China and researching in Oxford.

He founded the Chevin Chase cross-country race in 1979, one of the most popular running events in Yorkshire, and has published seven books including a novel, a book of poems, and two books of anecdotes and stories. He lives in Leeds, and has three grown children and five grandchildren.

Riding the rods of the Snowdon railway. *Photo: Eric Beard.*

An involuntary bathe. *Photo: Mike Dawson.*

Hand-traversing the bridge at Glen Nevis. *Photo: Godfrey Page.*

Dennis Gray leading *Z climb* at Almscliff.

Arthur Dolphin attempting what was later to be *Delphinus* on Raven Crag, Thirlmere. *Photo: Mike Dawson.*

Joe Brown, Eric Beard and Terry Burnell. *Photo: Dennis Gray.*

Above: Dennis Gray on the East Buttress Girdle, Clogwyn Du'r Arddu. *Photo: Gordon Smith.*

Above: Pete Greenall. *Photo: Dennis Gray.*

Above: Nat Allen. *Photo: Dennis Gray.*

Above: Paul Grainger. *Photo: Dennis Gray.*

Above: Slim Sorrell. *Photo: Dennis Gray.*

Above: Joe Smith and Dennis Gray. *Photo: Eric Beard.*

Above: Gordon Smith. *Photo: Dennis Gray.*

Above: Charlie Vigano. *Photo: Dennis Gray.*

Above: Ron Cummaford. *Photo: Dennis Gray.*

Above: Dez Hadlum. *Photo: Dennis Gray.*

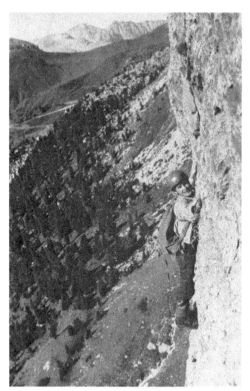

On the north face, Cima Ouest di Lavaredo. *Photo: H. Koehler.*

Above: The south face of Piz Ciaveses. *Photo: H. Koehler.*

Dez Hadlum on Solleder Route, Civetta. *Photo: Dennis Gray.*

Dennis Gray on Indrasan, 1961. *Photo: D. Burgess.*

On the road to Gauri Sankar. *Photo: Dennis Gray.*

Chosfel, the axe man. *Photo: Bob Pettigrew.*

Ian Howell on the rope move on Llithrig, Clogwyn Du'r Arddu. *Photo: Gordon Smith.*

The Gauri Sankar Expedition. *Photo taken by Ang Namgyal (Yum Yum).*

Gauri Sankar. *Photo: Erwin Schneider.*

Don Whillans on the 'Little Eiger': Gauri Sankar, 1964. *Photo: Ian Clough.*

A closer look at the knife-edge ridges of Gauri Sankar. *Photo: Erwin Schneider.*

Start of a Dovedale Dash at Ilam Hall, Derbyshire. *Photo: Dennis Gray.*

A climbing competitor out on the course. *Photo: Dennis Gray.*

Alpamayo showing the south and north ridges. *Photo: Erwin Schneider.*

Alpamayo reveals herself. *Photo: Erwin Schneider.*

Alpamayo with the north ridge in profile. *Photo: Erwin Schneider.*

El Capitan: Yosemite Valley. *Photo: Dennis Gray.*

Chuck Pratt making a mantelshelf on the Lower Cathedral Spire, Yosemite Valley. *Photo: Dennis Gray.*

Sonam Wangyal. *Photo: Dennis Gray.*

At the Polish climbers' camp in the Morskie Oko valley. *Photo: Dennis Gray.*

Manali Peak and Mukar Beh. *Photo: Bob Pettigrew.*

Jim McDowell and Jim McArtney climbing in the Polish Tatra. *Photo: Dennis Gray.*

Eric Beard and Stephen Dillon Gray. *Photo: Dennis Gray.*

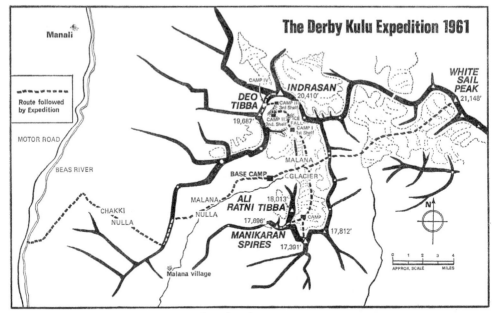

The Derby Kulu Expedition.

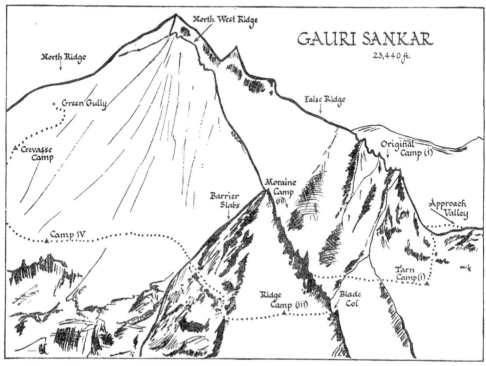

Gauri Sankar 1964, the route on the mountain.

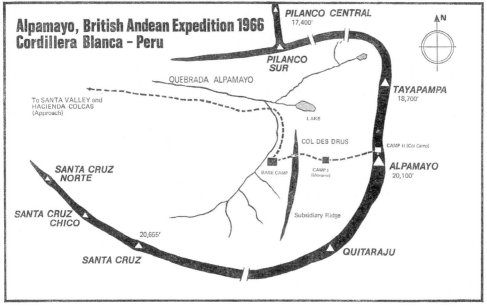

Alpamayo and the Cordillera Blanca.

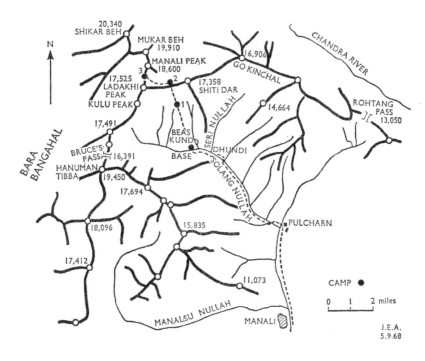

Mukar Beh.